The Mental and Social Life of Babies

Kenneth Kaye

The Mental and Social Life of Babies

How
Parents
Create
Persons

The University of Chicago Press

The University of Chicago Press, Chicago 60637
The Harvester Press Limited, Brighton, Sussex

Library of Congress Cataloging in Publication Data

Kaye, Kenneth.
  The mental & social life of babies.

  Bibliography: p.
  Includes index.
  1. Infant psychology.   2. Child development.   3. Parent
and child.   4. Parenting—Psychological aspects.
I. Title.   II. Mental and social life of babies.
BF720.P37K39   155.4′22   82-6965
ISBN 0-226-42847-8   (cloth)   AACR2
ISBN 0-226-42848-6   (paper)

For Lev Dylan Kaye
who had to ask three times
who the book would be "For"
before I understood

Contents

Acknowledgments

Many authors, in listing the colleagues and friends who helped them in significant ways, feel compelled to issue a disclaimer assuring the reader that those people should share only in the praise the book receives, not in any of the responsibility for its deficiencies. That is clearly fallacious. If the acknowledgees contributed to making the book as good as the author feels it is, then surely an even greater effort on their part would have made it even better. Consequently, it is fair to blame them for the book's weaknesses.

I am grateful to the talented and dedicated individuals who must share the blame with me. First, there are the former students whose names appear as coauthors of the investigations discussed: Alan Fogel, Janet Marcus, and Anne Wells. (Many other students assisted in those studies, as noted with thanks in the various journal articles we have produced.) Stephen Muka designed and implemented CRESCAT, our computer language. Dr. Richard Nachman, Dr. Daksha Patel, and the nursing staff of Columbus Hospital were invaluable colleagues in the recruitment of our sample of mothers and infants. And the Spencer Foundation, under Tom James's inspired leadership, paid for it all. It seems to me that all these people, because they believed in me, must be held accountable.

I have had many mentors over the years whose ideas have wormed their way into this work in devious ways. My first course in the social sciences was with Prof. George C. Homans, whose model of interdisciplinary rigor in studying the English villagers of the 13th century had something to do with luring me toward psychology. It was Jerome Bruner who actually made a psychologist of me and who declared that some of our questions about Man could be answered by babies. Berry Brazelton taught me all his secrets, and Martin Richards launched me on this course of research 13 years ago. Since so many of their ideas are presented in these pages as my own, I want to acknowledge their responsibility against the day when those ideas will be shown to have been unsound.

The book itself owes much to others. Large sections of the manuscript were read carefully by three anonymous reviewers (one of whom later identified himself as Kurt Fischer) as well as by Alan Fogel, Dan Freedman, and Michelle Perry-Barras, good friends and good critics. I disclaim responsibility for any flaws in the book that all these readers failed to bring to my attention, as well as for any that I may have introduced into it at their suggestion.

Some of the people mentioned so far might try to escape criticism by pleading that their tact or respect for my academic freedom led them to hold back some criticisms that occurred to them. There is one person, the center of my own mental and social life, who cannot use that excuse: My wife, Rosalind Charney, neither held back her criticisms nor gave me the freedom to ignore them. She is therefore most to blame for whatever measure of cogency and clarity the book still lacks. She is also responsible for many of the ideas and arguments found in these pages (perhaps the very ones the reader will disagree with). In her defense I can only plead that her motives were pure: scientific integrity, the deepest intellectual curiosity about human psychology, a phenomenal capacity for work, humor, and love.

1

Overture

The babe whose birth embraves this morn,
Made his own bed ere he was born.

Richard Crashaw, *Hymn of the Nativity,* 1652

At 2 weeks, Jessica lay on her back between her mother's knees, half-swaddled in an oversized flannel nightdress. The mother talked to Jessica and to the visitor at the same time. "You're quiet now, aren't ya? You should have seen her at 4:00 this morning. Yeah! Yeah! You weren't quiet then, were ya? No. No. No you weren't!" Jessica did not reply. Her eyes, not quite meeting the mother's gaze, flickered across her face as though inspecting one eye, then the other, then the mother's bangs, then the eyes again. Her mother had been playing with Jessica's hands. Now each small hand was wrapped around one of the mother's index fingers. "Could she know who I am already? The way she holds on to me." The baby's lips parted and seemed to make a round O. Her mother imitated this, then laughed. "Is that 'Yes'? Say, 'I know who Mommy is!' "

Amy, almost 4 months old, sat in her father's lap in a booth at the coffee shop. He was talking to a friend. Amy was teething on a hard rubber ring he had brought along for her. Her father supported Amy's back with his left arm, keeping his hand free. Twice he used that hand to catch the ring when it fell to her lap or his own lap. When Amy dropped the ring for the third time, he interrupted his conversation, said, "Klutz," picked it up and put it on the table. She leaned toward

1

it, awkwardly reached out and touched it, but was not able to grasp it well enough to pick it up. Her father had returned to his conversation, and this time without interrupting it (though he was glancing back and forth between Amy's hand and his friend) he tilted the ring upward toward Amy so that she could get her thumb under it. She grasped the ring and pulled it away from him. Absorbed in chewing on the toy, Amy did not look at him. He went on talking and drinking his coffee, paying no further attention to her until he felt the toy drop into his lap once again.

Dylan, at 9 months, played pat-a-cake with his grandmother. She held her hands up, ready to clap them together, and made a face as if to say, "Are you ready?" He reached toward one of her hands with both of his, but she clapped her hands together slowly, three times. Dylan stopped, in mid-reach. When his grandmother finished clapping, he started: slowly touching his hands together, separating them, touching them together again. Grandma tried to get him to clap his hands against hers, but he was distracted by the dog's barking. The doorbell rang and Grandma had to leave the house. When she came in the door 6 hours later, Dylan was sitting on the living room floor. He looked up at her, smiled when she greeted him, then grandly reached out his hands and clapped them together three or four times, without taking his eyes from Grandma.

At 17 months, Nathan was standing between mother and father, who were sitting in the kitchen. His father handed him a wooden block from a pile on the table. Nathan took it in his right hand, passed it to his left hand, and pointed with his right hand at the pile of blocks. His father handed him another. "Now you've got one in each hand, don't ya?" But Nathan added the second block to the one in his left hand, managing not to drop either of them. He pointed to the pile again. Father offered him another block. This time, holding two blocks in his left hand and one in his right, Nathan seemed to hesitate for a moment. Then he put the block that was in his right hand into his mother's lap, taking another block from his father. He held out the blocks in his left hand toward mother, who took them. Now he dropped the block from his right hand into his mother's lap, and she did the same with the two blocks she was holding. Nathan picked up one of those, looked at it, then pointed at the pile on the table, looked at his father, and grunted, "More." Father obliged. Soon Nathan had transferred all the remaining blocks to mother's lap, where he could reach them without help.

At 30 months Nikki, whom we were observing in her home, said to her mother, "I have to pee," whereupon she left the room. She turned on the light in the bathroom, pulled down her pants, sat down, urinated, stood up, pulled up her pants, turned off the light, and rejoined us in the living room. At that moment she truly seemed to have joined the community: independent agent, tool-user, aficionado of electric lights and toilets, respecter of domestic tranquillity and hygiene; socialized, intelligent; a person in her own right.

All these incidents have something in common: They are cognitive achievements in a social context. They illustrate the impossibility of drawing a line between mental life and social life at any age. And they raise some specific controversial issues about the psychology of infancy: Would substantially the same behavior have occurred without the parents' participation, perhaps in somewhat different form, but involving the same basic skills? Or do we have to use some notion of *communication* in any explanation of this behavior? Do we see an exchange of meaningful gestures between Jessica and her mother, or between Amy and her father, long before language development begins? If so, shall we say that later language development is merely a more complex level of gesturing, with conventional words and sentences taking the place of innate gestures?

This book replies "No" to all those questions. It argues instead that the behavior of these children depends as much upon preadapted adult behavior and universal human interaction patterns as it does upon the infant's intrinsic cognitive abilities. The kind of exchanges with adults that facilitate sensorimotor and later linguistic development require little from the infant at first except regularities in behavior and expressive reactions that parents tend to interpret *as if* they were meaningful gestures.

It surely is a miracle that the kind of creature a man and a woman can bring into the world by purely biological processes becomes (eventually) the kind of creature that possesses a mind and a sense of self, an unsurpassed intelligence and a personal identity in relation to society. The explanation has most often been given by pointing to man's superior brain. This book offers an additional perspective. It supports an argument that has been, until recently, a minority view. The evolution of the human brain alone, as the instrument of learning and thought, could not have brought about mind. Symbolic representation, language, and thought could not emerge in any species, and would not develop in any individual, without a special kind of fit between adult behavior and infant behavior. That fit is preadapted: It comes to each child as a birthright, both as a result of biological propensities and as a result of social processes learned and transmitted by each new generation.

Since the argument places social relations at the very root of mental development, it amounts to an extension of Vygotsky's theory and of his objections to Piaget, down to the first year of life. (Their debate actually dealt with the preschool years.) However, in the course of this discussion and in the light of modern evidence we can also refine the Vygotskyan perspective. This perspective reverses the tacit assumption of many authors, that communication is the felicitous by-product of a symbol-using mind. Like Vygotsky, I assume the contrary: that communication is the origin of mind. Yet this only raises the question: How does communication itself develop in an organism that still lacks a mind?

A great deal happens between birth and sometime around the middle of the third year (when, filled with pleasure and pride at that glorious accomplishment, we tell Nikki she is no longer a baby). The processes producing those changes are a great mystery in between two lesser mysteries. Before infancy, our mechanisms of reproduction and gestation, miraculous and mysterious as they are, are similar to other mammals. After infancy, human development is an elaboration of the intelligence, learning processes, and communication that all originate in the first 2 or 3 years. But human babyhood itself is practically without precedent: The uniqueness of our species is never more evident than in the extraordinary transformation from newborn to 2-year-old.

From the Mouths of Babes

Surprisingly, the psychology of human infancy has been a battleground for many of the great issues of the modern social sciences: issues about education (what must be taught? what is learned spontaneously? what is innate?), evolution (what distinguishes the infant homo sapiens from other primates that could explain its subsequent achievements?), language (how does it originate?), culture (how early do cultural differences affect the child, and by what means?), social class (are differences in ability hereditary or acquired?), sex roles (are sex differences biological or conditioned?), humanism (is man ever an animal? and if so, when does that animal change into a person?), theology (are we born innocent or cloaked in sin?), social reform (can we reduce poverty, retardation, drug addiction, etc., by early intervention?), and the relation between science and political ideology (does the asocial, socialized, or innately social character of infants tell us anything about how a society ought to be organized or governed?). In the past decade, each of these issues has been the subject of at least a dozen articles, sometimes of entire edited volumes. We seem to be turning to the young infant with questions our wisest old heads have not been able to answer.

Perhaps the practical importance of those questions is only a way of rationalizing an enduring fascination. Paul Tillich (1951) wrote that "man's ultimate concern" is the question of what lies ahead, beyond the death of the body. Personally, with no anticipation of a hereafter and with little confidence even in a tomorrow, I would be satisfied with a better understanding of what lies behind. The mystery of where we came from and the contrast between what we are and what we were at birth are at the core of man's ceaseless quest to understand nature. There are special obstacles in the way of understanding the part of nature that is man himself, but there is also a special aesthetic, a special energy that comes from confronting directly the most profound mystery of human life.

To participate in that quest and to develop a coherent theory, we psychologists have to avail ourselves (as well as we can) of biology, anthropology, philosophy, and sociology. We need to think about how evolution has provided man with the means to be opportunistic and adaptable while also passing along technology and culture. We need to think about the behavior of adults and children as they interact with an infant. We need to think about symbolic representation and the origins of mental life together with the acquisition of language and the way it transforms social relations.

This book has five main goals. First is to explore the nature of the human mind, self, and social relations, as all three of those gradually and simultaneously emerge in infancy. We shall be concerned with the intersection (not the union) of those three areas of work in developmental psychology. Second is to examine a set of critical concepts for the field, especially *system, communication, gesture, symbol, representation, intersubjectivity, imitation, socialization,* and *self-consciousness.* Third is to describe a new conception of the parental role in early development. Fourth is to outline a theory that saves the best features and abandons the worst features of what I call the "inside-out" and the "outside-in" views of how the human infant becomes an intelligent person. The theory is concerned with causal factors in development from a universal, species point of view. This turns out to be a different task from theorizing about the causes of individual differences in development. A final goal, between the lines, is to pose some major metatheoretical and methodological problems of developmental psychology in a way that is, while not definitive, at least challenging.

The substance of the book is in two parts. Chapters 2 through 6 deal with the problem of our unit or units of analysis. I shall first explore what we know about human action at the level of organism-as-system, then expand the perspective to that of two or more organisms functioning together as a system. At both levels, the fundamental constructs with which we must be concerned are the same: intention, attention, representation, coordination, and so forth. But we cannot simply equate the "parent-infant system" with the kind of system a single organism is. The mutual coordination of infants with adults changes in the course of their development together, and that change is nothing less than the development of human communication. Our task is to identify and de-

scribe the recurring units of organized activity, "frames" provided by
adults but fitted to the intrinsic features of infant behavior. These recurring frames serve at least three functions: They facilitate interaction
between parent and infant, they facilitate the infant's own exploration
of the world and practice of sensorimotor skills, and they provide means
of educating the infant about both the universals and the culture-specific
conventions of language.

All this is necessary groundwork for the second part of the book.
In Chapters 7 through 12, I shall derive a theory of the social basis of
symbols and the symbolic basis of socialization, attachment, individuation, and self-consciousness. At the heart of all these processes is imitation, the fundamental process of human learning. We need to sort out
those aspects of imitation that operate at every age and in all domains,
from the ways the process changes in the course of development and
the ways it differs across domains. Most important, we need to appre-
ciate the extent to which the infant's imitative capacity is matched by
the parents' presentation of models that are spatially and temporally
organized so as to be salient and imitable.

Since the nature of man and the nature of our quest as developmental psychologists are the most general questions to be kept in the
backs of our minds, we shall take them as our starting point in Chapter
2.

Part One

Construction of the Framework

Chapter 2 distinguishes between intrinsic and extrinsic functions, that is, between processes that are wholly within the developing child and processes that are essentially interpersonal. Most theories of cognitive development have treated it as a matter of intrinsic functions—for example, assuming that representation arises out of object permanence, or that the differentiation of means-ends schemas takes place somewhere inside the infant's nervous system. We shall see that this is as unnecessary as it is inadequate. Many of the concepts and models that we use to explain the action schemas within an organism will be extended, in Chapter 4, to the level of adult-infant interaction. An important assumption of this book is that extrinsic functions evolved, just as intrinsic ones did. Infants inherit certain aspects of their social environments as much as they inherit their nervous systems.

Chapter 3 argues that the term *mother-infant system* has been used too vaguely. Although mothers and infants in the human species have surely evolved together and are therefore preadapted to one another as a system in one sense, the individual mother and her infant do not satisfy certain elementary criteria of a true social system until the infant is at least 6 months old. The age is not so critical as our insistence that "system" be understood as a form of interaction that has to develop over time rather than as merely a rubric for "complex" or bidirectional effects.

Chapter 4 rejects the "inside-out" (orthogenetic) metaphor for infant development, finds problems with some forms of "outside-in" (conditioning) metaphor, and introduces a more appropriate metaphor, an apprenticeship. Adults provide an environment within which the infant's sensorimotor skills are adequate to certain tasks only because an adult breaks those tasks down and serves as the "memory" component of the infant's skill. In the second half of the first year, when infants begin to be part of a coordinated action system, their role is more like that of an apprentice who is only entrusted with certain subroutines while the "executive" remains the role of the parent.

Chapter 5 describes some different kinds of frames used by parents to guide and enrich their infants' intentional acts: the nurturant frame, the protective frame, the instrumental frame, the feedback frame, the modeling frame, the discourse frame, and the memory frame. It argues that these frames enable a parent to recruit the infant into a joint task, or to enter into a task in which the infant is already engaged, so as to provide practice, feedback, experience in turn-taking, and demonstrated solutions to problems on which the infant is working. The result is nothing less than "shared meaning" between infant and adult.

Chapter 6 is devoted to a specific temporal pattern that is characteristic of several types of frame: turn-taking. It shows that turn-taking occurs initially without any sense of being rule-governed, so far as the infant's participation is concerned; but that by the end of the first year the conventional ways of exchanging turns come to be expected, so that the infant both conforms to them and is aware when they are occasionally violated. Turn-taking has become rule-governed and itself becomes the means for introducing the more complex conventional rules of language.

2

Intrinsic and Extrinsic Functions

With all its eyes, the creature world beholds
the open. But our eyes, as though reversed,
encircle it on every side, like traps
set round its unobstructed path to freedom.

Rainer Maria Rilke, Duino Elegies, 1922

This chapter is about the kinds of theorizing that we must do when we attempt to encircle human infancy on every side. We shall begin with some comments on the nature of developmental psychology, a science whose goal is to understand the basic processes—"invariant functions"—that create the distinctive course of human development throughout the life cycle. Then we shall turn to the important question of whether those developmental functions are all to be found within the intrinsic equipment that infants bring with them into the world, or whether the species might have extrinsic (outside-the-organism) means of providing them for each new human candidate.

Humanism and Biology

Some special conceptual problems arise when we turn our eyes inward upon ourselves. Why should that be? Surely man obeys the laws of all matter and the laws of all living things. That he is unique among the animals is not itself remarkable, for every species has its own uniqueness. It would seem, then, that any science adequate to the other species ought to be adequate to our own as well.

One problem is that the generalizations we hope to make about man will apply to man alone. An entomologist often has only a utilitarian

11

interest in the particular species of grasshopper he is working on; his real interests may lie in the whole order *Orthoptera*, or in insects in general, even in fundamental principles of genetics. But that is not true of psychologists, anthropologists, and other social scientists. Our primary interest is in man for man's sake. The invariant laws of zoology are of little interest to a science of man. Our fascination is with just those qualities that are true of nothing else in "the creature world." Those psychologists who deny this, who take as their topic "the behavior of organisms," are not studying man. That is why the scientific study of behavior has acquired a bad name among humanists, as Wayne Booth illustrates in an essay on Kenneth Burke:

> The language of physical science and of behaviorism, . . . though indispensable in studying mere motion, gets its users into trouble when they try to apply it to the human drama. There is no place here for a tolerant bow to the behaviorists, saying "you explain the human drama in your terms, and we'll explain the human drama in our terms." Because for them there *is* no human drama, since there is no concept of *action*. Having reduced their language, for the sake of efficiency, to the language of motion, they deny in their terms what their own competitive treatises display: man's symbolic drama. Reducing action to motion, the behaviorists do not tell "a representative anecdote" when they tell us their stories about man-as-animal. Anecdotes about rats in mazes lack the "circumference" or scope needed if something like justice is to be done to the drama of man. [Booth, 1974, p. 19]

The concepts of *action* and of "man's symbolic drama" are central to this book, but we shall not equate them. For although *action* distinguishes the behavior of organisms from the *motion* of inorganic stuff, it does not distinguish man from other organisms. The difference between action and mere motion is intention, or purposefulness, which is seen as clearly in subhuman species as in our own. Defined objectively, it is no problem to a behaviorist: Intentional behavior is behavior that persists toward an end, as evident in the fact that when the end is reached it causes the behavior to cease. The organism often varies the form of the behavior until it is successful. Then the goal-directed behavior gives way to consummative behavior; for example, food-seeking gives way to eating. The early behaviorist literature was full of debates about the need for specifying goals when describing behavior, and whether it was even possible to do so without being circular (McDougall, 1912; Tolman, 1925; Skinner, 1938). We need not rehash those debates; the difference between saying an animal is searching for food or is driven by hunger is a matter of words. In either case, one is saying that the animal is responding to the absence of its goal, not to a present stimulus. For when it reaches the food (the previously absent goal), the hunger pangs (the present stimulus) do not cease. But the searching does cease, and the food is eaten. So the searching must have been a response to the absence of food, not to the presence of hunger. Similarly, if I teach my dog to bark when she needs to go outside, and she does so only until she sees me start toward the door, the stimuli to which she may be responding have not stopped (her bladder is still full), but her barking stops because it has achieved its intention.

Another important distinction, especially when studying infants, is between the intention inferred by a psychologist from someone's observed actions and the intention inferred by others who are interacting with that person. The actual participants in the behaving person's world are not restricted to the objective definition and reliable criteria of an observing psychologist; they make subjective inferences by projecting themselves into what they see the other person do. Whose interpretation, the psychologist's objective characterization of intention or the coparticipant's subjective one, comes closer to the "real" intention of the person observed? The former is more parsimonious, but only by virtue of ignoring information not externally verifiable. The participants' *internally* verified interpretations of one another's intentions are valid, to the extent they share a perspective on the world and share similar schemas for action. This is especially true if we are concerned with each one's conscious intention (what they think they are doing), for that is surely arrived at by a process more akin to the partner's subjective interpretation than to the psychologist's parsimonious one.

Finally, we shall be concerned with distinguishing between an intentional *act*, which may serve as a sign whenever another organism happens to infer something from it, and intentional *signs*, whose intention is precisely that the other should do so. Animals act intentionally when they build nests, search for food, flee from predators. Furthermore, they often act in concert with one another, communicate, and plan ahead. When two wolves chase a caribou herd toward where a third wolf waits in ambush, or when a swarm of ants occupies a dropped sandwich, there is a plan of action, and there is responding to various sorts of signs. (The rat in a maze is no more representative of those dramas than of our own.)

Man does dwell in a special province, though, with respect to the use of symbolic processes in organizing cooperative action and in planning individual action at a spatial and temporal distance. When other animals cooperate or plan, they do not use symbols (as we shall define them later). The origins of those special qualities of human action are the subject of this book. Our concern at this point is only to say that the mystery of symbolic communication does not remove man from the domain of biology. The problem is to develop a science of man that is adequate to the specialness of man, yet is still science. We must use the methods that have taught us so much about the rest of the universe, without reducing the human drama to terms that miss precisely what makes it human.

It is not a matter of choosing between man as animal and man as human. For both those perspectives are absolutely true. We must confront both simultaneously, with the same confidence in our inquiry that we would apply to any other species. The fact that a chameleon can change its skin color so as to blend with its surroundings, or the fact that a fly can walk on ceilings, does not lead us to attribute those powers to magic. So the unsolved mystery of how man can communicate about events past, future, and nonexistent should not lead us to be satisfied with religious or other magical explanations. The unknown is not necessarily unknowable.

It is true that the human drama has to be analyzed in uniquely human terms. It is also true that any science with which man might manage to explain the rest of the universe would still not be adequate to explain man. Our concern in this book, however, is understanding how humans can have come to be, in the creature world; and how it is that an infant can come to be a person. That coming-to-be is accessible to the student of infancy, for none of those processes which we regard as defining human superiority are present in the newborn.

Epistemology and Developmental Psychology

A theory of human development is a theory of what man is. The converse is also true: An analysis of grown men and women will always raise questions about how their behavior came to be. We isolate a particular phenomenon of adult behavior: for example, the ability to see a three-dimensional scene in a two-dimensional drawing. What mechanisms are involved? Immediately this leads us to ask if they are possessed by everyone in any culture. Are they there at birth? If not, at what age does the ability appear? How is it acquired? A *description* of what the perceptual system achieves as an adult is possible without the developmental perspective, but an *explanation* of how it is achieved requires us to know what the constituent skills are and how they work. These questions in turn force us to ask whether the constituent skills are organized by the very anatomy of the nervous system or whether they are learned and, if so, how?

The study of mind can be treated as epistemology, a branch of "pure" philosophy, without need of psychologists. But when I read any epistemology from Aristotle to Descartes to Chomsky, it always seems to me to be trespassing upon psychological ground. It is full of assertions or implicit assumptions about thinking processes, memory, and learning, yet without a theory of how those processes develop. We should not object to philosophers raising hypotheses about the nature of thought (quite the contrary, those hypotheses are the main use philosophy has to a psychologist), but it is futile to do so as if thought were born full-bodied from the head of Zeus. When Descartes, for example, deliberately doubted all knowledge and then sought to ascertain what could be deduced beginning from the indubitable existence of himself the thinker, the sequence of his deductions corresponded to logic but not at all to the order or the manner in which knowledge actually accumulates.[1]

Philosophers would agree that no description of a product of development can ever be a sufficient explanation of how that product comes about. Some have argued, however, that such a description is necessary prior to studying development; in other words, that we cannot understand cognitive development without a prior analysis of adult cognition, or social development without a prior analysis of adult social relations. There are two reasons for agreeing with that argument, but there is also a sense in which it is misleading. One reason it is right is that the analysis of the finished product, the epistemological analysis of formal reasoning, for example, specifies some of the components of that product and therefore the constituent abilities for whose antecedents and developmental causes we must look (Kaye, 1979a). The other reason is that the finished product is a major part of the explanation of why development takes place as it does: because of the adaptive value this result had in our evolutionary ancestors' environment.

However, it is a mistake to carry the argument as far as some do. The analogy has been made to a train ride, in which the very process of the journey is determined by its destination (Hamlyn, 1971; Toulmin, 1971). For example, it is not a satisfactory explanation of such a journey to say that I wound up in St. Petersburg because I was sitting on a train that went from Moscow to Tver, thence to Vyshni Volochek, etc. On the contrary, I explain my passage through those cities by saying that I was traveling to St. Petersburg. This point may seem to resemble the one with which we began this chapter: the difference between action and mere motion. But that is just the fallacy. We must not confuse the purposefulness of action with purposefulness in development. The train journey analogy, in fact, is an anecdote about action. It is not a good analogy for development, because it suggests that the child knows where

---

1. Philosophers have their own set of goals, which do not require psychological research for their achievement. However, my concern here is what use a psychologist is supposed to make of epistemology. Its inherently nondevelopmental approach severely limits its interest to anyone besides epistemologists.

he is headed.[2] It implies a theory about development that is probably wrong and certainly teleological.

If in fact a child simply wandered onto a train in Moscow and it happened to leave the station just then, the delights and elegance of St. Petersburg would have nothing to do with explaining his transportation thither. The explanation would lie in the tracks, or in the switchmen along the way, or in the judgments of kind strangers who took the child in hand at each station. These are just the kinds of events a developmental psychologist looks for and just the questions we must be sure not to prejudge. (We shall see in Chapters 4 and 5 that adults often do "take the child in hand" in guiding both his action and his development.)

Explaining natural phenomena by their final forms has an old and honorable history in philosophy. To Aristotle, "nature" (*physis*) consisted of those things that "by a continuous movement originating from an internal principle, arrive at some completion."[3] Interestingly, he urged this view in opposition to the evolutionary "survival of the fittest" views held by Empedocles. An appeal to evolution, however, is free of teleology. A natural selection process occurring in the past could well explain why it is that development happens to proceed in the way it now does rather than some other way. But this only concerns the *why*; it does not pretend to explain *how* the development proceeds, that is, what those actual mechanisms are that evolution selected. In Aristotle's teleological argument, the fact that a given child is to develop formal reasoning would be offered as an explanation of his development. Yet, at best it too can only explain why (by reference to the child's membership in the human species), not how the changes are able to take place.

The analysis of the destination of development is important, then, as an outline of what it is whose eventual appearance needs explaining. But we must not make the mistake of assuming that any features of that ultimate result are causally operative in the steps along the way. The ingredients of an explanation have to be found at the point of embarkation. What train does the newborn child get on and what luggage does he bring with him?

Innateness and Intrinsic Functions

Although this book focuses on the first 2 or 3 years of human life, age periods are not really a good way to approach the study of development.

2. For the sake of clarity and unobtrusiveness of style, I shall use the pronoun "he" to refer to any child of indeterminate or inconsequential gender. No offense is intended toward the female sex (by refusing to distract the reader with more than a thousand "he or she"s or "she or he"s that would be required) or toward males (by indiscriminate use of their pronoun).

3. Aristotle's *Physis* 199.

Even if it were possible to provide a description of what happens step by step in the course of a certain age period, then to put all the age periods together to make the life span, we would still have no more than a description. To understand and be able to generalize from a necessarily incomplete description requires the psychologist to postulate general functions at work throughout the life span. The goal of developmental psychology, then, is to close upon a short list of functions: just those that must be postulated or "given" to the human organism if we are to account for particular transitions in particular domains. With what features would one have to design a system so that it would develop (in all important respects) as we do?

Inevitably, that task brings psychologists to infancy and to babies as young as we can get our hands on. The postulated functions must be part of the equipment infants bring with them into the world. If we really understood infants and really understood the behavior of their environment, we should be able to account for their subsequent development. This is why human infancy is such a vital period for an understanding of the whole life span and the very nature of man and society. The task, however, is considerably more complicated than what is implied by the dichotomy of neonatal equipment and environmental effects.

In the first place, "innate" includes more than just "present at birth." Infants do not bring all their innate equipment into the world with them at birth. Some of their baggage has been sent on ahead. Whatever matures according to the designs of the genetic program is innate: crawling, walking, puberty, menopause. True, many extrinsic factors also affect these events, such as nutrition, exercise, and anxiety; but that is equally true of the innate behavior we see in the newborn (affected by the mother's nutrition, exercise, and anxiety during pregnancy). The innate endowment of the human organism includes many features of behavior (as well as, more obviously, anatomy) that appear at various points in the life span, always as an environmentally realized manifestation of a genetic plan.

Second, "innate" includes both specific behavior and the more general "invariant functions." There is a distinction to be made between equipment in the sense of building blocks (the built-in responses of the newborn), and equipment in the sense of developmental processes (abilities to adapt). It is analogous to the set of elements and the set of operations that together define a "group" in mathematics. A group is defined most parsimoniously when it contains the minimum set of operations necessary to generate all, and only, its elements from combinations of its defined operations applied to its defined elements. Human development would be explained most parsimoniously if we could explain the origins of all human behavior from the operations of a minimum set of invariant functions on a minimum set of innate behaviors. A developmental psychology should postulate, then, along with the building blocks that the infant brings into the world, the developmental processes he will apply to those building blocks. All psychological theorizing depends upon the assumption that a relatively small number of processes account for all the transformations that take place in the behavioral system from birth to the end of life. (We also assume that we are smart enough to investigate those processes and to understand them.)

In invoking broad explanatory principles we should be invoking generalizations that, while themselves not yet fully understood, are not so general as to be vague, empty, or undisprovable. To appeal to universalities of part-whole relations, for example, as Piaget often did, claiming to explain transitions in mental structure by analogy with purely mathematical structures (like the "group") or with structuralist analyses of society, history, and so forth, is to force the generality to a level at which, in the first place, we could make an analogy to anything; and, in the second place, we would have a theory about structures in general, not about human development.

On the other hand, while an invariant function like "assimilation" begs the question of its own explanation, at least it is a property of a specific class of things to which man belongs, the class of all behaving organisms. When one invokes the assimilation function, one is saying, "In this respect human behavior depends upon a very general property of organisms that we do not yet understand." And when one details the particular forms and circumstances of assimilation in the human species, one is using the function itself as a background against which to mark clearly how the particular development of man differs from other organisms.

The principles of *human* development are what we are looking for. Any general laws of development (such as would apply to societies, business institutions, salamanders, ant colonies) are either mere metaphors or too general to tell us what we want to know about man. If they are true of all open systems or all organisms, then they are of course true of man. But they are merely the point where the task of investigating human development begins.

What Precisely Is It That Develops? We referred above to "building blocks" and to a set of processes that account for their transformation. If we were studying anatomy, those units would be cells, tissues, or organs. What are the structural units of behavior?

By a "structural unit" we mean the thing that both endures in the organism and changes over time. An *act* is a unit of behavior, but it is only an event, a one-time occurrence. Where does the act come from and where does it go when it has been "executed"? Our real interest is in the regularity underlying a class of similar actions under similar circumstances. That regularity must be due to knowledge-of-how-to-act, stored in the organism's nervous system and subject to alteration by experience. The words *schemas* and *skills* are used interchangeably to denote underlying capacities of that kind. Skills do not consist of general-purpose movement patterns available for any purpose. The intentions for which each skill will be used are an integral part of it, and thus the *ends* can be transformed just as the *means* can, through learning and development. Just as the infant can learn to reach for attractive objects more efficiently, he can also learn to reach for other kinds of objects, reach in order to touch or to manipulate or to bring something to his mouth. The schema involved, in other words, is not "reaching," it is "reaching-for-an-objective."

The presence of a skill and much about its nature can be inferred from an organism's actions under specified conditions. Fortunately, psychology can describe and investigate skills without concerning itself with how they are stored and actualized in the brain. When we say that some person "has" a skill, we mean only that we have a model of the regularity underlying his behavior over a number of different occasions. Our model may be a vague one, so that all we are really doing is defining a class of equivalent acts and treating them as a recurring event, or it may be relatively detailed, so that we can predict the occurrence, form, and outcome of those acts. No matter how detailed the psychologist's model is, however, there will always be more details unknown. In other words, no matter how closely we model the processes involved in action, even if we were to pinpoint the very synapses involved and the timing with which they fired, someone could still ask, "But how does *that* work?" Our theory must always stop somewhere.

P-Models and C-Models. A skill or schema, then, is any class of systematic actions that an organism is capable of producing under particular circumstances. By "circumstances" I mean both "under particular conditions" and "with particular goals." When we say that an organism possesses a skill, we mean we can construct a model that accounts for the organism's behavior. Whatever we find necessary to include in our model can be considered a property of the skill that is actually stored somehow in that organism's nervous system.

However, some models come closer than others to the actual processes we believe occur in the execution of a skill, step by step. These are functional models, specifying in greater or less detail how the system works in real time. Other models are more abstract and analyze the products rather than the processes of skill; these are often called *formal models*. Elsewhere (in Kaye, 1979a), to avoid inconsistencies in others' usages of words like *functional, formal, process,* etc., I have suggested calling the first type P-models (P for *process*) and the second type C-models (C for *competence* in the Chomskyan sense). A C-model is only a statement of some formal properties logically requisite for a system to behave as the observed organism, person, language community, species, or computer does in fact behave. Figure 2-1, for example, is a C-model of infants' reaching skill at various stages. It represents the skill formally but not schematically. A list of specifications is a C-model.

An alternative way of representing the same information, a flow chart, would be a P-model (Figure 2-2). The basic observations come from a study that I did as a graduate student with Jerome Bruner (1971). If you place a small object within the arm's length of a 6-month-old, he will reach for it with whichever hand happens to be closest to it. If you move it away or conceal it, he will stop reaching. If you place a transparent barrier in front of the object so as to foil his reach, he will switch to the other hand. Without help, he can only repeat his direct reach with one hand, switch to the other hand, or stop trying. (Actually Figure 2-2 depicts an idealized infant who would keep trying to reach through the Plexiglas barrier some number of times depending upon his level of arousal, then try the other hand once, and then avert his gaze.)

The two kinds of models are complementary. An important use of the C-model is in specifying the features to be incorporated into a corresponding P-model, and vice versa. Since a P-model is never completely detailed, it always contains "black boxes" or nodes in the flow diagram, for which we have to be satisfied with mere labels or lists of properties without further modeling of their actual functioning. These black boxes are really C-models, perhaps rather vague ones awaiting subsequent

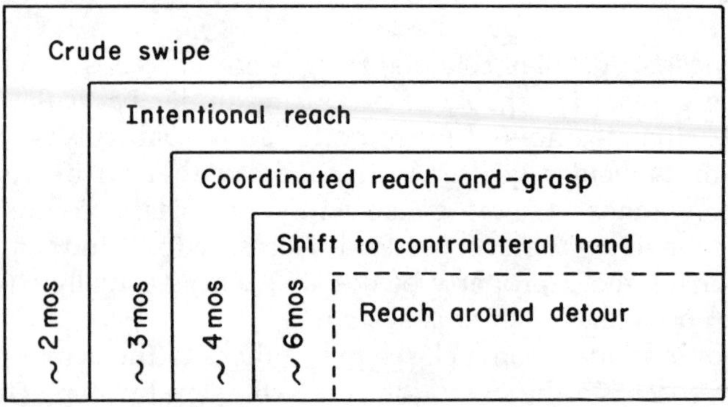

Figure 2-1. C-model of the reaching skill in infants (cumulative competencies).

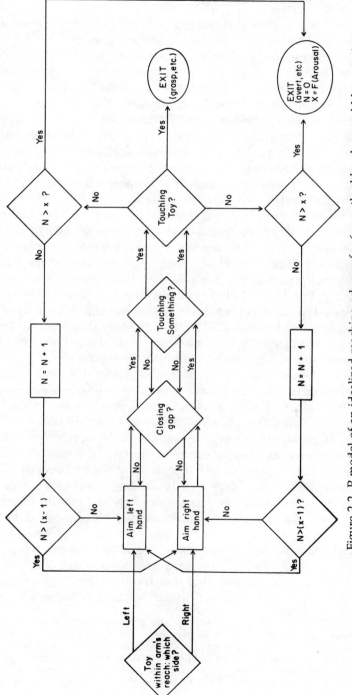

Figure 2-2. P-model of an idealized reaching schema for 6-month-olds who would keep trying to reach through a Plexiglas screen X − 1 times (where X depends upon their level of arousal), then try the other hand once, then avert their gaze. (From Kaye, 1979a.)

investigation. In describing skills and explaining their programmatic functioning, then, both kinds of models are important.

A major theoretical problem arises, however, when we move from the consideration of skills at one period of time to their development over time. For P-models and C-models are not equivalent representations of what it is that develops. When we characterize the behavior of a child during some age period and in some domain of performance, we are concerned with abstracting the significant properties of that stage and contrasting them with a previous or a subsequent stage. Stages, in other words, tend to be described in terms of their formal (C-model) rather than functional properties. Although this abstraction is useful, we cannot expect to explain transition from one stage to the next on the basis of change in formal models.[4] Formal structures do not develop. Skills do. P-models are models of the actual mechanism that develops, while C-models are not. C-models are models of what that mechanism can do or can produce at some period in the course of its development, but not of how it actually works. Yet it is just the "how-it-works," the *process* represented by the P-model, that must develop over time. When we say that skills develop we mean much more than the fact that we have one skill at one age and another skill later. It is really development in the fullest sense: A skill affects the experiences a child will have, and thus affects its own gradual transformation into something else.

When the infant averts his gaze from a task of this kind, it has an important effect upon the behavior of his mother, who usually intervenes at that point and elicits alternative responses in a number of different ways (Kaye, 1970, 1977a). Thus the temporal structure of the infant's skill at one stage affects the experiences that subsequently provide information and opportunities for accommodation in the transition to the next stage. The P-model captures this developmental property of the skill, whereas the C-model does not. It was important to discover that we could P-model the reaching process similarly at 9 months (Figure 2-3) to the way it was represented at 6 months. The precise difference between the two P-models, at a particular place in the process, constitutes a fairly specific hypothesis about the frontier along which this schema for reaching obstructed objects apparently develops. The fact that further investigations revealed that mothers tend to intervene at just that point in their infants' efforts at reaching (Chapters 3 and 6)

---

4. It is absurd to suggest that the development of formal classification skills in the child is explained simply by the transition from a grouping to group structure. It is also absurd to suggest that the development of language in the child is explained by logical progression in the grammatical rules accounting for the sentences produced by children at each age. The grammar may change, but it does not develop. Progressive grammars provide a description of the stages but no explanation of the transition from one stage to another.

gives empirical support to the developmental hypothesis that was deduced from the P-models.[5] C-models cannot be used in this way because the temporal structure of the skill is ignored.

The distinction between these two kinds of models applies to verbal representations of phenomena as much as to pictorial ones. In fact, most of the phenomena to be discussed in this book lend themselves more to written descriptions than to oversimplified and overly specific schematic drawings.

In summary, we need both C-models and P-models. The latter (especially if we try to represent them pictorially) have the disadvantage of becoming either simplistic or terribly unwieldy and specific to a given phenomenon. C-models help us to see the resemblance among disparate skills: to subsume them under general kinds of organization, for example, Piaget's operational structures. The danger, however, is that we reify those structures and treat them as though they were in the child rather than something we impose upon our observations. That in turn leads us to treat the structures as the things that develop. When instead

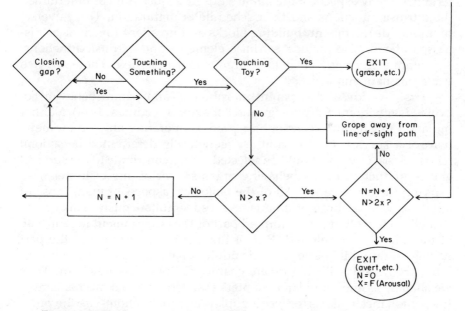

Figure 2-3. The lower right-hand section of Figure 2-2, with a new subroutine added (age 9 months). (From Kaye, 1979a.)

5. Detour problems have a long history in comparative psychology; they are one basis for concluding that dogs are more intelligent than chickens and that chimpanzees are more intelligent than dogs. We shall see in the next few chapters that what eventually makes the human 18-month-old more intelligent than a chimp is the way the human parent gets involved in the infant's problem-solving play.

we think in terms of P-models, although they be abstract and incomplete ones, we begin to specify what it is about the organism's behavior that leads it to the kinds of experience, including interactions with others, that will motivate and inform the development of the actual mechanisms of skills.

Extrinsic Functions

What I have just said implies that we should not expect to find the explanations of development within the child. We must not think of the world as a chaotic flux that the child organizes and reorganizes for himself because of an intrinsic quest for order or in obedience to universal laws regarding the genesis of structures. Instead, at least some of the responsibility for development lies with the adults who organize the child's experience in certain ways.

The difference between extrinsic and intrinsic functions is not the same as the question of nurture versus nature. The point about extrinsic functions is that much of nurture is, in fact, nature; evolution has determined many aspects of the infant's *experience* just as it has determined the intrinsic functions and their schedule of maturation. The "givens" of human development, building blocks and invariant functions as discussed above, also include extrinsic elements and extrinsic functions: An infant's environment is to a large extent inherited. There are two ways this happens.

First, we know that parent morphology and parent behavior co-evolved with infant morphology and behavior (Freedman, 1974). Neither mutation nor natural selection is a process operating only on the newborn of a species. On the contrary, genetically determined behavioral tendencies at any age should be selected if they contribute to the survival and reproduction of the behaving organism, or of any of its relatives carrying the same genes. All of the biological aspects of man, those of adults as well as those of infants, evolved simultaneously. This means that all such evolving traits formed part of the environment in which all of the others were selected. Part of the infant's environment, the part having to do with species-specific adult behavior, shares its own evolutionary history with the innate characteristics of the newborn. Thus we shall be assuming in later chapters that certain social mechanisms—interaction mechanisms for feeding, play, and instruction—are the products of evolution every bit as much as those features we think of as innate to the individual organism. In fact, it can even be argued that such jointly evolved social mechanisms are likely to be more stable, once evolved, than particular traits intrinsic to either the infant or the adult alone. The morphology and behavior of one are not free to vary without changes in the morphology and behavior of the other. A direct analogy is the relation between the shapes of orchids, whose anthers are deep within the flower, and the long proboscises of insects that fertilize them (Darwin, 1862).

Second, a good deal of the environment into which a human infant is born is a matter of cultural transmission and cultural evolution. The latter is a very different affair from biological evolution, since cultures experiment and pass along the fruits of their experimentation in Lamarckian rather than Darwinian fashion. (In essence, Lamarck believed in the inheritance of characteristics acquired by one's parents in the course of their lives, not just of random mutations that happened to have adaptive value. Although wrong with respect to the origin of species, Lamarck's model does fit cultural innovation and transmission.) It is important to remember that cultures are adaptations to the species. This is especially important with respect to developmental processes, which must have placed a great constraint upon cultural evolution. Culture—including, for example, language—consists of just those aspects of social life that survive from one generation to the next. Early man was not free (and neither are we despite all our technology) to design any system of life he could imagine. To survive, it had to be a system transmittable across generations. This meant that it had to be suited to the processes by which people educated their children or by which young adults learned from their elders. It also had to facilitate, not obstruct, the processes of cognitive as well as physical development that had evolved over a much longer span of time. For example, no culture could have arisen in which children were prohibited from imitating. Thus the universal aspects of infants' culturally transmitted nurturing environments turn out to be also a matter of nature.

Mutual Adaptation. We are here only foreshadowing the kind of reasoning that is to come in subsequent chapters, but it will be helpful to mention a few examples of what I presume to be the evolved fit between infant and parent behavior. Let us begin with maternal anatomy, where the point is most obvious. The newborn comes equipped for sucking with a suitably shaped mouth; strong buccinator muscles; rooting, sucking, and swallowing reflexes; and the ability to coordinate these with breathing. None of this would be of value if human mothers did not come equipped with nipples of appropriate size and shape for the newborn's oral cavity, suited to just the kind and amount of expression produced by the sucking movements, responsive to the range of suction pressures infants happen to create, and so forth. In the next chapter I shall make almost the same argument with respect to more global aspects of mother and infant behavior during feeding. Others have used the argument to explain the universal adult reaction to the obnoxious, unignorable sound of a child's cry.[6] The argument is really no more speculative in these cases than with respect to the anatomy of the mother's breast. In both cases we guess that the good fit between the two partners is more than fortuitous, that it actually resulted from mutual natural selection.

These examples have to do with basic survival mechanisms. But there is also a fit between the developmental functions intrinsic to the infant's *cognitive* mechanism and some extrinsic functions having to do with the ways adults will interact with him. For example, imitation is an intrinsic cognitive function, operating during most of the life span as a basic process in the development of skills and the formation of one's personal identity. It involves much more than the sensorimotor ability to assimilate another person's action to one's own schema, accommodate the schema, and reproduce the action. We shall see that the ability to imitate relies upon certain fundamental human interaction patterns involving turn-taking, self-repetition, and the fact that adults and older children systematically analyze the younger child's imitative attempts. They then emphasize the mismatch between those attempts and the behavior they are trying to model. Imitation, in short, depends upon the way behavior is presented by models as much as it does upon the intrinsic information-processing capacities of the learner. Along with learning ability, the human species evolved teaching ability. This is not to minimize the extraordinary learning capacities of infants; we merely assert that the whole story is not understood until we extend our psychological analysis to the larger system of which the infant is part.[7] While doing so, we remain within an evolutionary perspective.

A good example of this kind of fittedness comes from the work of Stern, Beebe, Jaffe, and Bennett (1977) on face-to-face play between mothers and infants. They found that the head, arm, and body movements of mothers in that situation, as well as their vocalizations, were highly repetitive. Variations were introduced subtly over a series of repetitions, as though mothers were holding down the variability so that their infants could tune in to the regularity. Gestures and vocalizations to older children and to other adults are much more variable: In fact, what mothers do and say to their babies would seem terribly monotonous to an adult interlocutor (Chapter 10). Stern et al. point out that

6. A good discussion of all the pertinent evidence on this topic is found in Murray's (1979) review. She shows that, whereas it is universal to react to the cry, there are differences in the latency of the response (Western mothers often wait 5 or 10 minutes or even longer, while hunter-gatherer mothers respond within a few seconds), and there is a whole spectrum of types of response ranging from feeding to murdering the baby. So an "evolved fit" is no guarantee that cultural change will not come into conflict with biology. But (at least up to the present) it has been culture that has had to yield. Biological limitations have always constrained the kinds of cultural variation that were possible.

7. As the next chapter will indicate, I am using the word *system* here only in the sense of parents and infants having evolved together.

this high degree of regularity and repetitiveness, with just a moderate degree of variation thrown in, is precisely the kind of stimulation we know from experimental research to be optimal for attracting and holding an infant's attention. Is this pure coincidence? Does each mother learn by trial and error how to capture her baby's attention? Or is the fit provided to at least some extent by the history of the species? In this example we have moved beyond just the matter of specific reflexes and schemas fitted for survival, as in the case of sucking/feeding and crying/responding, to more general aspects pervading several different modalities of behavior through a wide age period. Furthermore, the fit seems in this case to have more to do with guaranteeing the infant's cognitive growth than with his physical survival.

Opportunism and Culture

Any discussion of the uniqueness of our own species risks falling into anthropocentrism and thence narcissism. Impressed by our own special attributes, we may forget that all the other species are unique, too, in their own ways. After all, we cannot change our skin color to blend with our surroundings, fly under our own power, or glow in the dark. There is no criterion by which those abilities should be considered less remarkable than the ones we do possess. What is extraordinary about man, however, is that we are adaptable to so many diverse demands; that so much of our adaptation is left to learning, and thus to culture. The variability among human languages may be no greater than the variability among butterfly wings, but the latter is found genetically among different varieties of butterflies, whereas any infant from anywhere in the world can learn any of the world's languages. That fact is even more remarkable than the languages themselves.

The two facts are related: that we are a highly "opportunistic" species able to adapt our behavior to a wide variety of conditions and that we rely heavily upon cultural not just genetic transmission (Bruner, 1972). Both these facts obviously depend upon the learning capacity of the individual organism. Less obvious is the fact that, as those developmental processes evolved (i.e., the universal processes underlying the acquisition of culturally specific behavior), they did not have to be adapted to human cultures or to human languages. Just the opposite must have been the case. The specific cultures were made possible by the evolution of developmental processes. Man did not first evolve language and then have to evolve a set of learning mechanisms and parent-infant mechanisms that were capable of teaching young children its complexities. Instead, no natural language could have arisen that was not easy for young children to learn.

Thus we are looking at developmental processes as the crucial elements in the evolution of man. This leads to a more productive focus than previous generations of developmental psychologists have had. It should not be the business of a theory of human development to explain maturation. Maturation of functions universally[8] found in the species, which means maturation according to an intrinsic genetic program, is an important study in its own right but is not a question of psychology. Instead, our job is to explain what is universal about the process of development of skills that depend upon experience. Those skills themselves may be universal in the species because the experience is universal, or they may vary across cultures that offer different experiences. In other words, a theory of development will attempt to explain how all children acquire the knowledge and behavior (including language, beliefs, norms, values, etc.) of their own families and communities. To the extent that learning to walk is a matter of maturation—even if practice, exercise, and nutrition are involved in that maturation—to study it would be a counterproductive digression for psychology. The same might be true for the development of eye-hand coordination, if that were pursued for its own sake. Our more important task is to explain the development of behavior that cannot be guaranteed by the genotype.

As mentioned above, this approach does not pit biology against environment. Cultural differences as well as individual differences are produced over and above universals. They are, in fact, made possible by the biologically evolved infant himself.

Holism without Romanticism. All of the above considerations lead us to the right kind of holism. Keeping a reasonable perspective on the various kinds of evolution will help us understand the ways in which human infants are inherently social. Their mental and social life is all one, right from its beginnings. This does not mean, however, that the infant is a social individual, a person with communicative intentions like yours or mine. The infant does participate in interaction, but by no means as an equal partner.

As this argument unfolds, we shall be rejecting both the traditional and the currently fashionable views of infancy. We reject the view that infants enter into a social contract only after their development as cognitive isolates has progressed sufficiently for them to decenter and locate themselves in a relative space. That idea has its parallels in certain theories about the origins of human society (the theory that early man banded together into larger groups as agriculture permitted economic

8. By "universally" I of course do not mean to deny that there will be phenotypic variability as well as some few individuals entirely lacking the functions. I mean universal in the sense of not varying among cultures.

specialization), but there is no virtue in such parallels. Of course, culturally and biologically evolved social patterns must be intimately connected with basic processes of development operating at the level of each individual organism. These different levels, however—development, species evolution, and the history of culture—are related to one another in complex ways. They are certainly not mere recapitulations of any divine structural principle.[9]

The other view to be rejected is the romantic one, attributing to the newborn all the social impulses that define our species. It sees these social impulses as merely to be realized in a more differentiated way as the infant matures. That is the view of those who let ideology dictate their psychological conclusions; it is just not supported by evidence.

The human infant is born social in the sense that his development will depend from the beginning upon patterns of interaction with elders. He does not enter into that interaction as an individual partner, as both of the views just mentioned hold. The first suggests that interaction does not really occur until after some autonomous cognitive development. The second holds that the infant enters into interaction with parents, as an individual partner, at birth. I shall argue, instead, that interaction does begin at birth but that infants only become individual partners gradually, as a direct result of those interactions.

The best word I know for what the infant gradually becomes is a *person*. When we use that word in ordinary speech—even if we apply it figuratively to a pet dog or cat—we imply certain characteristics and social understandings that are normally attributed only to humans. I shall argue that from a psychological point of view the young infant, though human, is not yet a person; but I hope it is clear that this has nothing to do with his personhood from any moral or legal standpoint.

This prelude on the nature of explanation in developmental psychology has been necessary because the movement of the whole field up to the present has been toward a gaping rift between the believers in empiricism, who have unfortunately treated the child as the unit of analysis, assuming that forces act upon him and transitions occur within him, and those holists who have been all too ready to abandon science altogether whenever they could not produce empirical evidence to support their intuitions or ideological premises. One of the main points of this book is that a holistic explanation of human cognitive growth in its original social context requires a more scientific, rather than a less scientific, approach than has been the case in the past.

9. Skinner (1981) joins the structuralists in assuming, only for the sake of elegance, that the same principle (in his case, the principle of selection by consequences) must explain change at all levels.

3

The Mother-Infant "System"

I must create a system, or be enslaved by another man's.

William Blake, *Jerusalem*, 1804

Ten years ago, this chapter would have reviewed traditional descriptions of the young infant as disorganized, victimized by the "blooming, buzzing confusion" all around, and a passive recipient of nurturance; and then would have proceeded to debunk those myths by discussing the evidence then beginning to accumulate. The evidence indicated that infant behavior is organized in certain respects right from the start, that the newborn's visual and auditory apparatus bring a degree of order to bear upon the stimulus world, and that the behavior of mothers and other caretakers is influenced by their babies' behavior.

Now those recent findings have themselves become the prevailing myths that need to be at least partly debunked. We should try to do so without letting the pendulum swing all the way back again, for the truth lies somewhere in the middle.

The shift in fashion among infancy researchers in the 1970's was a benevolent one, for the most part. Pediatricians and nurses awoke to the psychological side of their patients, who previously had been too often treated as though all that mattered in the first year were their physical survival and growth. And psychologists began to realize that physiological state, arousal, parent-infant interaction and affect, rather than just being inconveniences in the way of proper experimental design, were among the phenomena to be understood. To most parents, it was not news to hear that young infants were interesting and personable creatures. Many, however, were relieved to hear it from the mouths of "experts." It relieved them from the conflict between their subjective impressions and some beliefs inherited from their grandmothers: that babies could not see anything in the early weeks, that a

30

smile was "just gas," etc. And for those who were more ambivalent about their roles—teenage unmarried mothers, for example—intervention programs could emphasize early emotional attachments and ways of eliciting optimal infant reactions that would reward the mother's efforts and thus combat her insecurity (see Epilogue).

In the long run, however, any benefits of these new ideas about infant capacities will depend upon their being true. An exaggerated view of the young infant's cognitive abilities or contribution to social interactions would be as detrimental to the goals of clinical practice and intervention programs as the opposite point of view was. In fact, it is already possible to see some unfortunate effects of the new attitudes. At a time when birth control, abortion, and social acceptance of unmarried mothers have reduced the number of newborns available for adoption to a small fraction of the number of couples seeking to adopt, it is a shame that some of these couples have been made to feel that they should not adopt an older infant because the first few months are so crucial for the establishment of normal parent-infant communication and attachment: especially if that hypothesis, which I shall call the Hypothesis of Critical Dyad-Formation in the First Few Months of Life, turns out not to be true.

Even more important than the practical implications of the new ideas is their effect on theory. The exaggeration or overinterpretation of infant capacities in the past decade has held back our understanding of basic issues in human development. It has amounted to something like a denial of the fundamental questions we have to ask. Instead of pursuing a theory of how infants learn to communicate, to share adult representations of objects and events, to have human minds rather than simply nervous systems, and to be individual persons in interaction with others, a number of investigators have concluded that all of these things are true at birth or soon become true by maturation alone. They choose to emphasize intrinsic functions. By exaggerating the levels of those functions at birth, they try to explain away some of the mysteries that developmental psychology has to deal with, the very mysteries that have led so many psychologists to begin looking at infants in the first place. I shall discuss the arguments of those authors and reach different conclusions.

Rapid strides began in the 1960's in two other fields, ethology (with its comparative and evolutionary implications for our own species) and linguistic philosophy. This work brought a new excitement to psychologists of development, motivating us to search for the origins of our species's uniqueness. Man's superiority to other creatures is clear by the second year of life but is far from clear in the first. We know that some foundations for language must be laid down in infancy: But what foundations? How are they established? To learn our parents' language, did we bring all the equipment we needed with us in the form of maturing brain functions, or did we have to derive some of it from experience with objects and with elders?

Those are the kinds of mysteries that began to be pursued in the 1970's. They encouraged broad theorizing, and they encouraged psychologists to read widely in all the different disciplines concerned with the nature of man. Powerful ideas from other fields in the social sciences were introduced into the literature on infancy. Two of these are central to the theme of this book: the idea that parent and infant constitute a "social system," and the idea of "intersubjectivity" or a shared understanding between individuals. Both notions are involved in communication and therefore in the origins of symbolic processes. Both can be viewed as only gradually coming to be true of the infant and his parents, and therefore as defining the problem for researchers: How do the parent-infant system and intersubjectivity develop? That is how we shall pose the question. We shall not assume that infants are born members of a system, that they already possess intersubjectivity, or that it emerges intrinsically. Instead we shall take a critical look at these two major concepts, with the purpose of pushing them toward more rigorous definitions so that it will be possible to say when they are and when they are not true of human infants. This chapter and the three following deal with the social system idea. Chapters 7 through 10 take up intersubjectivity.

The Social System

The concept of "system" entered the vocabulary of human infancy researchers in the mid-1960's, when many influential child psychologists, pediatricians, and psychiatrists (Ainsworth, 1964; Bell, 1968; Bowlby, 1969; Brazelton, 1963; Richards, 1971; Robson, 1967; Sander, Stechler, Julia, & Burns, 1969; Schaefer & Bayley, 1963; Schaffer, 1963; Yarrow & Goodwin, 1965) began calling attention to infant effects upon parental behavior. They also began analyzing the whole, the dyad, as somehow more than the sum of its parts. And they began to break down the traditional compartmentalization of cognitive, social, and affective development. For example, the sensorimotor period (which had been discussed primarily from the point of view of cognition) was the same period as that of attachment formation (which had at first been seen as primarily a social and affective phenomenon).

Using the word *system* to describe complex interactions would be justified only if they could not be represented adequately by the simple sum of infant responses plus parental responses. In other words, a real system is "more than the sum of its parts." However, none of these authors really had a strict criterion in mind. They were moved to refer to the "mother-infant system" just because of the bidirectional effects, mothers reacting to infants as well as infants to mothers, and because of the sheer complexity of those effects and the difficulty of analyzing them.

Meanwhile, the idea of a "social system" was treated more rigorously by other social scientists, as a type of "open system," which in turn had a well-defined meaning in General System Theory (von Bertalanffy, 1968). We shall see that, if the concept "mother-infant system" or "dyad" has any useful meaning, it must correspond to this rigorous usage, not to the vague implication of complexity or bidirectionality. And there are two distinct senses in which mother and infant may comprise a system, a sense having to do with the evolution of the species and another quite different sense having to do with the development of an individual mother and infant.

System theory originated in the late 19th-century revolt against reductionism, against molecular and mechanistic theories in physics, and eventually against using those theories as models of the mind and of human society.[1] What makes a system open as opposed to closed is its functioning as a unit so as to exchange energy and information with its environment. The functioning of the parts is subordinated (organized) to a goal or direction of the whole. By virtue of this organization, the second law of thermodynamics (entropy) is violated. Over the lifetime of the system there is "negative entropy," an increasing organization. Energy is brought into the system to counteract entropy, and information is created in the system. An important part of the theory is that this occurs at a decreasing cost: The system develops so as to function more efficiently vis-à-vis the outside world. (An automobile engine, over time, tends toward entropy. It is a closed system. As the interacting parts wear down and lose precision, the performance of the whole declines. A horse, over the same period of time, grows internally more complex— i.e., gains information—and performs more efficiently. It is an open system.)

All social systems, whether human or animal, are open systems; in fact, in a biological context the word *system* always implies *open* system, whether infraorganism (e.g., the cardiopulmonary system) or social (e.g., a hive, a community, an institution, or a small task force). Many social systems consist of dyads: husband-wife, employer-employee, pupil-teacher, or parent-child. However, not just any relationship between organisms is a system. Two paramecia in a drop of water interact with one another—the behavior of each affects the behavior of the other—but their joint action is only the sum of their separate actions and

1. The open/closed system contrast was a renewal of classical analyses of organic as opposed to inorganic nature. For a bridge from Aristotelian to 19th-century natural history, see von Humboldt (1849, e.g., "The Vital Force," pp. 401–410).

reactions. By contrast, a social system has a direction as a whole, to which the individuals are at least partly subordinated.

Figure 3-1 lists examples of interaction between organisms, all of which depend to some extent on the way the species have evolved (so all are systems in that sense). There are two critical distinctions to be made, and only those relationships that meet both criteria can truly be called social systems.

		(SOCIAL SYSTEM)
SHARED DEVELOPMENT	enemy armies horse and rider	husband and wife pupil and teacher two wolves
INDEPENDENT DEVELOPMENT	wolf and caribou two paramecia	strangers in elevator bees
	SEPARATE PURPOSES	SHARED PURPOSE

Figure 3-1. Levels of Interaction.

The first criterion is that of sharing a history. The relationships in the upper quadrants of Figure 3-1 all develop among the individual members; they are not merely inevitable because evolutionary histories were intertwined. As an example of the latter, take the Alaskan caribou and the wolves that prey upon them. These two species are complexly related parts of an ecosystem. Yet the individual wolf separating out an elderly or lame caribou from the herd is not responding to knowledge of the habits of that particular animal gained in the course of their relationship as members of a system. Their relationship is by virtue of their species, not their individual development. By contrast, a horse and its trainer can anticipate one another's behavior due to their experience in the relationship. Two opposing armies in a protracted war certainly do that. So do the wolves with respect to the other wolves in their own family. The difference between social mammals—wolves, whales, primates—and social insects like bees is the difference between two ways of knowing the other members of one's family. Social mammals know each other as individuals. They are able to anticipate one another's behavior because they have grown up together. Social insects know each other only as drone, worker, queen. Each one plays its role and is able to anticipate others' roles only through what is programmed into it genetically. The bees actually constitute a system only in the sense that drone and worker evolved together, with the selection of traits in each depending upon their adaptive value in an environment that included the traits of the other. They are not a system in the sense of relationships among individual members.

The second criterion is whether the members are working toward common ends. This criterion is independent of the first. The social insects do work together, despite not knowing each other as individuals. Similarly, two strangers in an elevator arrive at a satisfactory division of space without having to bump one another paramecium-fashion. This is because they share a common goal, as the bees do with one another and the wolves do with their family members but not with the caribou. (It can be argued that some horse-human or dog-human dyads are social systems, but these are exceptional; in most cases there is no real shared purpose, even when there is shared experience.)

Note that all four cells involve intentional or goal-directed behavior. However, only in the right-hand cells do members share the goals. On the left side they may accomplish ends that are mutually beneficial (e.g., population control) but those ends result only from their pursuit of independent or even conflicting goals.

The strangers in the elevator achieve their shared intention by signaling their intentions and anticipating one another's moves. Yet the relationship lasts less than a minute. Their ability to anticipate one another's behavior does not depend upon a history of shared development. The mechanisms of communication between them are partly innate, like those of the bees. But they depend also upon cultural conventions each has learned in interaction with others. In this respect they do have parts of their personal histories in common. In other words, their individual development as members of social systems—in their families, their schools—has prepared them to behave as social organisms even with strangers. Mothers and fathers have this advantage; babies do not.

What the Members of a System Know. My two criteria correspond to the way the word *system* has been used in sociology and social psychology, long before it was borrowed by students of infancy. A crucial aspect of social systems is the perception that individuals have of the whole and of their places in it. This does not mean that they consciously analyze it as the psychologist does. It means that each member behaves intentionally so as to capitalize on as much behavior of others as he can anticipate. Their behavior does not simply happen to fit neatly into a pattern of joint action, like that of the social insects. Members of a system know when other members are or are not performing their roles. And it is not enough for only one member to be responsible for that awareness: A mother and infant do not begin to be a social system until the infant, too, has expectations of how the mother will behave. These must be expectations based on experience together, not genetically programmed information like the expectations spiders have about the behavior of flies.

A softball team is a good example of a social system, and it illustrates how the performance of a role depends upon knowing how the other members will perform their roles. The pitcher who sees a grounder go past him toward right field runs to first base because he knows that the first baseperson will leave the bag to field the ball; the first baseperson, in doing so, is already preparing to throw quickly to first base, knowing the pitcher will be there. Furthermore, he adjusts his throw according to his knowledge of how fast the individual pitcher and hitter can run. The most important point is that the team improves in effectiveness and each member improves in his own role as a direct result of learning to anticipate the behavior of the other members (Mead, 1934). (We are not talking about certainty, about *knowing* how others will behave, but about guessing with greater and greater accuracy.)

How does a new member enter the system? More easily the more experience he has in similarly functioning systems. A team can assimilate a new first baseperson easily if that player has played first base for another team. The less knowledge the new member brings, the more the old members will have to accommodate to him, anticipating his limited ability to perform his own role. Conversely, the more ably the old members make the system function while the new member is learning, the more he can develop by socialization and the less he needs to be preprogrammed. This is exactly the situation with human infants. The issue is not only how soon is the newborn infant ready to play his role as a member of a system, but how capable is the system of functioning as if the infant were already playing that role while he is learning to do so? Research has provided some answers to both questions, and with the foregoing considerations in mind we can turn to the evidence.

Evidence of the Mother-Infant System: Microanalysis

Investigations of parent-infant interaction with the hope of testing the applicability of the concept of social system have mainly involved mothers rather than fathers or other caretakers. This does not mean that psychologists have assumed only the mother-infant dyad is a system;

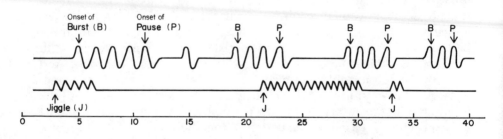

Figure 3-2. Organization of sucking into bursts, with mother's jiggling; first 75 seconds of a bottle-feeding, age 2 weeks.

but since the mother is the person with whom the vast majority of young infants spend the vast majority of time, that relationship seems like the best place to look for evidence of a system. The studies can be divided into two types: those based on microanalysis of interaction, discussed in this section, and those based on stability of variables distinguishing individual dyads across situations and across time, to be discussed in the next section.

The review of relevant studies is necessarily selective. I shall begin with some studies of my own, which will be referred to again in later chapters; then I shall discuss some of the most important findings and arguments of other investigators.

Neonatal Feeding. Unquestionably the most advanced behaviors in the newborn infant are those having to do with the coordination of sucking. The feeding interaction is more complex and quickly established at birth than anything else mothers and infants do together. Is this complexity sufficient to say that the dyad behaves as a social system?

In the first month of life, all human infants suck in bursts of 4–10 sucks at about one per second, separated by pauses of about 4–15 seconds. A burst-pause pattern has not been found in any other mammals including chimps (Wolff, 1966; Brown, 1973). All mothers who have been observed[2] try to intervene in the burst-pause pattern by jiggling either the baby (if breast-feeding) or the bottle. They do not do this in every pause, nor do they restrict their jiggling only to the pauses. But they do it significantly more often just after the baby pauses than at other times. This is illustrated in Figure 3-2.

The fact that we have seen this stereotypical jiggling response in the first pause the first time the baby was put to the breast, in mothers who had never fed or even held another baby, strongly suggests that it is an instinctive response to the baby's burst-pause pattern. In a series of studies, we investigated whether the jiggling really has the effect mothers think it has (Kaye & Brazelton, 1971; Kaye, 1972, 1977b; Kaye & Wells, 1980). Figure 3-3 shows the effect of jiggling upon the duration

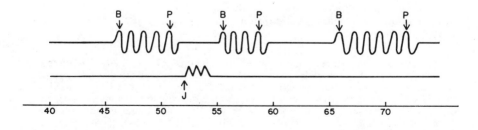

2. We can report only on British and American mothers, but discussions with anthropologists strengthen my faith that mothers everywhere respond in these ways.

of the pause.[3] Mothers' jiggling per se suppressed the likelihood of resumption of sucking (lengthened the pause), but *jiggling and stopping* did in fact tend to elicit the next burst. It will be important for the reader to understand the way this is demonstrated because we use the same method of analysis in other studies. The effect of the mother's behavior is expressed in terms of conditional probabilities, similar to a biostatistician's conditional mortality rates. Of all those pauses that have lasted at least x seconds, what proportion will end in the next 1-second interval, and is this likelihood affected by whether the mother has jiggled? After $x + 1$ seconds, a smaller number of pauses remain for consideration. How does the likelihood that they will end depend on whether the mother has jiggled? For any 1-second interval we were concerned with three conditions, as shown in Figure 3-3: segments of pauses in which

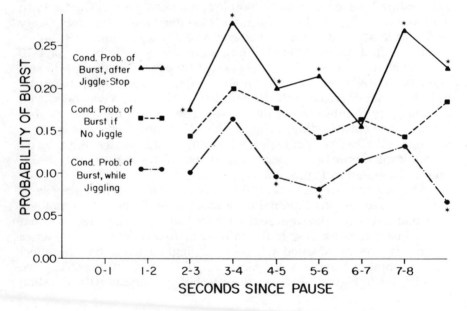

Figure 3-3. Probability of burst onset as a function of time since end of previous burst ($*$ = significantly different from baseline, $p < .05$). (From Kaye & Wells, 1980.)

3. Our data come from 52 mothers and their infants. Although all were white and English-speaking, they otherwise represented a diverse sample of families from all socio-economic levels and a variety of ethnic backgrounds. They were recruited for our longitudinal study during pregnancy or a few hours after delivery in a community hospital in Chicago. The same families participated in the various studies by Kaye and Wells (1980), Kaye and Fogel (1980), Kaye and Marcus (1978), Kaye (1977b, 1978, 1980b, 1980c), and Kaye and Charney (1980, 1981). They were observed in the hospital at age 2 days, and thereafter in their homes.

the mother had not yet jiggled and the infant had not yet resumed sucking; those in which she was jiggling; and those after she had started and stopped jiggling. Each point represents bursts-per-opportunities-to-burst at that point in time.

Kaye and Wells also demonstrated this contingency experimentally in 12 infants whom we fed ourselves, administering jiggles of different latencies and durations in a predetermined schedule. The effect, eliciting a resumption of sucking, was found only after short (1–2 seconds) jiggles, regardless whether those began immediately after the pause or a few seconds later. This is shown in Figure 3-4. Such a contingency would predict that mothers ought to learn to shorten their jiggling, and that is exactly what we found. Over the first 2 weeks, the average mother's median duration of jiggling declined from 3.1 seconds to 1.8 seconds, a result that was significant in a longitudinal sample observed both at 2 days and at 2 weeks as well as in cross-sectional samples.

All of these results held true in bottle- as well as breast-feeding, with experienced as well as inexperienced mothers, of boys as well as girls. Whether the change in mothers' behavior over time is actually due to the infant contingency shown in Figures 3-3 and 3-4 cannot be proved directly. What we do know is that the infant's pause tends to elicit the

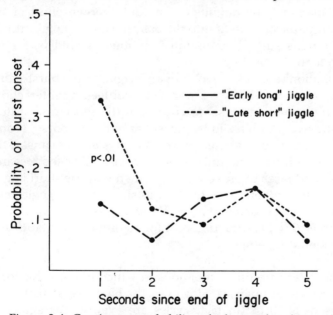

Figure 3-4. Contingent probability of a burst of sucking, after the end of a long versus a short jiggle. ("Early long" and "late short" jiggles were timed by the experimenter so as to end at the same time (5 seconds) after the onset of the pause.) (Data from Kaye & Wells, 1980.)

mother's jiggling and that the cessation of her jiggling tends to elicit the next burst. Thus we have demonstrated at birth the kind of two-way directionality and the evolved fit between infant and maternal behavior that had led other investigators to use the words *system* and *dyad*.

Despite the fact that this phenomenon is the earliest instance of turn-taking and of mutual contingency that has yet been found (and it is difficult to imagine finding an earlier instance), I do not consider it evidence of a social system. For the infant's bursts and pauses are a neurological phenomenon, susceptible to adjustment but not through any intentional modification or any anticipation of the partner's behavior. It is the mother who fits her intervention into the infant's activity in such a way as to have a predictable effect upon it. If she does not do so, the infant's pauses may be a little longer, but the bursts come eventually and the milk gets consumed. In fact, there is no satisfactory functional explanation for the pauses except in terms of their effect upon the mother. It can be shown that they are not for breathing, swallowing, or resting. Since they occur in bottle-feeding, they cannot be a response to the emptying of the milk sacs (though the emptying and refilling might have been involved in their evolution). Most remarkably, they appear to be a uniquely human phenomenon, while nursing itself is common to all mammals by definition. The only known effect of the pauses is to prompt mothers to fit into the baby's pattern, to take turns. Apparently, if infants sucked continuously mothers would take a far more passive role in the feeding.

If our speculations about the evolutionary origins of the burst-pause pattern are correct, then what we see in neonatal feeding interactions is a system in the evolutionary sense but not in the sense of a system developed by the two partners. To be present at birth, of course, it only has to be a system in the first sense. However, a mystery remains. If the interaction pattern is innate and universal—and we really need research in other cultures and races to prove that it is—then why are short jiggles not innate? Why do mothers have to learn to shorten their jiggles and learn it again with each subsequent baby? We shall postpone these questions until Chapter 6, where the different forms of mother-infant turn-taking are considered together.

Face-to-Face Play. There are other situations in which infant behavior is organized into bursts and pauses. However, the burst-pause pattern of sucking is present at birth (in fact, cycles are even more regular in premature newborns), whereas in other domains, such as facial expressions directed toward an adult, the temporal organization only emerges gradually.

A study by Kaye and Fogel (1980) helped to elucidate the temporal structure of mother-infant play. We videotaped our 52 mother-infant pairs in their homes at 6, 13, and 26 weeks. The infants were held in the mothers' laps, facing them, for 5 minutes of play ("Just try to get his attention and play with him as you normally do"). This situation has been more or less the standard paradigm for students of early communication over the past decade, though for the cameraperson's and coder's convenience other investigators have usually strapped the infant into an infant seat instead of asking the mother to hold him.

Our videotapes of face-to-face play at 6, 13, and 26 weeks were coded in an elaborate assembly-line procedure involving seven passes through each of 133 5-minute tapes, using a total of 25 categories. The occurrence of events in each category was recorded on a digital event recorder to a precision of 0.2 seconds, then stored in a computer. The details of this work are reported in a number of papers (Fogel, 1977; Kaye, 1977b; Kaye & Fogel, 1980), including our procedures for establishing reliability. Some of the tapes coded by one coder were randomly reinserted in the list for another coder to do; the coders did not know which tapes these were. In this way we ensured, not only in training coders but in the actual process of coding, that all our categories were agreed upon 85% of the time or better; and that nearly all events were coded within 1 second of their actual time of occurrence on the videotape (Kaye, 1980a).

At 6 weeks the infants' smiles, vocalizations, and wide-mouthed expressions were randomly distributed throughout the session. They were just as frequent when the infants were looking elsewhere as when they were attending to the mothers (eyes open and directed at mother's face). The expressions were also randomly distributed in time, with respect to each other; that is, there was no "clustering." This is shown in Figure 3-5, where the log-survivorship distribution of intervals between expressions by the 6-week-olds fits the straight line predicted by a Poisson (random) model (Cox & Lewis, 1966). By 13 weeks, however, the infants' expressions tended to occur in clusters, so that there were more of them within a few seconds of each other than would have occurred by chance. This is manifested by a steeper slope, in the log-survivorship distribution at 13 weeks, for interevent intervals less than 5 seconds. By 26 weeks there was a sharper clustering, especially when the infant was attending to the mother.

These data are representative of the fact that the "organization" loosely attributed by Brazelton, Koslowski, and Main (1974), Trevarthen (1977), and others to the young infant only appears gradually in modes of behavior other than neonatal sucking. The organization of sucking is an inborn organization. The organization of face-to-face expressions

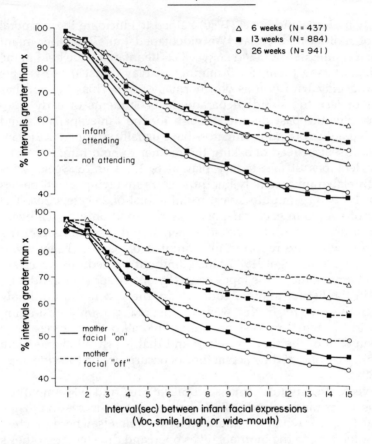

Figure 3-5. Log-survivorship functions showing clustering of infant facial expressions directed toward the mother and elsewhere (top), and as a function of mother's facial activity (bottom). Total number of events: 437 at 6 weeks, 884 at 13 weeks, 941 at 26 weeks. (Data from Kaye & Fogel, 1980.)

is decidedly not. And sucking is something the baby alone does, whereas infant expressions toward adults resemble the parents' expressions toward the infant. The 6-month-old infant, whose facial expressions are clustered into dialogue-like "turns," is an infant who has already done a lot of watching and imitating, hence could have begun to accommodate to the mother's way of behaving. There is no reason to suppose that any systematic interaction we see between infant and maternal expressions is inborn.

It would be wise, therefore, to look closely at the temporal relation between the infant's facial expressions and those of the mother. Figure 3-6 compares the likelihood of *spontaneous* infant expressions after attending to the mother (as defined above) with the likelihood of the same expressions as *responses* to the mother's having first smiled or opened her mouth wide, etc. By plotting the likelihood of the same class of infant behaviors under two different maternal conditions, as a function of time since onset of infant attention, we control for variability in the timing of the mother's greeting.[4] The change with age is apparent: At 6 weeks the infant expressions occurred as responses if they occurred at all; at 13 weeks they were much more frequent responses, and we also began to see some greetings initiated by the infants; at 26 weeks these spontaneous greetings were just as frequent as the responsive ones. In fact, at 26 weeks the mothers' greetings made no difference as elicitors of the infants': The infants were more likely than not to produce one of the criterion categories of facial expression within 8 seconds following the onset of attention (based on the fact that the cumulative probability over the function plotted in Figure 3-6 is 53%), regardless whether the mothers greeted them or not. In other words, the mothers' behavior changed from being necessary but not very effective at 6 weeks, to less necessary but more effective at 13 weeks, to neither necessary nor effective by 26 weeks.

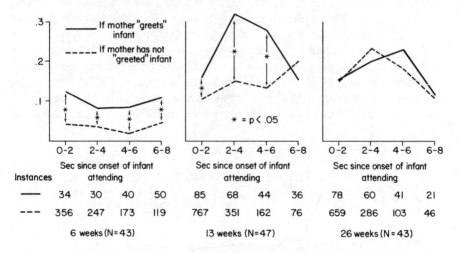

Figure 3-6. Conditional probability of infant "greeting" mother, as a function of time following onset of attention to her face, depending upon whether the mother first "greets" the infant. (From Kaye & Fogel, 1980.)

4. Each onset of attention is regarded as an opportunity for the infant to greet the mother under the dotted-line condition, up until the time she first greets him; thereafter it is treated as an opportunity for an infant's greeting under the solid-line condition. At any point, the mother either has or has not greeted her infant. When an infant greeting occurs, the opportunity has been taken and is not counted in subsequent time intervals.

The two sets of findings together give a clear picture. At first there is only a slight tendency for the parent to be able to elicit a smile or other positive facial expression, and this does not even depend on the infant looking at the parent's face. Slowly these expressions begin to be elicited more reliably during mutual gaze, and finally they no longer depend upon elicitation at all; they become "greetings" at the onset of mutual gaze, so that the infant has assumed some responsibility for performing a partner's role in face-to-face play. As we shall see later, a mother rarely fails to respond to one of these greetings as though it were a significant communication from the baby.

A Teaching Situation. In another study (Kaye, 1977a), with the infants sitting in their mothers' laps at a table and attempting to reach a toy behind a Plexiglas barrier, we again found mothers creating a turn-taking structure. The mothers, who had simply been asked to "help in any way you can," reached for the toy (to demonstrate the path around the detour, or to make the task easier by bringing the toy part way out) in response to a clear sign from the 6-month-old infant. Figure 3-7 demonstrates this finding in a previously unpublished replication of the original study. (The replication subjects were all of the Kaye and Fogel dyads at their final [26-week] session.) The contingency analysis shows that the sign consisted of a glance away from the task and then back to it. As a result, infants were able to watch a demonstration, make their own attempt, and elicit another demonstration (Kaye, 1977a). This does not mean, however, that their "signs" were intentional. In the terminology we shall dwell upon later, they were merely *indices* of the failure

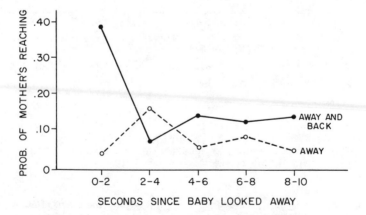

Figure 3-7. Probability of mother's reaching, as a function of time since the infant looked away, depending upon whether the infant first looks back to the task. (Previously unpublished data.)

of goal-directed reaching, to which the mothers responded systematically. As in face-to-face play at the same age, some of the responsibility for the interaction now rested with the infants, but only because their mothers structured their own behavior around those signs.

Other Evidence. A large number of close studies of young infants and mothers, mostly in the face-to-face situation, have produced some consistent findings about the complexity and bidirectionality of effects in adult-infant interaction. None of these findings, however, justify calling the mother-infant dyad, in the early months, a "system" in the sense defined above.

One group of studies shows different behaviors in infants when they are with their mothers as compared with other women (Bronson, 1972; Campos, Emde, Gaensbauer, & Henderson, 1975; Carpenter, 1974; Turnure, 1971), with fathers (Parke, 1979), other babies (Field, 1979; Fogel, 1979), or inanimate objects (Trevarthen, 1977). The reasonable conclusion from these findings is that infants, from birth, are responsive to differences in stimulation. There is nothing remarkable about that. They also fixate more on moving versus still faces (Carpenter, 1974) and talking versus silent faces (Freedman, 1974). The strong form of the system hypothesis requires something more: that the infant differentiate behaviorally between his mother and another person *given the same behavior on the part of the other*. Contingency functions like those in Figure 3-6 should be different for mother-infant versus stranger-infant. (It can be argued that this would still not be sufficient evidence, because the fact that the stimulating behaviors produced by mother and stranger happened to fall in the same category would not mean they behaved identically, but it certainly would be *necessary* evidence.) Apparently Fogel (1981) is the only investigator who has attempted a contingent analysis of that kind. He found no differences at all in 2-month-olds' behavior with mothers versus strangers in the face-to-face situation.

If an infant's behavior with mother only differs from his behavior with a stranger because the mother and stranger themselves behave differently, then the interaction does not depend upon knowledge and expectations of the partner, acquired in the course of the "shared development" discussed above. Knowledge and expectations imply something more than the fact that the infant can *discriminate* between stranger and mother, which can be inferred from the infant's behavior as early as 2 months (Carpenter, 1974) by such criteria as proportion of time attending or latency to smile. Instead, we are asking about differences between the contingent patterns of interaction with mother and those found in behavior with others. That kind of partner-specific behavior does not exist in the early months. In the second half-year, when attachment to the mother as a special person becomes evident in proximity-seeking behavior, it is hard to resist the conclusion that a system has been formed. But I shall argue in Chapter 12 that proximity-seeking alone could be accomplished merely by the fact that some characteristics of mothers in general and some characteristics of babies in general co-evolved rather than by mutual exchange of specific signals. To see a true social system in action, we must wait for the use of conventional signals, which the infant will begin to acquire between 9 and 12 months.

Another kind of evidence commonly cited in justification of the "system" idea is that infant behavior and parent behavior are both contingent upon one another, moment by moment. No better example of this can be found than in our study of neonatal feeding, but there are also many similar reports in the literature on early vocalization (Strain & Vietze, 1975), gaze (Stern, 1974), smiling (Emde, Campos, Reich, & Gaensbauer, 1978; Fraiberg, 1974), state of arousal (Brazelton, Koslowski, & Main, 1974; Korner, 1974), crying (Bernal, 1972; DeVore & Konner, 1974; Wolff, 1969), to list only a few. This work has long since laid to rest any one-way models of behavioral effects, if indeed anyone ever really held such a model. However, those mutual contingencies are provided by evolution, not by the shared experience of the individual mother and baby. So this body of evidence, too, falls short of what is required by the rigorous meaning of system.

Finally, there are some important experiments involving violations of normal behavior. Spitz and Wolf (1946) found that 3-month-old babies smiled to nodding wooden model heads as well as to actual faces but that they would not smile to profiles, real or wooden. Tronick, Als, and Adamson (1979) asked mothers to stare blankly at their infants for part of the session, then to show their profiles instead of the head-on view. Babies as young as 10 weeks reacted with marked cessation of activity, a suppressed rate of smiling and vocalizing, and a "worried" look.[5] Trevarthen (1977) reports similar results, when a few mothers were uncomfortable in his laboratory situation (see also Mundy-Castle, 1980). These studies all show that the infant expects face-to-face interaction to proceed in certain ways. But what is the nature and origin of those expectations? Their origin is an innate response repertoire that is effectively suited to some kinds of adult behavior—the kinds adults normally produce—and poorly suited to others, which adults do not normally produce. In other words, those expectations do not depend upon the development of a dyadic relationship with a particular caretaker.

---

5. It is interesting that this procedure does not produce distress in the infant; he merely seems to be adjusting to the level of arousal that the mother establishes, and this may be a means by which different cultures socialize different modal levels of affect (Tronick, Ricks, & Cohn, 1982; see Chapter 10).

Furthermore, despite the studies just mentioned, it is possible to violate the rules of normal interaction in what to an adult is a startling fashion, yet not disturb the infant so long as one has not interfered with his ability to engage in mutual gazing, smiling, and vocalizing. Bower (1974) used mirrors to present infants with three identical images of their mothers, each interacting with them "live." Up to 6 months, the infants did not seem at all surprised or disturbed, interacting normally with one image and then another. Bower's infants only began to show Stage IV object permanence with their mothers—that is, recognition that a mother's face should only be in one place at a time—shortly before object permanence with inanimate objects. The mother's face was apparently the first object to become "permanent"—*in the seventh or eighth month.*

What do all of these studies, and the many others with similar findings, tell us about the mother-infant or parent-infant system? They show that the infant's attentional preferences are well fitted, "pre-adapted" to just the kind of stimulation normally provided by parents' faces. They also show an increasing ability of adults to get reactions from the infant comparable to the kinds of response the adults have been making to him. That increase is very gradual, only beginning at about 3 or 4 months and not approaching anything like symmetry. The results also show an increasing expectancy on the baby's part of what normal adult behavior consists of, without any evidence of specific expectancies about the parent as opposed to others. And they show an increasing initiative on the baby's part to greet the adult on a reciprocal basis—but only after age 5 months or so.

Perhaps most important, they show that the first stimuli the infant learns to recognize as familiar are parts of the mother. He habituates to her face, with the result that he fixates longer on other faces (Carpenter, 1974); he recognizes her voice, so that hers is more effective than other voices at coaxing a smile out of him (Wolff, 1963; Fraiberg, 1974). None of this is sufficient to satisfy the criteria for a social system, but it does tell us something about the context in which the infant's earliest schemas begin to differentiate.

In the first half year, parents and infant undergo a shared history. The process, which is only possible because human adults and infants coevolved as a system, leads—eventually—to the infant becoming part of the parents' social system. This can only happen, however, to the extent that the infant accommodates in the long-term sense, involving representation in the form of schemas for social interaction. The latter are not the same as built-in preadapted mechanisms well suited for survival, as in sucking, or for bonding the parent, as in smiling and eye contact. Nor do I mean by accommodation merely moment-to-moment contingent responses. Accommodation means change in the underlying competencies for behavior, that is, modification in schemas, not just in action. All these issues remain to be considered further in later chapters.

Referring back to Figure 3-1, it is important to emphasize that none of the studies of interaction in the earliest months show shared purpose between infant and adult. There is intentionality in the infant's behavior itself. There is also some sharing by the parent of the infant's intentions, to the extent that the parent can make correct guesses about those intentions. Later, in the second half-year, these correct guesses plus the baby's imitation of the parent's actions upon objects will introduce the first glimmers of mutually shared purpose.

Evidence of the Mother-Infant System: Individual Differences

In the foregoing section we used microanalytic studies of interaction at different ages to address the notion of the mother-infant system, specifically to see how early shared intentions appear and when the young infant makes use of knowledge of the mother gained from their shared experience rather than from the species' genetic endowment. For those studies, data from many dyads were pooled together. But the system idea also leads to a strong hypothesis about continuity in differences among dyads. This was the reason we did all our microanalytic studies with the same longitudinal sample. We considered the hypothesis to be more than simply the idea that infant behavior and maternal or parental behavior were evolutionarily adapted and mutually fitted to one another in the species. If they were systems, individual mother-infant dyads would develop together over time so that at some point they would depend upon knowledge of one another's behavior as individuals, not just wired-in schemas anticipating the behavior of any mother or any baby. The question is how early that point is reached.

Since the experimental method (swapping babies among parents) was impracticable, our longitudinal project with its microanalytic studies of different domains of interaction in the same large sample of families would have been the most promising approach to test the Hypothesis of Critical Dyad-Formation in the First Few Months of Life, that is, the idea that mothers and babies adapt to one another very early as individuals, not just in the species-preadapted sense. If mothers and infants begin to learn to be a dyadic system soon after birth, then the experience of an individual mother and baby together in the various domains of interaction—feeding, play, and instruction—should matter a great deal. Learning how to interact in one task should transfer to another task, especially if both tasks require turn-taking, monitoring one another's behavior, and so forth. Therefore individual differences in the separate studies should be reliable over time and across tasks. When we designed this project, we hoped that the measures derived from our fine-grained analyses would prove to be more sensitive longitudinal predictors of the child's development than traditional infant assessments had been. Our reasoning was that we had assessed contingencies between the partners as they behaved with one another, and thus we were coming closer to tapping actual developmental processes than if we had made assessments of the infants alone. Longitudinal predictability is, in essence, a matter of transfer from one domain of interaction to other domains.

There were indeed individual differences in this sample within each separate domain of interaction. For example:

——Kaye and Wells (1980) found that the likelihood of a mother's jiggling during a pause (as opposed to her infant's resuming sucking before she jiggled) differed among the subjects and was a reliable characteristic of their feeding interactions between 2 days and 2 weeks.

——Kaye and Fogel (1980) found individual differences in the mothers' abilities to elicit a "greeting" from their infants in response to their own greetings (smiling, nodding, vocalizing) when the baby made eye contact.

——The content, length, and repetitiveness of the mothers' utterances to the babies in the face-to-face task all showed highly reliable individual differences across the sessions at 6, 13, and 26 weeks (Kaye, 1980b, 1980c).

——In the detour-reaching task, while the mothers' likelihood of intervening was always higher immediately after the infants glanced away from the barrier than while they were actually trying to deal with it, still the mothers' quickness to intervene varied considerably. The mean likelihood of a mother's reaching for the toy behind the barrier within 3 seconds of her infant's glancing to the side was 27%, with a standard deviation (SD) of 18%. This means that mothers 1 SD above the mean intervened about five times as frequently as mothers 1 SD below the mean (27% + 18% = 45%; vs. 27% − 18% = 9%).

——Furthermore, as we had also found in the original study (Kaye, 1977a), the different types of intervention—whether to demonstrate how the toy could be obtained, to attempt to push him toward it, or to simplify the task—were used with different frequencies by different mothers.

The hypothesis of most concern to us, however, was whether these individual differences within each of the several situations we studied would be related to one another. For this purpose we restricted our analysis to just those 48 variables that had been interesting enough in their own right to have been defined and discussed in our published studies of the separate domains of interaction. The list, though only a small selection from among the variables originally measured, would

yield 1128 first-order correlation coefficients. Of those, 788 were correlations over time, predicting from one situation to another.

Before analyzing those predictive associations we removed a common source of variance that many of the variables shared, the socioeconomic variance as measured by mothers' education. This was
significantly related to 12 of the 48 variables; other demographic break-
downs (by marital status, family size, infant's sex, etc.) showed very
few differences in our sample. Consequently we partialed the effects
attributable to mother's educational status out of the 788 longitudinal
correlations, and the results were quite clear. Only 50 of the partial
correlation coefficients, or 6.7%, were significant beyond the .05 level;
hardly more than one would expect by chance.

What mother's education represents, in a sample like ours, is social
class. It is important to acknowledge this. Partialing out mother's education not only removed any significant continuity from our measures
of dyadic interaction; it also left us with no continuity in those variables
that an earlier generation of investigators might have considered to be
assessments of the infants alone (e.g., crying during sessions). The same
result is found in projects more intensively devoted to infant assessment
and much longer-term follow-up, especially where the predictions attempted are cognitive ones (Kagan, Lapidus, & Moore, 1978). Educational (or economic) status of the family accounts for practically all the
stable variance one can find among individual infants. This does not tell
anything about the relative importance of middle-class parental behavior
versus middle-class genes. It does, however, so far absolutely fail to
justify the belief that to predict infants' developmental success we have
to observe the interaction of the "system" as opposed to grosser assessments of the parents alone.

Considering that many of these tasks and contingency scores were
selected deliberately because of their structural similarity to one another—that is, their face validity—the lack of continuity among the measures is remarkable and compelling. Beyond the social-class differences
within our sample, we found practically no relationship between the
individual performances of our mothers or infants in any one situation
and their performances in another situation at another age.

Other Evidence. Nor has such evidence emerged in any other studies of
this kind. Of course, most studies have either been microanalytic studies
with an *N* of 1–5, or employed grosser variables (e.g. frequency of crying,
time spent feeding baby, etc.). Only a few longitudinal studies of sizable
samples have been relevant to the question of the mother-infant system.
Thoman, Acebo, Dreyer, Becker, and Freese (1979) found reliable individual differences among 20 pairs observed at home for 7 hours at 2, 3,

4, and 5 weeks. The exceptionally long observations and the fact that they were only 1 week apart undoubtedly accounted for the stability Thoman et al. found. But it also should be noted that their subjects were observed in the same situations each time. We, too, found stability within tasks; neither they nor we found evidence of any sort of system enduring across different situations. The Thoman et al. study is a good illustration of how much the variability of infant behavior must be smoothed over long observations in the full range of states of arousal, before reliable measures appear.[6] It does not, however, show enduring or pervasive characteristics of the mother-infant pair as a "system" because the continuity can be attributed to continuity in either of the two separate individuals (perhaps in the mother alone).

A large longitudinal study that found continuity over the first 9 months and from that period to a follow-up at 2 years was conducted at the University of California, Los Angeles (Beckwith, Cohen, Kopp, Parmelee, & Marcy, 1976; Cohen & Beckwith, 1979; Sigman, Cohen, & Forsythe, 1981). The study involved 50 preterm infants and their "primary caregivers" (usually but apparently not always their mothers), and the interaction behaviors were of the checklist, 15-second time-sampled variety. The continuity that was found was neither continuity of interaction nor of dyads. Although interactive behaviors were involved, they did not seem to have predictive stability after partialling out variables assessable in the mothers themselves. The authors realized that what they had found was consistency in mothers, not in dyads:

> The study suggests that it is possible to identify early in the first year those caregivers who are engaged in and are likely to continue to engage in a low level of social interaction with their preterm infants. Such a low level is then predictive of lowered infant competence at age 2. [Cohen & Beckwith, 1979, p. 775]

Essentially the same conclusion emerged from a study by Clarke-Stewart and Hevey (1981), using longitudinal data between ages 1 and 2½. Even after dyadic behavior patterns are well established, the literature shows far more continuity in maternal behavior differences than in children. Dunn and Kendrick (1980), for example, studied mothers' interactions with their firstborn 1- to 3-year-olds before and after the birth of a second child. Despite gross changes in frequencies of behavior (increase in negative, restrictive behaviors and decrease in positive, nurturant behaviors), Dunn and Kendrick found that individual differences among the mothers were highly consistent. They retained their relative

6. This is shown also in our own study of Brazelton assessments (Kaye, 1978), and more generally in personality assessment (Epstein, 1980).

rank orders in nearly every category observed, while there was considerable change in the individual differences among children.

Looking at the literature as a whole and taking account (so far as one can) of the vast number of correlation coefficients that have been computed, it is clear that any stability in observational measures is merely stability in certain variables of maternal behavior (mostly variables accounted for by socioeconomic status, mother's age, ethnicity, etc.) or in a very few infant variables. The latter, in fact, are so few in the first 6 months and so far from being replicated across studies (except for differences between preterm and full-term infants, Caucasian and African and Oriental infants) that we should beware of any analysis of parental behavior in relation to so-called infant variables. Parents' behavior does vary as a function of the infant's age, sex, state of health, and mood at any given moment, but these variables are different from the sort of stable characteristics of the parent-infant relationship that are implied by the concept of "system."

This conclusion is consistent with our data showing that the relationship gets off to a new start in each new domain of interaction. We also showed that whatever continuity exists is found in the maternal measures rather than in the infant or interaction measures. To the extent later competence is predictable at all from behavior in the first year, it is predictable from parental variables, not from any "system." There is, in fact, no evidence of stability in the relationship between individual infants and parents in the first half-year of life.

Conclusion

The widespread use of the notion of a mother-infant interaction system has simply not been based on rigorous evidence. As mentioned above, it came into vogue as a result of several lines of argument. One was the idea that the feeding interaction, for example, must constitute a system beyond the sum of its parts simply because it is so complicated. This idea we have rejected because it is the mother alone who goes beyond the sum of action and reaction.[7] The infant, of course, is an active partner having definite effects upon the behavior of caretakers. But we must distinguish between an infant's effect and an infant's intention to produce an effect (an issue to be treated at length in Chapters 7 and 8). We must also distinguish between the effects of infants in general, upon caretakers in general, and the effect of individual infants upon their individual parents in some lasting way so that their relationship is itself a developing system. The latter idea followed only as a hypothesis from

---

7. It only takes *one* to tango, as Fred Astaire showed in his famous dance number with a hat rack (*Royal Wedding*, 1951).

the former. The Hypothesis of Critical Dyad-Formation in the First Few Months of Life has not been confirmed.

Other justifications for talking about a mother-infant system are based upon the evolutionary rather than the individual-experiential sense of the word. It is certainly true that parental and neonatal behavior have evolved for one another. But this does not automatically have implications regarding the relationship between individual adults and their offspring.[8]

Nothing that I have said in this chapter is to deny that critical processes of adjustment to the infant, and of emotional attachment, and of self-concept redefinition, take place in mothers right after giving birth (e.g., Sander, 1962; Klaus & Kennell, 1976). What I am denying is that these processes are to be located within the dyad and, hence, that they are a matter of communication. The extent to which adjustment has to occur in parents, as a precondition for the infant's learning to be a member of their system, is the principal theme of the next few chapters. We shall find a great deal of asymmetry in the relations between parent and infant, so that the temporal structure that eventually becomes a true social system will at first only have been created by the parent, making use of built-in regularities in infant behavior rather than actual cooperation or communication.

Another way of stating this is that evolution has produced infants who can fool their parents into treating them as more intelligent than they really are. I shall argue that it is precisely because parents play out this fiction that it eventually comes to be true: that the infant does become a person and an intelligent partner in intersubjective communication.

The conclusions of this chapter have strengthened the arguments of the preceding one: that we need to take a holistic view placing much of the explanation for human development in phenomena external to the child himself, that this in turn requires us to understand that parents have evolved along with infants, and in particular that there is nothing to be gained by a romantic and dogmatic faith in the innate capacities of the newborn. But the chapter has also shown that we still lack a theory of the actual processes by which an infant becomes a symbol-using, communicating person.

8. Chappell and Sander (1979) have emphasized the biological system of mother-fetus and felt that naturally this system must continue to exist after parturition. But the mother-fetus system in fact does not continue—it is cut off with the umbilicus. The prenatal physiological system is much the same in other mammals. The *social* system is a different matter. It has evolved from a fairly brief relationship in many species, through more and more prolonged childhood dependencies, with man at the extreme. Furthermore, in all these species postnatal care of the young depends upon completely different behavioral patterns than those of reproduction and gestation.

4

The Apprentice

Man is the only one that knows nothing, that can learn nothing without being taught. He can neither speak nor walk nor eat, and in short he can do nothing at the prompting of nature only, but weep.

Pliny, *Natural History*, ca. 70 A.D.

We are now ready to integrate the topic of Chapter 2—"What is it that develops in the developing individual?"—with that of Chapter 3—"What is the nature of the system that develops between individuals?" Are these separate and independent kinds of development? Are they two ways of looking at the same process? Are they two processes, one of which is necessary and/or sufficient for the other to occur? Or are they simultaneous processes, mutually dependent?

Inside-Out and Outside-In

Every developmental theory assumes, at least implicitly, some relation between the systems within and the systems outside the organism, that is, between the skills and representations within and the social relations without. Theories differ as to whether the course of development is inside-out or outside-in. Does cognition unfold according to an intrinsic plan and then affect the child's relations with others? Or do those relations somehow develop first, then shape the development of skills and, in effect, mental life?

The most thorough exponent of the inside-out view of infancy was Piaget, whose theory we shall discuss in this and later chapters. I shall argue that it contains two unsatisfactory features: first, instead of explaining the development of human infants by specific processes, it falls back upon broad structuralist principles which are not explanations; and, second, it implicitly assumes that adult behavior is not universal

54

and therefore cannot contribute to the universal aspects of infants' cognitive development.

The leading exponent of the outside-in view, Vygotsky, as well as other authors who view the mind as an internalization of language and culture, unfortunately begin their analysis at the end of the period we are considering. They assume the availability of a symbolic code by means of which the child gains access to the powerful but culturally constrained categories of thought, either through the medium of language itself (e.g., Whorf, 1956) or through dialogue with adults (e.g., Vygotsky, 1962). But they tell us nothing about how the child comes to be able to grasp the meaning of that code in the first place.

Since the inside-out and the outside-in theories have in fact focused upon different age periods, they are not necessarily incompatible, and the obvious temptation would be to accept Piaget's account of how symbolic processes develop, arguing that the direction is inside-out in infancy and then outside-in once the child shares the language of his community. However, we would still have to meet the objections to Piaget's theory that I just mentioned. An alternative temptation, which we shall discuss in Chapter 8 because some authors have succumbed to it, is to dismiss the problem of developing communication and shared meaning by claiming that it exists almost from birth: If the infant is innately social and innately communicative or "intersubjective," then there is nothing to explain. Unfortunately, these claims are either romantically vague or empirically unsupportable.

The conclusion to which the rest of this book leads is that the outside-in view can, in fact, be extended down to infancy. When we take into account the social context with which adults surround infants, and when we accept the principle that parental behavior is every bit as much a part of infants' innate endowment as their own intrinsic processes are, we can derive a theory of how communication itself develops and how it culminates in a symbol-using mind.

A metaphor for this theory, which I offer at this point so that the reader can judge how well it fits the more concrete considerations I shall introduce, is an apprentice in the shop of a master craftsman. The apprentice learns the trade because the master provides protected opportunities to practice selected subtasks, monitors the growth of the apprentice's skills, and gradually presents more difficult tasks. We can see this basic parental role in many domains, at all ages. Sometimes it is more obvious than at other times. When my father taught me to swim, he backed away as I paddled toward him. I can remember crying that it was unfair—but 25 years later I did the same thing to my son. It may be less obvious when parents teach children to weave, to hunt, to count, to read, to do geometric proofs, and now to write computer programs, but in each case the main thing we do is pose them manageable subtasks, one step at a time, and gradually pull that support away from them as their competence grows.

In Chapter 5, I shall describe various concrete forms of that relationship during infancy. Here, let us begin to consider the kinds of changes that take place in the infant's skills and in the relations between those skills and the adult system.

A Skill Is an Open System

I have pointed out that an organism is the very model of an open system, with all its parts interconnected and with its genetic code repeated in every cell but distinct from every other organism; yet the basic open-system properties of goal-directedness, reorganization, and negative entropy (von Bertalanffy, 1968) are found in intraorganism systems (the circulatory system, the pulmonary system) as well as interorganism ones (families, governments). All have in common the capacity to bring about modifications in their own situation, which is essentially the definition of action. Planets, rivers, and basketballs, which are closed systems, move but do not act; hearts and lungs and families do act. Thus the same distinction between organic and inorganic is imbedded in the concept of action (Chapter 2) as in the concept of open system (Chapter 3).[1]

We turn our attention now to those intraorganism systems called skills or schemas. Our purpose is to link what we know about the structure of skills, in P-model terms, to what we shall find to be true of the interaction between infants and adults.

Skill, the regularity underlying action, is an open system for the accomplishment of ends by variable behavioral means. Action can take a variety of paths depending upon circumstances, recognizing when specified ends have been attained. Alternative paths, or means, generally develop through a splitting called *differentiation*, by analogy to cell division in embryology. The results of varied trials will lead to a decision that affects the way the system operates in the future. Skills, as open systems, develop; they become organized so as to deal more efficiently with whatever factors have to be controlled in the attainment of particular goals. As soon as we choose to describe human activity in terms of intention, we are choosing an open system model of skill.

In fact, behavioral evidence requires us to choose such a model. The subject persists in the face of failure or obstruction, varies his movements nonrandomly in a direction to circumvent obstruction, initiates

1. The same need for intellectual unity across all levels, from infraindividual to suprasocial, was met a century ago by the concept of evolution, and in the 16th and 17th centuries by the "spheres." Such unifying descriptions are aesthetically satisfying but not logically defensible. We cannot be satisfied with them as *explanations* of phenomena.

or resumes his activity in the absence of any external stimulus, and ceases his activity when the goal has been reached. We can see all these features in infants' actions, for example, in the detour task. However, we can also see something else. The persistence and directedness of a sequence of acts is due to the hierarchical organization of skills. This involves some basic concepts, which we shall discuss in some detail before returning to the social framework "outside" the infant.

Hierarchy, Intention, Coordination. All plans, strategies, and skills are characterized by hierarchical organization, with subroutines embedded in larger routines (von Uexkull, 1957). Miller, Galanter, and Pribram (1960) described this structural characteristic as the Test-Operate-Test-Exit (TOTE) unit. The flow of signal-processing must be characterized by nested loops rather than by a sequential chain. While engaged in Plan X, we initiate Subplan Y (which in turn may require Subsubplan Z), and when Subplan Y has been completed we continue with Plan X. When we reach for an object, for example, many different component acts are involved: raising the upper arm, extending the forearm, opening the hand, orienting the fingers, etc. Instead of happening all at once or in random order, the component responses and the sensory control that monitors them are organized hierarchically like a computer program with subroutines to be called in at appropriate points. A theory of skill, therefore, has to account for the relation between skills and subskills, not just the relation between acts in sequence.

In Chapter 1 I described how Nikki, a 2½-year-old, went off to the bathroom by herself. "She turned on the light in the bathroom, pulled down her pants, sat down, urinated, stood up, pulled up her pants, turned off the light, and rejoined us in the living room." That chronological account disguised the true structure of her action:

> leave others
>   turn light on
>   pull pants down
>   sit down
>   urinate
>   stand up
>   pull pants up
>   turn light off
> return to others

What is it that maintains Plan X after the execution of Subplan Y? It is clear that the concept of purposiveness really implies not only the original intention but also a kind of memory for the direction of the whole. It is due to the purposiveness of behavior that an actor can descend into nested subroutines and return again without getting side-tracked. When an infant is reaching for something, and activates a schema for hand orientation or for grasping, the latter might be expected to distract him from his reach. Because it does not, we can say that the infant has not forgotten his intention. In other words, his memory in this case is sufficient to maintain a programmatic pattern of behavior, organizing means toward an end.

We may ask of the infant at any age, for what ends does he have organized means? In other words, what intentions can he carry out? What skills does he possess? We may find that the 1-month-old's hunger cry is well-organized in terms of TOTE units but that his tracking of objects is not. A month later, he will have the skill of tracking but not reaching. At any age when the infant cannot yet carry through an intention with a particular level of complexity, there is always the possibility of some external supporting framework making some of the subskills unnecessary. A "walker" chair does that for the 9-month-old who cannot yet stand alone. The intervention of adults can provide a similar framework in other situations. For example, the 2-month-old cannot swipe effectively at a mobile hanging above his crib, but if we tie a string around his wrist and attach the other end to the mobile, he can make it dance. What we have done is to make the visually guided reaching TOTE units unnecessary and to make the circular reaction of arm-shaking effectively a mobile-shaking skill.

At a later age, Nikki provided an example of hierarchically organized behavior involving more than her own intentions and more than her own skills. The purposiveness in that sequence was supplied to a great extent by her mother. Originally, it was not Nikki's intention to use toilets at all. Once she had accepted that goal, she needed no instruction in what to do once seated in the proper place, but it was her mother who had pulled down the training pants for her and who pulled them up again afterward. Later, when those steps were added to Nikki's own routine, it was still her mother who took care of the light switch; even when Nikki began to turn it on herself upon entering the bathroom, she would not have remembered to turn it off afterward. And it was the mother who was vigilant for signs that it was time to go, who excused herself and Nikki from company and went along to help her. At 30 months when we happened to be there to applaud that momentous achievement, the mother was still helping with the vigilance; Nikki was capable of all the rest.

At every step of the training process Nikki's mother had to be a placeholder and pathfinder. The differentiation and coordination of means-end schemas depends upon this frame, extrinsic to the child. Examples of such framing behavior are rare in other species, and always much more limited in complexity, lacking the frame-within-frame-within-frame quality seen constantly in humans. When we do see complex hierarchical action patterns in other species, we find them either in unlearned action patterns, such as a spider's weaving, or in animals trained by humans in the circus or in the laboratory. We do not see it in behavior that animals acquire through ordinary experience. (I do not know whether one could *train* a rat to pull a bag out of a garbage can, fill it with edible treats, then drag the whole bag away. Left to its own devices, however, the rat will eat the food or carry it off one item at a time. It will never learn on its own to save trips by using a container.)

I suggest that what makes embedded plans a largely human affair is more the way skills are *taught* by humans than the way they are learned. Furthermore, despite the enormous variation in specific techniques of instruction—including demonstration, operant shaping, verbal explanation, cue enhancement, and combinations thereof—one constant feature of human teaching is the way the possessor of the skill serves as repository of memory for the learner, ready to bring him back to the appropriate place when a given subskill has been executed. This is as true of a parent helping a child with homework and a professor helping a graduate student organize dissertation research as it is of a mother helping her infant retrieve a toy or use the toilet.

Feedback. Although in principle purposive action is possible without the use of feedback en route to the goal, many kinds of action must require periodic tests both in order to facilitate adjustment and in order to know when an intermediate goal has been reached so that the next step can begin. These periodic tests are TOTE units. The behavior of a toddler trying to stay near a moving mother is similar in this respect to the behavior of a singer who has to sustain a constant note, or of a skier, or of a gull flying in the slipstream of a ship. Nearly every kind of animal alters some of its actions as a function of movement-generated feedback.[2] In addition to its guidance function, this kind of feedback seems to be important for learning. Certain kinds of environmental information will either not be attended to, not be processed, or not be stored by organisms unless the information is generated as feedback from voluntary action. In the classic study by Held and Hein (1963), for example, kittens who had been reared entirely in the dark and then walked through a pat-

2. The experiments proving this involve deprivation or distortion of feedback produced by action (Hinde, 1969). Feedback control loops also play a central role in models of human skill developed by Deutsch (1960), Bernshtein (1967), and Welford (1968), and the analogy with computer programs has been with us since before the first electronic computer was built (Craik, 1943). Neisser's (1976) reformulation of his theory of perceptual processing, stressing the cyclic as opposed to linear relation between stimulus and perceiver, emphasizes the feedback control loop.

terned arena developed the appropriate depth reflexes; while each kitten's partner, whom it towed through the arena sitting passively in a little cart, was significantly retarded in visual perception of depth. The development of these reflexes apparently requires experience with the visual consequences of voluntary movement. With human subjects, corroborating results have been found for both perceptual and motor learning (Held, 1965; Holding & Macrae, 1964).

The need for feedback, information generated in the course of action, helps us understand why infants and children resist attempts at teaching them new skills by pulling or pushing their limbs. For example, in the detour-reaching situation that has already been discussed, many mothers tried once or twice to push the infant's hand around the Plexiglas barrier to help the infant discover that the toy could be reached that way. This seems a sensible idea, but the infants usually tensed and sharply flexed their arms at all three joints (shoulder, elbow, and wrist). We noticed that mothers tended to resort to the pulling-and-pushing teaching strategy mainly out of frustration, when they thought the babies were close to a solution or when an infant was already crying (Kaye, 1977a). Otherwise, the preferred method was to time the interventions to the breaks in the infant's own trials; in other words, to work on building a sequence of systematic trials, allowing feedback to do its own work on the component skills.

The use of feedback to guide action depends upon the fact that the action has a goal and that the schema provides for systematic monitoring and correction of acts in relation to the goal during execution (Bernshtein, 1967; Boden, 1972). The word *feedback* can be extended to include reinforcement by the consequences of acts as well as the response-contingent information used en route to a goal. We should simply regard the consequences of a completed act as feedback in a higher-order program for improvement of the skill in question. In other words, reinforcement is information used en route to the goal of competence (White, 1959). Again, however, this is not just a motive in the child. It is shared by the parent. The parent is the one with the clearer image of what it will mean for the infant to be competent in a particular skill.

Putting Subskills Together. Piaget's notion of the sensorimotor schema is the same thing we call a skill, and its hierarchical organization is an important aspect of Piaget's theory (in fact, it is the "structure" of sensorimotor intelligence). The result of having a schema is a programmatic action sequence. Just as the organization of a skill is such that other skills can be embedded within it, the substructures that Piaget calls schemas are embedded within one another (1951, 1952, 1954). The schema for reaching-for-objects, for example, includes a schema for hand orientation. Piaget uses the word *coordinated* to include the meaning of *hierarchical*, that is, the fact that schemas do not come into play sequentially. Like the TOTE unit that forms the "Operate" phase of another TOTE unit, the second schema comes in service of the first, embedded within it. The coordinated use of schemas begins slowly over the course of the first 2 years. Piaget (1952) considers that coordination (intentional coordination, i.e., as opposed to the built-in neuromuscular coordination found at every level) can first be seen at the end of the first year, in the fourth stage of sensorimotor development. But this only applies to co-ordination accomplished by the infant on his own behalf. If we extend the idea to actions organized from outside, by other people, even the very first schemas (the ones involved in feeding) are coordinated.

The programmatic organization of schemas depends upon the generic nature of experience. If each event were entirely novel for the child, there could be no assimilation or accommodation of schemas, no hierarchical coordination of schemas, no progress toward complex organization, no development at all. It is only because new events and objects, though always more or less novel, are never absolutely novel, that they can be assimilated to particular existing schemas and those schemas in turn accommodated to them. Having reduced the adaptation process to assimilation and accommodation, and having implicitly postulated a law of similarity, Piaget's model describes the progressive hierarchical coordination of sensorimotor schemas. The ultimate forms of these substructures, the operations of intelligence, obey the formalized laws of the logical grouping (Piaget, 1950). (At that later period, the conditions of associativity and transitivity are expressions of the same hierarchical, recursive quality we found in the TOTE unit and the sensorimotor schema.)

It is, in fact, the ability of schemas to become coordinated on the basis of their common factors that allows us to attribute meaning to the schemas, and meaning to the child's experience of objects and space. (The word *meaning* here refers to the simplest form of representation, as we shall see in Chapter 7. This explains why the same word *schema*, referring to a sensorimotor skill, can also denote a representation of an object upon which the child can act.) The coordination and integration of two schemas with one another, which involves embedding not just chaining, depends upon both schemas being activated by some common contextual feature, because if both were not activated at the same time there would be no reason for them to coordinate with one another. In other words, schemas accommodate (adapt to the environment) for the same reason they assimilate (interpret the environment as fitted by particular existing schemas), and for the same reason we say more generally that skills transfer to new situations. The assimilation and accommodation of schemas hinges upon the correspondence between certain features of objects in the world and certain features of particular schemas, and also between the features of one schema and another. Furthermore, since a conception of reality is constructed through changes in the schemas underlying action, what we call *meaning* only arises through the reciprocal assimilation and coordination of schemas.

All of these observations about the relation between skills and subskills, and about the origin of meaning in the coordination of schemas, become important when we realize that the executive role in an action can be performed by an adult, while the infant is only entrusted with a subroutine. To the extent the adult can coordinate their jointly produced action, infant and adult share meaning with respect to the object world.

Attention and the Course of Skill Acquisition

We have emphasized that skills are organized hierarchically, or programmatically, referring to the fact that the attainment of a goal often requires certain subgoals along the way; subskills are nested within other skills. This same organization that has to do with the execution of skills is also important in their acquisition. The subskills that we can identify in performance often turn out to be separate units of the "curriculum"; they must be learned separately, then combined. At first, the learner has to attend to the component movements. With practice, these require less attention, which can then be focused upon the higher-level coordination. This point, stressed by William James (1890) and demonstrated by Bryan and Harter's (1899) classic study of how telegraphers learned the Morse Code, is a motoric parallel to the idea of "chunking" of information in perception and memory (Miller, 1956). As emphasized by Bruner (1971) in connection with infant sensorimotor development, it involves the assumption that attention is a limited resource. However, adults can compensate for the infant's limited attention capacity.

The principal need for attending to components comes from the use of feedback or "Test" within each TOTE unit. In this connection, Lashley (1917) first pointed out that skilled behavior does not always utilize feedback; the pianist has gone on to subsequent notes in less time than it would take to monitor and respond to the notes he hears. When typing rapidly, I sometimes know that I am about to make a mistake before I type it—but too late to prevent myself. This is because monitoring and execution go on simultaneously as various steps in the planned sequence are in various stages of preparation and execution. In order to put the parts of the skill together, therefore, one has to be able to negotiate each component with less than full attention. In fact, the less monitoring required for each of the constituents, the more attention can be focused upon the way they are put together and upon the goal to be reached. The pianist's eyes are further ahead of his fingers the more proficient he is and the better he knows the piece.

Gibson (1966) gave a good illustration of the extent to which we attend to the aims, not the components, of our skilled actions: Imagine yourself cutting with a pair of scissors. What do your fingers feel? Not the handles of the scissors but the blade slicing through the paper. It is the mastery of "chunks" or subroutines that enables us to project our attention forward to our goals rather than having to attend to our own movements.

Bruner (1971) found that children under 2 mastered discrete "modules" before learning to combine them smoothly. Elliott and Connolly (1973) noticed the same sort of modularization in children between 3 and 6, with the game of "Tilt" requiring bimanual control of a tilting, perforated board so that a marble could traverse it without falling through any of the holes. The children intuitively broke the task down into its constituent skills, which they mastered one at a time. Common experience tells us the same thing about our mastery of skills as adults. As she becomes more skillful, the tennis player will devote less attention to tossing the ball up in the air, and thus will be able to devote more attention to aiming her serve. The good player concentrates on where the ball is going to go, and her windup and swing somehow take care of themselves.

The infant, however, whose most basic motor skills (orienting, tracking, reaching, manually exploring) are still so crude as to require attention, yet whose memory is quite limited, has a real conflict when it comes to attending to goals versus means. That function is served by adults' placeholding and pathfinding, to which Chapter 5 is devoted.

One of the feedback loops in a P-model of the young infant's reaching skill is enlarged in Figure 4-1. This is a TOTE unit, with the rectangle representing the "Operate" component and the diamond the "Test." The feedback loop can be seen in the infant's reaching behavior at 3 or

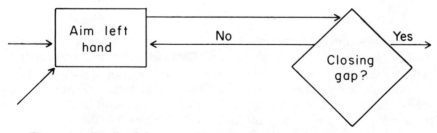

Figure 4-1. Feedback loop (a TOTE unit from Figure 2-2). (From Kaye, 1979a.)

4 months, when he sometimes glances back and forth between hand and object (Piaget, 1952). Later, he does not seem to need to monitor his hand visually—he can attend to the goal alone. Thus instead of having to carry out a series of tests by looking back and forth between hand and object, the 8-month-old will be able to integrate information from several modalities very rapidly and essentially automatically.

This takes the process of skillful action out of the realm of conscious control, so that what we think about are only the images of goals and of intermediate states en route to goals. This is why an instructor can help even though he or she has no P-model of how the desired skill is really performed. The instructor has a representation of the desired outcome and of appropriate benchmarks along the way. Theoretical knowledge of the physics and physiology of throwing a spear, weaving, reading, or playing tennis is not important in teaching someone how to do those things. The same is true in training an infant: A parent knows virtually nothing about how any of the infant's skills (reaching, finding hidden objects, naming things) are actually performed. Nonetheless, the parent facilitates their acquisition by storing representations of where the infant is and where he is supposed to be going.

So far, I have emphasized the programmatic organization of skills: the hierarchical relation between skills and the subskills of which they are composed. I have also said that skill development involves the smoothing of the lower-order constituents, the subskills (or "subroutines" in analogy to computer programs), so that they can be executed with little or no monitoring and so that attention can be devoted to the higher-order combinations. These too then gradually become more automatic, until the highly skilled individual is one whose conscious attention is devoted only to strategies. The feedback process still goes on at all levels, but it requires relatively little attention, and therefore each component of the skill does not have to wait for conscious monitoring. All this is characteristic of human skills and of human development; yet none of it would work if the human infant were an autonomous organism.

Systems Concepts and the Infant's Development

The various concepts discussed above—hierarchy, intention, differentiation, etc.—come from analysis of the individual organism as an open system. Taken together, they imply a way of looking at skills that has a considerable consensus in the psychological literature. That the terms are invoked by a broad range of theorists may be due to the fact that these notions still provide wide latitude with respect to the mechanisms of development. Differentiation, for example, can proceed according to a genetic plan, inside-out as it clearly does in embryogenesis, or according to the shaping forces outside as it clearly does in learning the nuances of a particular language. A theorist who is partial to the inside-out view can emphasize the importance of integrating constituent schemas in an intrinsically ordered hierarchy. One who is overly partial to the outside-in view might decide to ignore intrinsic factors and emphasize the role of environmental contingencies in shaping means-ends schemas. A more reasonable theory would grant the intrinsic functions but suggest that the alternative ways of differentiating are externally guided, that the feedback comes from the social not just the physical world, and that this feedback is more like a staged curriculum than a shaping by accidental contingencies.

How does the concept of system relate to the inside-out versus the outside-in metaphors? There is no doubt that the infant himself is a system, for the organism is the principal model for the definition of an open system. However, part of the definition of an open system is that it interacts with its environment and then reorganizes internally so as to deal with the environment more efficiently. Energy is conserved and information is created (referred to in systems theory as *negative entropy*). The infant's environment is, in great part, the maternal one. That is why in Chapter 3 we asked when the infant and mother together begin to comprise a system. But there is something in between being just an organism system and being an active member of a social system. The evidence reviewed so far suggests the idea of *apprenticeship*.

An apprentice to a social system would be one who is treated in some respects as a member but who does not share the other members' expectations and their knowledge of what is expected in his role. This notion can only be suggested at this point, for its elaboration is to continue in the rest of the book. Thus far I have merely pointed out that the hierarchical organization described above, besides being intrinsic to skills within an individual, can also be true of the way a social system functions. The relation of a skill to a subskill is embodied in the relation between a skilled system member, such as a parent, and a less skilled apprentice, such as an infant. The adult can take over the planning of a skilled action and have the infant perform those subskills of which he is capable. The parent-infant interaction routines that we began to discuss in Chapter 3 can be viewed as the parents' use of anticipatable regularities in infant action, as "subroutines" toward grander ends: for example, the establishment of an interpersonal dialogue, the differentiation of the infant's skills, the induction of the infant from apprentice to full partner in the system.

There are several stages in this process, stages in the loosest sense of the word: periods when particular agendas seem to be dominant. These periods, with each new level of interaction overlaid upon prior achievements rather than supplanting them, can be distinguished by different relationships between the infant's activity and the parents' enterprise. (Later I shall indicate how these periods correspond with many other authors' developmental benchmarks, which have been given other names when the emphasis was upon the infant's cognitive development alone, social development alone, parent-infant attachment, or some other agenda.)

First is what I shall call the period of *shared rhythms and regulations*. From birth to about 3 months the parent capitalizes on inborn regularity in infant behavior—cycles of sucking, attention, and arousal—to build the semblance of a dialogue. One could say the mother is entrained by the biological rhythms of the infant, but it is just as correct to say that the mother uses these rhythms to entrain the infant into patterns of dialogue that characterize the adult world. The insightful psychoanalyst Rene Spitz saw it this way:

> . . . my proposition is that the mutual exchanges between mother and baby consist in a give and take of action and reaction between the two partners, which requires from each of them both active and passive responses. These responses form series and chains, the single links of which consist in what I call "action cycles," each completed in itself and at the same time anticipating the next link. I designated these seriated response exchanges as the "precursor of dialogue," as a primal dialogue. [Spitz, 1964, p. 774]

We have already explored some of those precursors beginning with the first feeding of the newborn. Later, this dialogue framework becomes the meeting ground between what is inherited genetically (the innate behavior of the individual partners) and what is inherited through interpersonal developmental processes (the consequences of dialogue). That makes it tremendously important, because it makes the dialogue also the meeting ground between what is fixed and what is free to vary between cultures, what has evolved genetically and what may evolve culturally.

The second period, beginning around 2 months (each period overlaps the prior one), is that of *shared intentions*. Again the sharing begins as a unilateral responsibility. Adults guess at the intentions underlying the infant's activity. In doing so, they nearly always go beyond the literal meaning of the infant's goal-directed act. Mothers and fathers attribute to the infant more specific intentionality, more elaborated plans, more accurate memory, more subtlety of affect than can ever be demonstrated objectively. Intentionality is indeed there: Baldwin (1895) showed long ago how it arises from reflexive activity via circular reactions. But until recently we have missed the importance of the way parents take over these indices of intention and interpret them as if they were messages.

The "he says" phenomenon is the purest illustration of this interpretive process. Before their infant is born, parents often tell each other what "he says." As they feel his intrauterine movements, one parent translates their meaning:

"He says," explains the parent, " 'No more beans, please!' "
"She says" (if their fantasy is a girl), " 'Let me out of here!' "

After the baby is born, one parent says to the other:

"She says, 'I'm hungry, Mom.' "
"He says, 'I'm sleepy Daddy, don't bounce me so much.' "

Indices of physiological state—hunger and pain cries, or the restless movements associated with fatigue—are interpreted as if they were signs of intention to do something about the state—to eat, to escape, to sleep—or requests to the parent to do something about it. Soon the infant begins doing things that are unambiguously intentional: smoothly tracking a moving object by eye, reaching and grasping, searching for an object that has disappeared. The "he says" phenomenon continues:

"He says, 'That tastes good. I want to put that in my mouth.' "
"She says, 'Where'd it go?' "

Even without the phrase "he says" or "she says," parents have many ways of speaking for the child. We shall have a good deal more to say about this phenomenon. What the parents are doing is integrating the new child into their already existing social system.

By 8 months or so, the sharing of intentions—through guessing at what the other's actions mean—has become a two-way process. The infant's schemas, differentiated through experience in certain behavioral frames imposed by adult behavior, allow him to anticipate the most likely direction of that behavior. Thus he shares the adult's intentions for the first time. Once this occurs, and he begins to comprehend signs, a new level of parent-infant relations becomes possible, characterized by *shared memory*. The mother, father, or other caretaker (such as the grandmother in our observation of Dylan in Chapter 1) can begin to rely on the fact that the infant has memory of certain experiences that they have shared. For example, they give him a certain stuffed toy to which he has demonstrated an attraction, and they assume that this toy has a specialness for the child and that he remembers its previous appearances. Or they say "No-oo-oo!" in a certain tone of voice, conventionalized on prior occasions. Word and gesture signify those prior occasions to the parents themselves and are assumed to signify them to the infant.

The signifiers for salient "signified" events are stored and presented repeatedly by the parent, so that differentiating the signifier-signified relation in general requires nothing more (and nothing less) than the ability to anticipate what the adult partner will do next.

The fourth period is the beginning of language proper, *shared language*, when the child participates (albeit crudely at first) in the true medium of social discourse and, ultimately, of internal discourse as well. Although Nathan (Chapter 1) used only one word, even his nonverbal behavior demonstrated an ability to marshal the help of others for his own ends. He could gesture, anticipating the responses his gestures would elicit. As we shall see, that is what it means to say the child has language.

In each of these periods, parents treat the child as more mature and more of a partner than he really is. Admittedly, there are real cues from the child that show he understands more than he did last week or last month. But the higher forms of interaction into which the adults slip are inevitably more advanced than what the child is actually capable of at the time. Thus parents are constantly drawing the child forward into a more challenging apprenticeship, eventually into a full partnership.

Apprenticeship Is a Human Privilege

There is a hierarchical or means-end structure, then, in the social process of skill transmission just as there is in the acquired skills themselves. The subassemblies being put together in the early months of sensorimotor development include essential features of a social matrix within which all subsequent development will take place. If human development occurs in ways fundamentally different from what we see elsewhere in biology, and depends upon empathic processes that we would not attribute to other species, it is only because we have evolved special developmental processes adequate to the task of becoming human. An important component of those processes is the behavior of those who already possess the skills in question. This kind of behavior is not specifically maternal or parental. We see it in any adult, even in children, whenever they interact with another person lacking their own level of competence in a particular situation. It is a basic birthright of the human species, and a remarkable one from the point of view of behavioral evolution. It is remarkable because its adaptive value, the reason this set of behavior patterns evolved, is directly related neither to the individual's survival nor to reproduction. Instead, its raison d'être is education, bringing up the young.

We can find behavior in other species that serves to educate the young. For example, the white-throated nunbird, instead of feeding its fledglings in the nest, brings an insect to a perch up to 100 feet away, then waits for the juvenile to fly up and take the food from its mouth without alighting. This provides excellent target practice while guaranteeing that the prey holds still (Skutch, 1976). But in all such examples we always find fixed action patterns involving particular times and circumstances, specific behavior of the adult, and specific developmental outcomes. In fact, it seems always to be a matter of facilitating the young animal's practice of maturing skills.

Maturation plays a role in the human infant's sensorimotor development, too; but the recurring modes of adult facilitation we shall discuss in the following chapter are different from anything other animal parents do. These behaviors are unusual for the width and indeterminacy of their application as well as for the way they are recapitulated throughout the child's development, with appropriate adjustment to his higher levels of skill. Furthermore, the establishment of particular communicative skills and conventions facilitates subsequent instruction. As a consequence of the child's adoption of those conventions, he comes to behave more and more as adults expect a communicating person to behave, permitting them to introduce additional meaningful modes of expression.

5

The Parental Frame

"You see, really and truly, apart from the things anyone can pick up (the dressing and the proper way of speaking and so on), the difference between a lady and a flower girl is not how she behaves, but how she's treated. I shall always be a flower girl to Professor Higgins, because he always treats me as a flower girl, and always will; but I know I can be a lady to you, because you always treat me as a lady, and always will."

George Bernard Shaw, *Pygmalion*, 1916

Everything I have said thus far about the organization and modification of schemas is subsumed by the general truth that a schema is an open system. It is one of many adapting systems that are particular properties of organisms. But the whole organism is also an open system. So is an interacting pair or a small group. So are larger collectivities and cultural institutions. We need not look within the schema or within the infant for the guiding principle of sensorimotor development, for the infant is in many respects an apprentice under close supervision. That supervision is informal and universal, conducted by older children as well as adults. Perhaps because it is largely unconscious and not labeled as "instruction," its importance has until recently been missed. The inside-out theory predominated; psychologists looked to the schema system for its own development. But nature is kinder to infants than that.

This chapter will add some more observations of interaction between infants and adults. I shall try to show that infants learn to play the roles of system members because adults place them in situations where the skills they lack are performed for them. Parents, especially, keep up many of the essential features of their own side of the interaction despite the infant's deficiencies as a partner. By taking his role for him, they

70

also demonstrate that role. Gradually, they relinquish it to him as he shows signs of being able to take it on.

Shared Meaning through Joint Doing

In the recent literature on mother-infant interaction some intriguing consistencies appear. The observations made by many investigators, across a variety of situations and ages, call attention to the way parents organize time and space for their infants:

> After eight weeks or so when social smiling is well estab-
> lished, the mother may spend long periods eliciting smiling in
> her infant. During such periods the infant is held on the
> mother's lap facing her and supported by her arms or is placed
> in an infant seat. The mother smiles and vocalizes to the infant
> and moves her head rhythmically towards and away from his
> face. The infant first responds by rapt attention, with a wid-
> ening of his eyes and a stilling of his body movements. Then
> his excitement increases, body movements begin again, he may
> vocalize and eventually a smile spreads over his face. At this
> point he turns away from his mother before beginning the
> whole cycle once again. Throughout this sequence the mother's
> actions are carefully phased with those of the infant. During
> the infant's attention phase the mother's behavior is restrained
> but as his excitement increases she vocalizes more rapidly and
> the pitch of her voice rises. At the point when he is about to
> smile her movements are suddenly reduced, as if she was al-
> lowing him time to reply. However, not all mothers behave in
> this way. Some subject their infants to a constant and unphased
> barrage of stimulation. The infant is given no pauses in which
> to reply and he seems totally overwhelmed by his mother. In-
> stead of playing this game for long periods, he is quickly re-
> duced to fussing and crying and shows sustained and prolonged
> turning away from the mother's face. [Richards, 1971, pp.
> 37–38]

This example shows how the successful mother creates a microcosm or "frame" within which schemas can function. All parents do this in one form or another much of the time, but since none can do it perfectly all the time difficulties will sometimes arise. (Clinical implications are discussed in the Epilogue.)

It may seem contradictory to say that mothers organize the world for their infants and also to say, as Richards says above, that interaction is a matter of mothers' adjustment to their babies. Yet this is not a contradiction. The consequence of that adjusting is that the infant ex- periences a mirroring and magnifying of his arousal, attention to his vocalization or facial expression, and then a reaction to it. When a parent fails to be responsive in these ways, the infant experiences no differentiation of the message-sending and message-receiving roles. When adults do allow their own behavior to be temporally organized by the infant's, they are really assimilating his cycles of attention and arousal to the adult world's cycles of speaking and listening, gesturing and observing. So the adults' adjustment is in fact a form of socialization. They construct a consistently organized social world around the infant, teaching him to punctuate the flow of experience.

Alan Fogel (1976), in a case study of one mother's face-to-face play with her son in 12 videotaped sessions from 5 to 13 weeks, found that the mother's continual gaze was a kind of frame within which her infant's gaze could wander and return. This is the same kind of frame a mother uses in holding her infant at the breast while he sucks and pauses (Kaye, 1977b), and later when the toddler returns to the mother after each exploratory foray into the wider world (Ainsworth, 1967). Within the periods of mutual gazing, Figure 5-1 shows Fogel's findings regarding the relation between baby's and mother's mouth movements, which prompted our analysis of mutual "greetings" (Figure 3-6).

The larger study by Kaye and Fogel (1980) mentioned in Chapter 3 confirmed what Fogel had concluded from his case study: When the mothers did not have their babies' attention, they typically waited. They continued talking to the infants and watching them. They provided a temporal frame within which infants were free to shift their attention away from the mothers and then back again. The babies' periods of attention-to-mother then provided a frame for their own expressive behavior as well as for that of the mothers. Over the period from 6 weeks to 6 months, we saw three clear changes: (1) The babies spent a smaller proportion of time looking at their mothers (i.e., the "on" to "off" ratio declined within the frame provided by mother) (Figure 5-2). (2) Mothers, rather than trying to resist this trend, became even more selective about

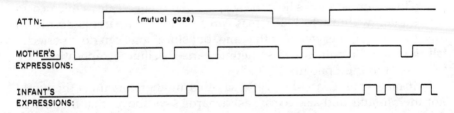

Figure 5-1. "Framing" relationship of infant's attention, mother's exaggerated facial expressions (smiling, nodding, raised eyebrows, etc.), and infant's vocalizations, smiles, wide-open mouth, etc. (Diagram adapted from Fogel, 1976.)

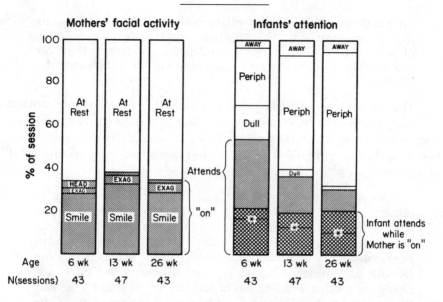

Figure 5-2. Proportions of time mothers spend in different facial activities, and proportion of time infants spend attending to mothers' faces, in the face-to-face play situation (☆ = level the cross-hatched area would have been equal to, by chance). (From Kaye & Fogel, 1980.)

fitting their own expressions within the frame of the babies' "on" time (also seen in Figure 5-2). (3) Babies began to take the role of initiators of greetings during these frames-within-frames rather than merely responders (Figure 3-6). In summary, by adjusting to the on-off cycles of infant attention, mothers succeed in creating consistent, recurring mini-sequences of events, which the infant in turn responds to and comes to anticipate in consistent ways. Intrinsic processes (the cycles of attention and arousal) provide one level of organization, but adults use that to create a deeper level of organization that is extrinsic, social, and communicating—long before it is understood.

What happens when the frame is removed? This was revealed by Tronick et al. (1979) in an experimental study. Instead of their normal active, attentive behavior, mothers were asked to violate the "rules" in specific ways. For example:

> When the mother is in profile the infant acts differently. The infant sits and watches her. He seldom smiles but makes cooing, calling vocalizations and often leans forward in his seat. He also may cry but the cries seem faked. This vocalizing is interspersed with long periods of intense looking at the mother. The infant's orientation remains straight ahead and with gaze fixed on the mother throughout the whole period. The infants

do not go into the greeting phase and they often get fussy as the session proceeds. Our mothers report that a similar type of performance often happens while they are driving their car and unable to maintain an *en face* position with their infants. [P. 364]

These frames are spatial as well as temporal. The behavior of mother and baby during the time frame takes place in a segment of space, and conversely the space marked off by their gaze directions constrains their behavior during a segment of time. Here are some more examples of behavioral space-time frames created by mothers:

To apply the name "Give and Take" to the exchange of objects between a mother and her three-month-old infant is somewhat of a misnomer. For early instances of Give and Take are more properly glossed as "offering and grasping" and appear notoriously one-sided: the burden of the exchange resting heavily on mother. Characteristic of this early period of exchange is mother's utilization of an array of attentional devices that make up the "offering" and "giving" phase of the Give and Take. This phase is often quite lengthy with the mother (M) maneuvering the object in a space approximately 12 to 24 inches in front of the child (C). M's manipulation of objects is frequently accompanied by verbal highlighting, primarily in the form of interrogatives and tag questions: "Do you want this?" "You want your rattle, don't you?" Moreover, the object being offered provides an additional source of stimulation for C. With the brightly coloured, noisy rattle, for example, M has an ideal object with which to capture and sustain his attention. Frequently she is observed shaking the rattle, looming it close to C's face, gently rubbing it up and down C's stomach—such endless variety in technique has the common purpose of activating C and, perhaps more importantly, M "sees" him as taking his "turn" in the "game." [Bruner, 1977, p. 283]

Mothers appear to have a good idea of whether the pointing gesture is meaningful to their infant. Many mothers of nine-month-old babies (and also of younger ones whom we brought to the laboratory) reported that normally they simply do not attract their babies' attention to objects at a distance but rather bring them to the child. This resulted in two mothers being replaced in the sample, because throughout the session they repeatedly got up from their seats for long periods in order to attract the baby's attention to toys by playing with them and by pulling them towards him, despite instructions to remain seated.

An attempt to observe mothers of much younger babies (four–six months) was abandoned because, when obliged to attract the attention of babies at this age to distal objects, the mothers pointed in a completely different way. They spent a lot of their time placing a finger in front of the babies' eyes, clicking their fingers, and slowly drawing the hand towards the object. It was observed that, in desperation, these mothers might even physically turn the babies' head in the direction of the finger. Such behavior we termed "cueing," i.e. providing additional cues to the point. . . .

The mothers of 14-month-olds cued less and the cues they used tended to be of a less forceful nature. Their behavior largely consisted of a quick tap on the hand or arm—a very effective method of indicating to a child that his mother is about to do something to which she wants him to attend. [Murphy & Messer, 1977, p. 334]

At 0;9 (16) [9 months, 16 days] [Jacqueline] discovers more complex signs during a meal than previously. She likes the grape juice in a glass but not the soup in a bowl. She watches her mother's activity. When the spoon comes out of the glass she opens her mouth wide, whereas when it comes from the bowl, her mouth remains closed. Her mother then tries to lead her to make a mistake by taking a spoon from the bowl and passing it by the glass before offering it to Jacqueline. But she is not fooled. At 0;9 (18) Jacqueline no longer needs to look at the spoon. She notes by the sound whether the spoonful comes from the glass or from the bowl and obstinately closes her mouth in the latter case. At 0;10 (26) Jacqueline also refuses her soup. But her mother, before holding out the spoon to her, strikes it against a silver bowl containing stewed fruit. Jacqueline is fooled this time and opens her mouth due to not having watched the move and to having depended on the sound alone. [Piaget, 1952, p. 249]

With babies in the second and third month, most mothers we have filmed played games that involved touching the infant's body, like pat-a-cake with the hands, bouncing the legs, shaking the cheeks, prodding the nose or stomach. Gradually, it would seem the mother herself is accepted as a game object as she mirrors the infant's acts of expression. After this the play incorporates objects that the infant has accepted as foci for interest. We found that by 6 months these games via objects, or with parts of the mother's body treated as objects, became the infant's preferred form of play. Then, at 9 or 10 months, they started the deliberately co-operative form of interest in objects which transforms play into exchange of acts of meaning. [Trevarthen & Hubley, 1978, p. 212]

The parade of examples could go on and on. I will conclude with an author who has traced explicitly how joint symbolic reference to objects, "shared meaning," is made salient to the 1-year-old child because of a framework of exchange established by parents.

> In the primitive phase, the reaching of the child is effective through the mother's acting upon her interpretation of its significance, but the child has no cognizance of this essential role that the mother plays and of those aspects of his own behaviour that are instrumental in securing her co-operation. In passing from the primitive phase to the gestural the child becomes *aware* of the communicative aspect of his own behavior, which has always been there in reality. In other words, whereas before there was co-ordination of activity, i.e., communication, the child was not aware of the relation between his own activity and his mother's monitoring of it. In a far-reaching cognitive restructuring he gains insight into the consequences of his own activity and the "mechanics" of the situation he finds himself in. A gesture, in this case the reach, emerges as a gesture because it is not simply produced in order to get an object, but in order to produce an effect on another in order to get an object. [Clark, 1978, p. 249]

Some of the points raised by these examples will be discussed in later chapters. Our concern here is with the role that all of the mothers just described seem to have been playing with respect to their infants' differentiation of skills. So we return to the different theories discussed in Chapter 4: the inside-out and the outside-in theories.

The parental frames help us to be more specific about our outside-in metaphor. The parents do not work on the infants' skills with pruning shears or with much contingent reinforcement. Actual praise and criticism are surprisingly infrequent, and when they occur they may be quite nonspecific or even contradictory. The same is true of verbal instructions. Instead, the parent relies on the infant's intrinsic abilities to differentiate his own skills gradually, as needed. However, that does not occur orthogenetically either. It occurs as a result of the way parents organize the world of objects and events. The differentiation process itself may be intrinsic, but the order to which the schemas adapt is only one of many possible orderings of the world. It is an ordering selected by parents to a greater extent than psychologists have realized.

Some theories have emphasized the early construction of a mental reality in adaptation to physical reality—to universal, logical truths about things—and some have discussed the socialization of children into cultural norms, especially after they begin to use language. What we have only recently come to understand is that the physical world too—the world of objects, motion, time, and space—is presented to infants in a socially structured way. The "social construction of reality" is not only a social consensus among language users about how things should be described and conceptualized. It is literally a construction, by social means, of microcosms that are the physical reality to which infants adapt. The spatial settings and anticipatable temporal patternings provide essential frames for cognitive development.

Types of Adult "Frames" for Child Behavior

Contrary to Watson's (1925) classic boast, the parent does not have unlimited power to shape the child into any kind of adult imaginable. There are plenty of intrinsic constraints upon the course of development. But contrary to Werner and Kaplan (1963) and to Piaget, those intrinsic functions fall far short of orthogenesis. The possible paths are varied and world-dependent. Growth depends upon the reduction of a potential chaos to an assimilable order, with just moderate degrees of novelty and variety.

There are many ways in which parental behavior structures the world so as to facilitate the infant's own processes of differentiation. The idea of frames is borrowed from Goffman's (1974) analysis of the context-dependency of social interaction and from Fogel's (1976) analysis of the multiply-imbedded levels of behavioral contexts in the mother-infant face-to-face situation. We can identify a number of different types of frames that adults provide for children. These types can be defined and exemplified functionally, without reference to specific modalities of behavior, ages of children, or situations.

In the *nurturant frame,* adults nourish, comfort, clean, console and fondle infants. As obvious and non-controversial as these functions are, they have occupied an inordinate amount of attention among students of child development. Perhaps this is because parents have been found to differ, across and within cultures, in the time and energy they devote to these various activities. However, performing them at some level is universal and unavoidable.

An important point about nurturance in the early months is that it often carries its own guaranteed concordance between parent and infant goals. So long as the mother realizes that her newborn is hungry, no formal communication is required in order to establish a cooperative endeavor (he does not have to be told to suck when she puts him to the breast). To some extent, this continues to be true. The toddler frightened by a stranger or injured by a fall finds immediate consolation without having to explain his problem. The nurturant frame is perhaps the most reliable channel for parent-infant intersubjectivity.

The *protective frame* is one that adults provide in a general sense by keeping the infant within earshot and by keeping dangerous objects out of his reach, as well as in a very specific sense by creating bounded spaces within which new accomplishments can be tried. For example, few parents would try to teach a child to dive by standing beside him at water's edge, urging him to plunge in. We stand in the water, an inch or two beyond where the child will hit, and promise to catch him. The child's daring depends upon trusting the adult, and the child's survival (psychologically if not biologically) depends upon the adult keeping that promise.

It is interesting to note how varied are the forms that the protective frame takes. There are the physical restraints of high chairs, playpens, cradle boards, etc. But there are also the ways in which adults restrict their discussion of certain topics, alter the rules of games so as to give the child an edge, and control the behavior of older siblings if the latter themselves do not spontaneously adopt a protective frame.

As with nurturance, protection is a dimension of cross-cultural and individual variation. But again as with nurturance, despite variation in the extent of protectiveness of any particular kind, the existence of the protection function in general is universal. It is merely expressed differently in different families and cultures. Protection is always relative. Parents do not normally try to protect the child completely—that would mean keeping him out of the water, not letting him play with older children, etc. We are as quick to condemn each other for being over-protective parents as for being underprotective. This fact shows that the function of the protective frame is to allow the child to go a little way, just not too far, beyond his competence.

We can also see examples of this frame in animals. Sometimes it comes close to human forms. I watched an orangutan mother in the Lincoln Park Zoo play a tickling game with her 2-month-old. As he hung by one hand from a horizontal bar, she made an elaborate show of being about to tickle him under that arm. When she did so, he would double up his body and switch to the other hand, sometimes getting hold of the bar and sometimes missing it but catching the mother's forearm. This went on for 15 minutes. I noticed that the mother always had one hand below her infant, not touching him but close enough to grab him when (as happened only once) he let go before getting a good grip with the other hand. The adaptive value of this maternal caution was obvious, for there was nothing else to catch the baby's fall but the concrete floor 30 feet below.

In the *instrumental frame,* an adult carries out what appears to be the infant's intention. For example, left to his own devices a 3-month-old swipes ineffectually toward a rattle placed upon a table. However, should he happen to be seated in someone's lap, within a minute or so the rattle is likely to be moved closer to his hand or turned so that his finger will hook its handle on the next swipe. The important difference between this kind of intervention and either the nurturant or the protective frame is that here an adult is acting on behalf of what she perceives as the infant's own goals, whereas nurturant or protective frames are merely for his benefit, without regard to his goals.

The instrumental frame, then, consists of the adult monitoring the infant's behavior (usually in relation to objects), interpreting the infant as having a certain intention, and partially or completely fulfilling that intention. Perhaps it is not immediately apparent that this is important for the development of the infant's skills. In fact, it may seem to be counterproductive, "overprotective," for it would seem to prevent the infant from learning to do things for himself. Let us postpone that question for a few moments.

The same parental act can serve several different functions. We can see in the very earliest nurturant activities the beginnings of the instrumental frame: In nursing her baby, while obviously providing nourishment and pleasure, a mother also closes the gap between her breast and the infant's rooting mouth, just as she will later close the gap between the rattle and his groping hand. In addition to providing a nurturant and an instrumental frame, the nursing mother encircles her baby protectively with her arm and simultaneously tries to prevent his swallowing too much air or breathing too little.

The *feedback frame* provides more consistent or more salient consequences to the child, for his own action, than the physical world itself would provide. For example, touching an electric cord or playing close to the fire do not usually result in pain. But the parent's "No!" serves to shape the infant's behavior so that the potentially dangerous consequences need never be felt. On the positive side, praise or parental delight can signal success in a task where the actual performance was not really good enough to attain its objective. Or the parent, by putting the rattle nearer the infant's hand, can make an inadequate reach a successful one, leaving its refinement for later. This is one way, then, that an instrumental completion is instructive: when it reinforces one or more constituents of the needed skill.

The feedback frame often overlaps with the instrumental frame; from the considerations in Chapter 4, this is just what we should expect. We discussed the importance of practicing subschemas until they become automatic. When they can be performed with minimal attention, the skill learner can focus upon the problem of combining subskills into higher-order skills. We see adults breaking tasks down into manageable subtasks all the time; one example already discussed was the detour task, in which most mothers brought the toy out to the open area at least once, as if to suggest to the baby that the hand on that side should do the reaching instead of the hand that was blocked by the plexiglass. We have seen 24-month-olds use a similar strategy in teaching 18-month-olds how to obtain a cookie from a puzzle box (Poppei, 1976), so it is clearly not a "maternal" frame so much as a natural human reaction to another person's incompetence.

The effectiveness of both the instrumental and the feedback frame may depend as much upon timing as upon consistency. Experimental studies of infants' ability to learn the contingent effects of their own behavior show that, when feedback is delayed by as little as 3 seconds, infants are unable to learn the contingency. This is true even of 6- to 8-month-olds (Millar & Watson, 1979). Behavior modification techniques, whether used by operant psychologists in the last 20 years, circus trainers in the last couple of thousand years, or human parents for perhaps a million years, involve the instrumental frame (simplifying the task) as much as the feedback frame (reinforcement).

In the foregoing examples, more is involved than the parent merely making the physical consequences of certain actions salient to the infant. The most important thing is that social consequences are introduced even into nonsocial actions. "Good girl!" someone shouts, and a simple product of maturation and solitary practice is marked as a social occasion. Similarly, parents' "No!" or "Hot!" when the child approaches too near the fire (which must occur a hundred times for every one time a child actually gets burned) does more to build the edifice of approving and disapproving caretakers, and to lay the foundation for perception of self, than it teaches about physical safety.

The *modeling frame* occurs when an adult performs some action and then waits for the child to try to imitate it. As we shall see, this can and does occur in a turn-taking pattern, alternating many trials by the infant with many demonstrations by the adult (Pawlby, 1977), or it may involve isolated trials on different occasions. Imitative attempts will often elicit feedback. On the other hand, inadequate goal-directed actions will often elicit adult demonstrations. In fact, when the adult carries out some action the infant seems to have been attempting, this instrumental frame provides a model for imitation whether the adult was intending to do so or not.

To illustrate, let us go back to the example of the rattle. I am holding a 3-month-old in my lap. She stares at the toy about 6 inches in front of her on the table. Her fingers scrabble on the table surface, then she extends her arm toward the toy but, with her fist closed, knocks it a few inches away. I reach for it and move it back to where it was. I have no lesson plan, in fact I act without really thinking. I don't care much whether the baby succeeds. I enjoy watching her clumsy failures, but I cannot do that when the toy is out of her reach. So I move it back. Yet in doing so, I have demonstrated the correct way to reach and grasp the rattle. Adults perform dozens of demonstrations like that for infants every day without realizing it. And when I watch quietly for the next attempt, though not thinking about it as a matter of imitation because I have not thought of what I just did as having provided a model, I am nonetheless providing a modeling frame.

Patiently waiting for the infant to make a trial might seem unlikely to be effective, in view of what I said above about the infant's short-term memory problems. However, his very short memory for contingencies—failing to see event Y as contingent upon X unless it comes within a second or two of X—is not due to any deficiency in short-term memory in general. In habituation, classical conditioning, and object permanence, all of which processes are involved in imitation, short-term memory increases greatly from 2 to 6 months (Watson, 1967; Millar & Watson, 1979; Fitzgerald & Brackbill, 1976). The result is that imitation becomes more powerful than operant learning, and consequently adults prefer trying to show the infant how to do things as opposed to "shaping" his behavior.

The modeling frame serves social functions at the same time it suggests new ends and means to the child. Given the opportunity to play with an object being manipulated by an adult or with an identical copy of it that is closer to him, the infant passes by the copy in favor of the one that seems to interest the adult (Eckerman, Whatley, & McGehee, 1979). So he is not merely imitating; he is allowing the adult to establish joint focus upon a common topic (Bruner, 1977). At the same time, he makes himself into a person among persons; imitation ceases to be a matter of assimilating features of isolated acts and begins to be an exchange of roles in a continuing dialogue with others. (We shall examine this process from different perspectives in the next seven chapters.)

The *discourse frame* creates a conversation-like exchange, not necessarily involving vocalizations. Discourse begins when the two partners' actions are still not equivalent in any respect. If the parent discovers that blowing "raspberries" or puffing air at baby's tummy will elicit a laugh, and if the parent then repeats the action, which then elicits another laugh, what results is a dialogue. The structure it has in the parent's mind or seems to have to an observer can lead us to ascribe more sophisticated interacting to the infant than is really warranted by the facts. All he is doing, at first, is laughing in response to each tickle.

Of course, the longer sequence soon becomes the routine, so that the 5-month-old expects and anticipates the parent's repetition in response to his own laugh.[1] This expectation is revealed in his reaction, a questioning look and a tentative chuckle, when the parent does *not* do the next trial. So the infant has some expectation of the normal sequence. But he is still not the one responsible for it. And, as we shall see in the next chapter, long after he is taking turns in a verbal conversation it will still be up to adults to ensure that those turns constitute connected discourse.

One of the ways the discourse frame is used is to manipulate the child's play. Adults pose demands in the form of questions and indirect suggestions, so that the child's turn in the turn-taking sequence can often take the form of demonstrating comprehension, of mastering a toy, and later of using language (Schaffer & Crook, 1979; Garvey, 1977; Kaye & Charney, 1981).

Finally (though I do not claim this list is exhaustive), there is the *memory frame*. To the extent the parent has shared experiences with the infant—knows what objects have intrigued him, what he has been able and unable to do with them, what he has imitated, what feedback he has received from objects and from people—the parent can use that information in making choices about what to offer, what to do for the infant, what to demonstrate, what kind of feedback to use, and so forth. In short, the adult's memory, especially to the extent that it is a *shared memory* with the infant, itself provides a frame organizing the infant's subsequent experiences.

By shared memory I do not mean that the information is encoded or represented in the same way, nor that it has the same meaning to both people. I mean that they have shared experiences, which usually take different forms in their different memories. That is precisely why the adult's memory provides a useful frame for the infant's activity, because the adult has often a symbolic representation of what the infant represents in a sensorimotor schema. We shall take this up in Chapters 7 and 8.

Any of these frames can, but need not, take the form of a *game*. I have avoided the term, because besides the connotation of conscious enjoyment, it also suggests that the two (or more) participants take turns and that they follow rules. In adult-infant interaction, a game is any routinized interaction in which the *adult* takes turns and pretends that

1. Because the discourse frame is used from birth and because it involves alternation of responses that are mutually imitative as well as mutually reinforcing, it has lent itself to adoption as an experimental paradigm by theorists both for and against "social conditioning" views of how communication develops. It is a good demonstration of the fact that infants and their parents do not feel compelled to subscribe to any one paradigm of learning.

the infant is taking turns, follows rules and pretends that the infant is aware of them, and acts as though they both are enjoying it.

Although games, strictly defined, account for a relatively small proportion of mothers' time with their babies (Gustafson, Green, & West, 1979), they have been the subject of dozens of studies in recent years. The reason for this interest is that what is true of the readily identified games like "peek-a-boo" or "pat-a-cake" is true of parental frames in general, or at least true of a great many activities that cannot be called games in any specific sense. The next chapter focuses on one of the threads that tie together games, discourse (verbal as well as preverbal), my own studies, and much of the literature on the interaction of infants with their elders.

6

Taking Turns

Clov: What is there to keep me here?
Hamm: The dialogue.

Samuel Beckett, Endgame, 1957

In the ordinary course of life, we take turn-taking for granted. The rules governing smooth exchange of turns are not apparent until they are violated; then they suddenly assume great importance. One is aware when one is interrupted, and one is aware of a partner's failures to respond. With babies, as we shall see, there are no "rules" in the same sense; but adults devote themselves energetically to getting the baby to behave as a good turn-taker should.

The latter point has received much attention in recent years, and there is a danger of overstating it at too general a level. The purpose of this chapter is to fill in some specific details about the changes we find in turn-taking over the course of infancy. In all our own studies, we observed infants and adults one-to-one in a situation that lent itself to, but did not necessarily require, alternating of turns. This allowed us to see how the turn-taking naturally arose in each situation.

We also could see how it developed from each domain of mother-infant interaction to the next one we studied. I shall show that mother-infant interaction is characterized by turn-taking right from the first, but the roles of mother and infant in managing the turns are highly asymmetrical. The infant's role is determined by built-in rhythms and contingencies. The mother's role is a matter of fitting in to those rhythms so as to produce a semblance of dialogue for which she alone is really responsible. Gradually the roles become more symmetrical, but adults continue to lead and manage dialogue with children until the children themselves become adults.

Along with moving toward symmetry there is the matter of learning to obey the rules that govern the exchange of speaking turns between adults. Although those rules can be broken, both partners are aware and uncomfortable when that occurs. When someone extends his hand in an offer to shake yours, you are not *forced* to offer your own, but you feel you *have to*. The rules for speaking turns are a bit more complex: For one thing, there are devices to "repair" ruptures caused by inter-ruptions and other violations. But it is still true that when one partner yields the floor, and only then, both partners feel that the other has to take it up. "There is a moral necessity but no mechanical necessity for the act" (Mead, 1934, p. 178). This consciousness of obligatory behavior is a critical part of the definition of a rule, as we shall see later in this chapter.

When conversing with a child, however, adults allow significant violations of the rules. They also use certain devices to make those violations appear only to have been optional variations. The younger the child, the less his taking and giving of turns is really a matter of following rules. With the young infant, in fact, the regularity that a mother takes advantage of is *stochastic* in nature, which is quite different from what we mean by rule-governed. But I shall postpone discussion of this issue until after the phenomena themselves have been described in sufficient detail.

The four areas of our research program traced turn-taking from birth to the third year. First were the complex effects of mother and infant upon one another in the very first feedings. The burst-pause pattern had been described in detail by other investigators and had not been found in any other mammals. We discovered that it has effects upon mothers' behavior and vice versa, as reported in Chapter 3. Here we shall discuss those mutual effects from the point of view of turn-taking.

Next were the studies, by many investigators, of mothers' and infants' control of their own and one another's gaze, arousal, and greeting behavior during face-to-face play. We were able to describe some of these processes in terms of contingent effects upon stochastic rates.

Third, we looked at parents' systematic attempts at teaching, from 6 months onward. The detour study mentioned in Chapters 2 and 3 led to a series of studies of imitation to be treated in Chapter 9, and to the discovery that infants' imitative abilities are optimized under just the kind of turn-taking frames that parents create.

Finally, we moved ahead to verbal exchanges after the children's speech was well underway, in the third year. These, too, have been studied in detail by many investigators in recent years. The young child's competence in discourse has often been pointed out. However, our own findings to be reported below indicate that parents continue to play a leading role in the construction and maintenance of these "dialogues."

I shall try to make the connections among these phenomena apparent by treating them in chronological sections, each of which ends in a summary of the progress up to that point.

Neonatal Feeding

In Chapter 3, our studies of feeding in the first 2 weeks were reported in order to make the point that an extremely complex interaction, including effects of both partners on one another, need not imply that they are members of a system. Complex interactions with an adult can result from rhythms and contingencies built into the newborn's nervous system. We shall now look at those rhythms and contingencies more closely.

Figure 3-2 showed a schematic representation of the burst-pause pattern of neonatal sucking. Individual sucks (normally including buccal suction as well as squeezing of the nipple) are rhythmical, but only within bursts.[1] The durations of bursts of sucks, and the durations of the pauses between bursts, are *not* rhythmical; they appear pretty much as a random distribution. This means that, once the infant begins sucking, there is a given probability—call it S—of each suck's being followed by another suck roughly 1 second later. That makes the sucking highly rhythmic within a burst, while the length of the burst is a random variate. A process like this is called *stochastic*, which means that all we can determine is a probability, because the process itself has random elements. The burst ends whenever a suck is missed, which has probability $1 - S = P$. Then a pause ensues. In other words, the burst-pause cycle is a simple binary switch: on or off. When it is on, there is a stochastic probability (in each second) that it will turn off; when it is off, there is a stochastic probability of its turning on. Let us define B as the probability of a resumption of sucking within the next second, that is, the onset of a burst. This simple stochastic switch has rather fancy consequences: rhythmic bursts of variable length separated by pauses which are also of variable length.[2]

1. When milk is flowing quite rapidly, as from a bottle with too large a hole in the nipple or from a breast engorged with milk, the infant sucks without pausing. After a minute or two on the breast, the burst-pause pattern will begin (Kaye, 1972).

2. The pauses contain isolated sucks, which can be conceived of as a burst of one. The stochastic model I am proposing makes direct predictions with respect to the distribution of the number of sucks per burst, including these "bursts of one." Our coders going by eye, concentrating upon the onset and offset of sucking, were not always precise about the number of individual sucks. Hence I have not been able to test the prediction on distribution of sucks per burst as I have on pause durations. Such a distributional analysis needs to be done in one of the laboratories where sucking is recorded automatically. Our concern was the natural interaction between baby and mother, so we shunned

An interesting fact about newborns is that, when they are left to themselves on a mother's breast, an artificial nipple, or a pacifier, but without being jiggled or otherwise interfered with, these probability coefficients *P*, *B*, and *S* do not change as the seconds tick away (until the infant is satiated or needs to bring up a bubble, or the flow of milk stops). The likelihood of another suck after the 20th in a row is about the same as the likelihood of a suck after only 2 or 5 or 10 in a row. In other words, the sucking mechanism need not keep track of how many sucks or seconds have elapsed since the burst began. The same is true of a pause: Its likelihood of ending, *B*, is independent of how much time has elapsed since it began.[3]

The phenomenon shown in Figure 3-3 is an effect of mothers' behavior, jiggling the baby during pauses, upon the value of *B*. For it is *B* that is plotted on the y-axis of that graph. Under the baseline condition, when the mothers did not jiggle, we can see that the probability of a new burst was fairly constant as time passed (x-axis) since the end of the last burst. But while the mothers were jiggling *B* was suppressed, and when they stopped jiggling it climbed much higher than its baseline value. It climbed, in fact, about half-way between the baseline value of *B* and the value we computed for *S*, the likelihood of a suck being followed by another suck.

Recall that we replicated this effect in a subsequent experimental study (Kaye & Wells, 1980), feeding the babies ourselves and administering jiggles according to a predetermined random schedule. So there was no possibility of the contingency's being an artifact of anticipation by the jiggler.

The foregoing model could be expressed in schematic form looking something like Figure 6-1. The model represents the two decision points for the baby's sucking system (neurological decisions, of course, not conscious ones): whether to start sucking, then whether to go on sucking. Those two decisions are stochastic functions of the parameters B and S, respectively. We have shown that the nervous system decides randomly how to proceed at these points, for the distribution of lengths of burst-pause cycles seems to fit the negative-exponential curve predicted by a Poisson model.[4] The system does not check first to see if the

---

the sophisticated apparatus that Sameroff (1967) and others had developed for precise recording of sucking.

3. The lengths of adjacent bursts and pauses are also independent of each other, a fact that indicates the pauses are unrelated to the amount of work done in the preceding burst and do not have a direct linear effect upon the amount of milk available in the following burst (Kaye, 1977b).

4. Some preliminary data that I reported in Kaye (1977b) suggested the opposite, but I now suspect that was an artifact of counting only clusters of three or more sucks as bursts (see note 2).

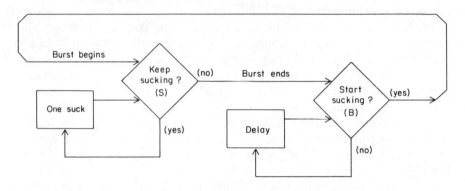

Figure 6-1. P-model of the burst-pause cycle in neonatal sucking.

mother is jiggling before it decides whether to resume sucking. Instead, as the model shows, it always has some probability (*B*) of resuming sucking at any moment, and the way the mother's jiggling-and-stopping has an effect is by altering that probability.

Now look at the other decision point, the decision to keep sucking, with probability *S*. When we say a particular baby in a particular feeding sucked in bursts containing a mean of *X* sucks, *X* is simply the result of the parameter *S*. Once we know *X*, we can compute what *S* must have been. Or, if we happened to be given *S* instead of *X*, we could generate the exponential distribution of burst durations and compute their mean. For example, an *S* of .75 will produce bursts of, on the average, 3.60 sucks; an *S* of .90 will produce bursts averaging 8.78 sucks. However, there are some external events that may affect *S*. For example, at some point the infant checks that the nipple is in his mouth and also that his breathing passage is clear. Do these TOTE units affect *S*, or do they simply cut off the sucking cycle entirely? Since our analysis excluded all bursts that ended in withdrawal of the nipple as opposed to a pause on the nipple, we do not know the answer to that question. So the P-model remains incomplete in that area and points the way to further research.

Why Did These Processes Evolve? The foregoing section showed that we can represent the mechanism involved in this contingency as a simple stochastic process with no awareness in the infant of any interaction with another person. However, that is not how a mother herself (or any adult feeding a newborn) sees the matter. She feels the infant was involved in feeding, then "got lazy" or "dozed off" or "stopped paying attention to what he was doing" and had to be jostled back onto the job. She is not aware (as we know from asking dozens of mothers) that her jiggling actually lengthens the pause and that only jiggling-and-stopping is an effective way to hasten the next burst. She does feel, though, that her intervention is important, that she is doing something active and necessary to keep him sucking.

This effect upon mothers' perceptions of their role in feeding assumes significance when we realize that it is the only known effect of the pauses. They are not necessary for breathing, resting, swallowing, or the let-down of milk into the aureolar sacs. And they are apparently unique to humans. All mammals feed their newborns by lactation and sucking—that is part of the definition of a mammal—and substantially the same physiological mechanisms are involved in the different species. But no other mammal has been found to pause during sucking with the nipple still in the mouth, as human newborns invariably do. We have suggested, therefore, that the function of the pauses is precisely the effect we have observed: to bring the mother into the feeding as an active taker of turns with the baby. As I have already suggested and shall show in more detail later, turn-taking plays a special role in the cognitive development of human infants.

The baby's sucking pattern is innate. So is the mother's lactation, of course, so we have no reason to doubt that her jiggling could be innate too. But it could also be attributed to experience. For in responding to the infant's pause a mother is doing the same thing she does in response to pauses in conversation. When a partner stops talking, one feels obligated to say something. Maternal jiggling may be a special case of an even more general phenomenon, the tendency to respond to any disruption of an ongoing stimulus. The mother only *tends* to do so; she often does not jiggle. Her behavior, like the baby's, is stochastic rather than obligatory, though we know less about the factors affecting its probability. Short jiggles are effective in eliciting a new burst: effective in the sense of a significant contingent increase in probability. Given this contingency, and given that it is only the *cessation* of the jiggle that the infant reinforces, we predicted that mothers should learn to shorten their jiggles after the first 2 weeks. That is exactly what we found. As was reported in Chapter 3, on the average across the mothers in our sample, the median duration of bouts of jiggling declined from 3.1 to 1.8 seconds over the first 2 weeks. This difference was significant when we compared two different subsamples at 2 days and at 2 weeks, and also when we compared the median jiggling durations of individual mothers from whom we had data at both ages.

Why should mothers' behavior have to be modified in this way by experience? Why were the jiggles not programmed innately to be short in the first place? This cannot be separated from the question of why mothers jiggle at all, or the question of why human infants pause at all.

Neither the jiggling nor the shortening of the jiggling would have arisen without the burst-pause pattern. The function of the pause seems to be, then, both to involve mothers and to give them something to adjust to. The fact that mothers adjust to babies' burst-pause cycles may have adaptive value for our species for no other reason than mothers learning that they can fit turns into the babies' natural cycles. At present, we have no evidence suggesting what else the burst-pause pattern's function might be.

If our current understanding is correct, the whole evolved system can be summarized along the following lines: Babies come equipped with rhythmic sucking and nonrhythmic burst-pause cycles. Mothers, too, have behavior that is switched on and off: variable stochastic probabilities of jiggling (J) and ending a jiggle (E). Some jiggles will seem to elicit a resumption of sucking and some will not; therefore there is no systematic reinforcement to increase J over the course of many feedings. However, those jiggles that *end* relatively soon tend to be reinforced because they increase B, while the long jiggles suppress B. This conditions the systematic increase in E over the first couple of weeks. Since mothers come equipped with the ability to adjust E, rather than with any particular value of E itself, the accommodation is only a temporary one applying to a mother's experience with the present infant, with no carry-over when she bears another baby. Its main result is to make her take turns with this baby, by increasing the frequency of his responding when she stops and decreasing the frequency of his having to resume sucking when she is still jiggling. Only because that turn-taking is not quite built-in do mothers have the opportunity to achieve it *by adjustment*, and thus to begin organizing the infant's world through sharing his rhythms and regulations.

I do not suggest that this relationship between maternal and infant behavior in feeding is the one crucial phenomenon upon which all of human development hinges. On the contrary, I believe it will turn out to be merely one example of many such relationships waiting to be discovered. Its importance is that it makes us think in a new way about the evolved mechanisms specific to human development. The argument builds as we look into subsequent forms of turn-taking between mothers and babies.

Face-to-Face Play

As mentioned in Chapter 3, our observations of face-to-face interaction at 6, 13, and 26 weeks revealed a burst-pause pattern of a different kind. This pattern was not a matter of organization built into the infants' behavior, as the sucking pattern was. Instead, at 6 weeks their smiles, vocalizations, and wide-mouthed expressions were still randomly distributed throughout the session. In terms of the model described above, it is as if there were only a stochastic probability, corresponding to B, of an expression's occurrence at any moment; there was no switching into a higher probability corresponding to S, which would produce more expressions in close succession to the first. So there were no bursts of facial expressions at 6 weeks to compare with the earlier bursts of sucking. The clustering into bursts began to be seen at 3 months and became more evident some time between 3 and 6 months, as shown in Figure 3-5. I pointed out in that chapter that these facial-expression behaviors, only gradually acquiring a nonrandom temporal organization, are the kinds of behavior that are comparable in form to maternal behaviors toward the infant. In other words, the question of the role of imitation in the organization of these behaviors has to be raised. Sucking is a different kind of behavior, specific to the baby's side of the interaction. Its organization is inborn, whereas facial expressions *become* organized in the modeling frame, in a process that has barely begun at 6 weeks. By 26 weeks, when the infant's facial expressions have begun to cluster into dialogue-like "turns," he has been watching and imitating for months. The modeling frame, in fact, as much as the discourse frame, induces alternating runs of expression between mother and infant.

The clustering of an infant's behavior into "runs" (Fogel, 1977) separated by "pauses" does not in itself constitute turn-taking. Like the burst-pause cycles in feeding, it only makes the exchange of turns easier; it provides a natural point of entry for the mother. The process is far from being a simple exchange of turns.

Figures 6-2 through 6-4 summarize the Kaye and Fogel mothers' stimulating behavior in relation to, on the one hand, the infants' attention and, on the other hand, the infants' expressive behaviors. Each of the three schematic polygraphs depicts a different age group, incorporating the mean proportions, rates, overlaps, and contingencies from our sample. This means that each figure summarizes the analysis of about 200 minutes of interaction in terms of an average 40 seconds. The choice of 40 seconds for the illustration simply corresponds to the length of a complete cycle of infant attention at the youngest age. (I emphasize that the total data constituted a stream 300 times as long as that represented in the drawings; so we have confidence in the reliability of these findings.)

As the infant gets older, his attention to the mother's face declines both in proportion of time (as also shown in Figure 5-2) and in the length of the cycles. As for the mother's proportions and cycles of visual stimulation (bursts of smiling, bobbing the head or making faces), there is no change over these months. What does change is that the placement of the mother's expressive activities corresponds more and more to the

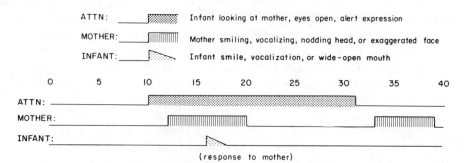

Figure 6-2. Typical temporal relation among infant's attention, mother's facial expressiveness, and infant expressions, in the face-to-face situation at 6 weeks. (Diagram adapted from data of Kaye & Fogel, 1980.)

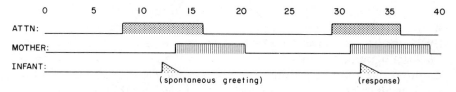

Figure 6-3. Temporal relation of face-to-face behaviors at 13 weeks. (Also from Kaye & Fogel data.)

Figure 6-4. Temporal relation of face-to-face behaviors at 26 weeks. (Also from Kaye & Fogel data.)

infant's attentive phases. The infant attends to the mother less but gets more stimulation from her when he does. (The mother also no longer uses vestibular stimulation when the baby is not looking at her—bouncing, touching, etc.—as she had done with the younger infant.)

We have therefore to explain two changes: (1) in the baby's timing, which could be due either to intrinsic changes or to adjustment to the mother's average duration of activity cycles; (2) an increasing overlap between baby's attention and mother's visual stimulation, which could be due to the baby's adjustment or to the mother's. Clearly, if the baby were going to adjust, that is, shorten his attention cycles to fit the mother's stimulation, the simplest way to do so would be to attend to the mother only when she is doing something. The mother's activity, then, would "frame" the baby's attention; but that is not what Figures 6-3 and 6-4 show. On the contrary, we found that the mothers' stimulation was not particularly effective in attracting their infants' attention. The infants were more likely to orient to them when the mothers were holding a relatively still face than when they were smiling or making exaggerated faces. These maternal expressions were greetings, reactions to the infants' attention rather than elicitors of it.

So the mother lets the baby's attention frame her displays, rather than the other way around. Additional studies will be needed to confirm this picture, but it looks as though a mother's ratio of "on" to "off" time and her mean duration of an on-off cycle remains relatively unchanged over the first 6 months, while the placement of "on" time with respect to the infant's attention time is enabled to be more accurate by the fact that the infant's attention cycles change to a more easily fittable average duration. The cause of this change on the infant's part remains unknown, but, whatever combination of intrinsic and extrinsic factors bring it about, we can see how it would be adaptive for the infant: His horizons widen to include more of the world beyond his mother's face, yet the quality of his interaction with her, during the time he devotes to that interaction, becomes richer.

A surprising and significant feature of the infant's cycles of attention and of the mother's cycles of stimulation, at all three ages, is that they are random, not periodic. Exactly as we found with the burst-pause cycles in sucking, the probability of looking at the mother is not a function of how much time has passed since looking away from her, and the probability of looking away is not a function of time since the onset of the gaze. Similarly, the probability of a mother's beginning to produce some display is independent of the passage of time since the last display. The durations of these displays, too, are randomly distributed. This means that there is nothing rhythmic about the two partners' cycles, and thus that they cannot anticipate one another's behavior by any kind of temporal "entraining" (though they might anticipate shifts of attention or of expressive behavior by means of other behavior that they have learned typically precedes those shifts).

The changes we see in Figures 6-2 through 6-4 in the infant's attention cycles, then, are really due to increases in stochastic parameters just like those we dubbed B and P in describing the sucking cycles. As for the mother, whose B and P do not change, how can we say that her displays depend upon the baby's attention and yet are "random"? This sounds like a contradiction in terms. The answer is that we are only saying the mother's cycles are not a function of *time*. (Respiration is an example of a process that is a direct function of time; as is the rhythmic sucking within bursts, whereas across bursts there is no rhythm at all.) Yet the mothers' cycles are contingent upon what the baby is doing, and this too is independent of time.

This distinction between rhythmic and arhythmic is an important one for students of interaction. A cycle that takes, on the average, 15 seconds might be very regular, so that every cycle is between 14 and 16 seconds in duration. Then it would be rhythmic; when 13 seconds had elapsed since the last event in the cycle one could be quite sure another occurrence was about due. However, it is possible for a cycle to have a mean of 15 seconds and even for that mean to be quite robust over subjects, ages, and situations, yet to have a negative-exponential distribution of cycle durations, so that knowing how much time has elapsed since the last event tells us nothing at all about when the next event will occur. As I explained in connection with sucking, the probability remains unchanged as the seconds tick away. (Time series analysis describes this as a matter of zero autocorrelation.)

Vocalizations within an adult dialogue also happen to have this Poisson-process quality (Jaffe & Feldstein, 1970). We can describe each partner's contributions to the dialogue in terms of their mean length of turn (a function of intrinsic "personality" factors but also of such external conditions as the person with whom they are talking, their relationship, and the topic [Siegman & Feldstein, 1979]). Yet the individual turns will fluctuate in length randomly (negative-exponentially) around that mean, so time cannot be used as a cue by the partner in knowing when to take the floor.

Human infants do not have to learn to produce arhythmic cycles, for they are endowed with at least one at birth: the burst-pause pattern of sucking. They do have to learn to recognize signals to be used for the exchange of turns. But some such turns are built in; for example, the onset of a new burst of sucking is contingent upon the cessation of a brief bout of jiggling by the mother. Figure 3-6 showed the gradual development of a contingent greeting to the mother, an example of turn-taking that is not built in. I have described these contingencies as a matter of one partner's affecting the value of the parameter on which the other partner's decision to shift is stochastically based. Is that what we mean by "rules"? I shall argue that it is not, that there are fundamental differences between a contingency of interaction and a social convention, and that only the latter is a rule. We postpone this issue to the end of the chapter.

Let us turn to the infant's expressions as shown in Figures 6-2 through 6-4. The infant's vocalizations and facial expressions increase in rate, especially when attending to the mother.[5] The conditional rate in fact is quite high (5.8 responses per minute of attention), but this has a diminished effect upon the effective rate (the number we see in an average time sample) because the baby is attending less.

As I placed the infant expressions in Figures 6-2, 6-3, and 6-4 in accord with their conditional rates depending upon the states of attention and maternal activity, the sequential relation between infant's and mother's greetings simply fell into place as a mathematical consequence. There was an increase in the likelihood of responsive greetings to the mother after she would greet the infant, then an increase in the likelihood of spontaneous greetings to the mother upon looking at her and before she greeted him (Figure 3-6). Notice that the question of "likelihood" as portrayed in a contingency function includes not just how many times a certain condition leads to a response but how quickly it does so; the higher proportion of maternal activity in the infant's attentive periods at 26 weeks means that the infant's greeting has to be quicker if it is to count as a spontaneous one. However, in Figure 3-6 we controlled for that by computing the likelihood of a greeting as a function of time since the onset of attention, as a proportion of the opportunities actually available to the infants given their mothers' behavior.

Alternation or Synchrony? Two partners can take turns by alternating with one another, or they can switch between "on" and "off" together. Synchronous or significantly overlapping cycles, such as we saw in the infants' attention and mothers' facial activity in Figure 6-4, require just as much organization as alternating cycles do. Neither type of coordination can occur over any significant length of time by chance; at least one of the partners must be adjusting to the other.

Within the same interaction, some behaviors can alternate while others overlap and others do neither. That is in fact what we have seen. The face-to-face interaction is a mixture of some alternation and some synchrony. The synchrony or "framing" relationship between infant's attention and mother's visual stimulation is clearly adaptive. She wants her baby to see those displays. This also accounts for the alternation in transitions: Although it is far from perfect, there is a tendency toward "baby attending, mother on, baby away, mother off."

Within the periods of infant attention, we might expect to see an alternation between the mother's expressions and those of the infant, something like conversational turn-taking. In fact, a mother could achieve alternation if she would always wait for the baby to take his turn

5. These figures do not show the clustering into bursts evident by 6 months, because on the average we would not see even one cluster in a 40-second time sample.

(to smile, vocalize, etc.) and only take her turn when he was quiet. But then she would often have to wait a long time, so there would be considerable portions of the attentive period when neither of them was taking a turn (as is the case when the baby is looking elsewhere). The maternal strategy, therefore, is to produce as much alternation as she can, but to err in the direction of synchrony rather than silence.

Synchrony takes two principal forms. One is what Duncan (1972) calls "back-channels," like "uh-huh" or a nod of the head, which do not interrupt the speaker who has the floor. When the infant begins to smile, the mother can mirror his smile back to him, even exaggerate it, without that constituting an interruption of the baby or an attempt to take the floor away from him. The same is true of vocalizations. In other words, these kinds of expression do not require alternation of turns in the way that verbal utterances do. Processing what another person is saying conflicts with producing one's own speech, but processing another's smile and smiling oneself do not conflict.

The other main form of synchrony is "chorusing." The word has been used for prolonged simultaneous vocalizing (Schaffer, Collis, & Parsons, 1977; Stern, Jaffe, Beebe, & Bennett, 1975; Strain & Vietze, 1975) but applies just as well to nonvocal expressions. The difference from "back-channels" is that here the mother tends to coax the simultaneous behavior from the baby rather than injecting simultaneous behavior into the baby's turn; thus the synchrony is prolonged.

Anderson, Vietze, and Dokecki (1977) gathered a large body of data from 24 3-month-olds and their mothers, based on 90 minutes of normal awake time per subject, not necessarily in face-to-face play. Their results support our generalization from the face-to-face analyses of Fogel (1977) and Kaye and Fogel (1980). Anderson et al. found that *both* the mother and the infant were significantly more likely to vocalize when the other was vocalizing (i.e., to "interrupt" the other) than when the other was silent. However, these contingencies were small compared with the differences between mother and infant, in the likelihood of vocalizing regardless of the other's behavior (mothers much more likely to do so) and likelihood of ending a vocalization regardless of the other (infants much more likely to do so). If chorusing had depended on the way the infants sang their parts, there would have been no chorus.

The results from the face-to-face studies lead to the same conclusion as the earlier feeding interaction. Any time the infant happens to do anything that can be interpreted as a turn in a conversation, taking the floor and then yielding it, his mother (or any adult) will treat it as such. But the next best thing is either to take his turn for him or to try to coax one out of him. In the face-to-face situation, adults' imitation of the infant and the construction of a modeling frame for the infant begin to play major roles in this turn-taking process.

Turn-taking in Teaching Situations

When human adults train their young, and consequently when any person trains another person, there is a strong tendency for tutor and learner to take turns. If this seems obvious and trivial, we had better take a look at the kinds of training that occur in other species. Whales, for example, can be said to teach their infants to swim; the mother pushes her baby to the surface for a breath within a few seconds after delivering. She then nudges him along just below the surface and prevents his straying from her side. But this training is completed in a matter of hours or even minutes, because it is only a matter of getting the right organs to exercise and inducing the appropriate sensations; maturation and practice take care of the details. The same can be said of mother ducks, who "teach" their ducklings to swim by leading them down to the pond and hopping in. In this kind of training, which can be characterized as induced exercise within a protective frame, there is no turn-taking. When do turns become necessary? In the feedback frame mentioned in Chapter 5, the parent has to monitor the child's behavior so as to respond with instructive consequences. In the modeling frame, the child has to watch the parent's demonstration. The parent also typically watches the child's attempts so as to make critical features more salient in the next demonstration.

The feedback frame and the modeling frame are extremely rare in other species. We might call it feedback when an adult baboon bites or chases an offending infant baboon, but it is not a structured "frame." And there is no sustained series of turns; it happens one event at a time. Similarly, chimpanzee or gorilla infants may imitate adult behavior, but the adult will not have presented a model deliberately or repeatedly, with pauses for the infant's trials.[6] Imitation may occur in other species (by processes that do not necessarily have anything in common with human imitation) and may even result in the learning of "conventional" signals. For example, Japanese macaques have been found to learn the habit of washing sand off crabs by observation of their elders (Kawai, 1965). But the fact that monkey A imitates monkey B does not mean that B has *taught* A. Teaching by demonstration and instruction does not

6. Exceptions may be found in certain song birds, where pauses occur between calls as fixed action patterns. Other species, however, even where imitation or at least exposure to the specific call is necessary for its acquisition, do not take turns. There are no valid generalizations to be made across species about song learning; every imaginable theory is probably true of at least one species (see Hinde, 1969).

occur at all in other species, occurs in hundreds of ways in our own, and necessarily involves turn-taking.

The borderline cases are the laboratory apes. It is interesting that they can learn so much more by imitating humans than by imitating each other. As they do so, their way of interrupting trainers shows that they are not really programmed to expect to be taught (Terrace, Petitto, Sanders, & Bever, 1979). That should tip us off to the fact that our uniqueness is more a matter of our teaching ability than of our learning ability: Human methods of teaching can be effective to some extent with subhuman learners. The evolution of human teaching has come about in the form of the instrumental frame, the modeling frame, the feedback frame, the discourse frame, all of which share one principal feature: turn-taking.

In the detour situation mentioned in Chapter 3, the mothers watched their infants' attempts, usually waited for them to avert their gaze from the task, and then intervened. Sometimes that intervention consisted of modeling the effective way to get the toy, reaching around the screen, shaking the toy, and putting it back. But sometimes, as I have said, it took other forms, such as pushing the infant's arm or moving the toy to the other side where it would not be blocked by the Plexiglas. So the turn-taking frame was a basic one, available for many instructional methods, only one of which was imitation. Although mothers concentrated on one strategy or another, they generally used some of all three. It is important to realize that part of what they were teaching the infants was how to take turns. The infants would come to expect trials to alternate with consequences, imitations with further demonstrations. A major feature of a mother's interventions, whatever else she did, was to attract the baby's attention to the mother's hand, to the toy, or to the edge of the Plexiglas. In other words, as much as she was involved in watching the baby during his turn, the mother also tried to get him to watch her during her turn. Their alternation was far from perfect; there were many "interruptions" on both sides. Nonetheless, the mothers significantly fit their demonstrations into pauses in the infant's attempts (as they did with their jiggling in the early feeding) and pretended the turn-taking was much more smooth and mutually managed than was really the case (as they also did in face-to-face play).

Other teaching situations that one observes more informally, including the ubiquitous games that combine demonstration with manipulating the baby's hands or limbs (like pat-a-cake), show this same turn-taking structure. As noted in connection with face-to-face play in general, the alternation structure may be masked by the fact that the mother sometimes takes her own turn, sometimes the baby's. But it is not lost on the baby. It induces him to act, then watch, then act, then watch. That pattern becomes a habit and a way of life.

Parent-Child Speech

Once the child begins to utter words, his turn-taking is suddenly nearly perfect. Interruptions drop to only a small percentage of all turns. Why? Because what each participant is doing is either signaling to the other, which requires getting the other's attention first, or responding to signals, which requires attending to them until the whole message has been processed. It turns out that this is not so easy for sign-language-using apes to learn to do. They are terrible about interrupting, in fact, which Terrace et al. (1979) argue is a major reason for the meagerness of their linguistic accomplishments compared to humans. They have acquired surprisingly large vocabularies but have not progressed to producing long sequences of signs. This may be because as soon as they recognize a sign or two they respond, and as soon as they produce one they expect a response. Human children expect their turns to be monitored and responded to as a whole, and expect to monitor and respond to the whole turn of the partner.

That certainly does not have to be learned *after* the onset of speech. It is an expectation already established in the human infant. How much its establishment depends upon turn-taking experiences such as those I have described is something we have only been able to speculate about. We shall continue those speculations shortly, after following the mother-child verbal dialogues a little further.

Turn-taking is smooth in these dialogues, if smoothness is defined as the relative absence of interruptions and of simultaneous starts (Bloom, Rocissano, & Hood, 1976; Garvey & Berninger, 1981). However, that smoothness may make young children appear to be more skilled as conversationalists than they really are. A study by Kaye and Charney (1980, 1981) distinguished turns that are really responsible for the flow of discourse from more isolated kinds of turns, which, though usually falling in a dialogue-like sequence of alternation with the partner, only relate to the partner in limited ways. This study shows that in creating and maintaining a semblance of true dialogue, mothers continue their leadership role from the period of nonverbal play with infants well into the time when the child can construct complex descriptions, questions, and requests.

The study involved sequences of turns transcribed and coded in the following way:

Mother		Child	
1. [Points to a picture] What is that one?	(M)		
		2. Kitty cat	(R)
3. Well what is it?	(RM)		
		4. Kitty cat	(R)
5. Well, I know there's a kitty in it; what's he in?	(RM)		
		6. Huh?	(RM)
7. What's he riding in?	(RM)		
		8. Airplane.	(R)
9. Right.	(R)		
		10. [Turns page]	(U)

The codes in this transcript (M, R, RM, and U) illustrate the four basic categories into which all turns were assigned. A "turn" was not necessarily a verbal utterance, as #10 above shows. Some turns consisted of two or more utterances strung together without a pause between them (e.g., #5), others contained an utterance with accompanying gestures (#1). Transcribers of videotapes achieved acceptable reliability as to the segmentation of turns.[7] The subjects themselves made this easy: Less than 3% of the mothers' turns and less than 5% of the children's were interruptions. Furthermore, in 70% of the interruptions the person who was interrupted yielded the floor immediately.

There can be two turns in a row by the same partner. This happens whenever he or she pauses for more than 2 seconds (an arbitrary criterion) and the other fails to take the floor. It is most common, however, for the mother and child to produce long sequences alternating turn for turn, adult fashion.

The question now is whether the *content* of those turns really forms a chain of connected discourse. In the example above, turns 1–9 are a chain. What makes them a chain is that 2–9 are all *responses* (R) to the partner's preceding turn. Some turns may respond only nonverbally (e.g., looking where the other has pointed, or pointing at something the other has named). A response need not have been requested or required (e.g., #9). Coders have no difficulty achieving reliability with this category. (In other words, human beings readily agree on whether a turn is a response or not: Otherwise, how could we communicate?)

7. Two coders agreed on the exact segmentation of 83% of the turns in eight sessions that they each transcribed independently. Reliability of the coding categories assigned was 85%.

   Since half the responses in this chain are made by the child, his
contribution would seem to be equal to that of the mother. But closer
analysis showed something different. Why did the child not respond to
turn #9? The answer is that children of this age are far less likely to
respond unless the mother's turn is a *mand* (M), which #9 is not. Mothers
respond whether the child's turn is a mand or not.

   Mands were defined as turns to which, in adult discourse, it would
be rude not to react in some way. Again, the feature on which this
judgment was based could be either a speech act (e.g., a question or
request) or a nonverbal act (e.g., pointing). Turns were coded as mands
or not, irrespective of whether they were responses. Those that happened to be both (RM in the transcript above) we called *turnabouts*. (U
stands for "unlinked" to the partner's turns, neither a response nor a
mand.)

   The data came from 28 children whom we videotaped at home at
age 26 months and again at 30 months. At each age, they sat with their
mothers at the kitchen table. The analysis involved three situations for
5 minutes each: a Richard Scarry picture book; a toy tea set with two
cups, two plates, etc.; and a Fisher-Price play family with table, chairs,
dog, car, etc. The example above comes from one of the picture book
segments.

   Two sessions by three tasks by 28 children by 5 minutes yielded
more than 20,000 turns, so that we are confident about the results shown
in Figure 6-5. The two ages have been combined in this figure because
the effect of age (both partners increased in the proportion of their turns

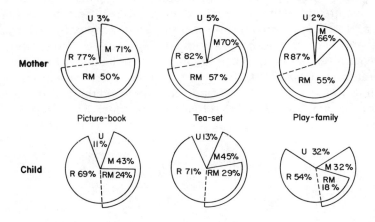

Figure 6-5. Proportions of turns that were responses (R), mands (M), and
unlinked (U), in three different mother-child play situations. Overlapping
wedges (RM) show the proportion of turnabouts. Data are averaged across
sessions at 26 and 30 months. (From Kaye & Charney, 1981.)

that were responses) was relatively small. There were some differences among the three tasks, but the major difference was between mothers and children. The fact that mothers produced many more mands, combined with the fact that children's proportions of turnabouts were significantly less than the chance combination of responses and mands would have predicted (i.e., the children tended to *either* respond or mand but not both), led to 70% of all turnabouts being due to the mothers.

In principle, turnabouts are not necessary for long chains of connected dialogue. Each link of the chain need only be a response. When two adults talk to one another, there are nowhere near as many turnabouts as the 50%–57% levels produced by our mothers (Figure 6-5). In practice, however, when one is talking to a 2-year-old, turnabouts are crucial if one wants to extend the chain. The reason appears in the first column of Table 6-1 and was exemplified by the transcript above. The mother's mand greatly increases the likelihood of the child's continuing the chain. Her turn also has to be a response if she herself is to continue the chain. Therefore what one has to do if one wants dialogue with a 2-year-old is both respond and mand, that is, produce turnabouts. And we know that the semblance of dialogue is just what mothers do want to create, for they have been creating it in one way or another since their infants' birth.

As we have seen, mothers use their newborn infants' pauses as occasions for jiggling. They learn to keep their jiggling brief so that it fits into the pauses and receives an "answer" in the form of the next burst of sucking. Jiggling, then, is a turnabout; so in a sense the mothers of 2-year-olds are still jiggling. Treating the child as if he were participating in an intelligent conversation is a prevalent activity in maternal caretaking and play (Newson, 1979; Snow, 1977). Recall that in the early months, whenever the infant gave his mother any behavior that could be interpreted as if he had taken a turn in a conversation—anything from smiling to rude noises—she made that interpretation; and when he did not, she often pretended that he had. The effect of this enduring discourse frame is to involve the infant in dialogue that is always beyond

Table 6-1
Probability of Response to Other (%)

	Response by Child	Response by Mother
Following other's mand	71.4	90.0
Following other's nonmand	41.9	77.7

his own capacities for intentional discourse. His efforts are interpreted and expanded, so that they become more effective communicative acts than they were quite intended to be.

This is likely to be a significant factor in language development, and its importance has been recognized by a number of students of child language. Brown (1968) discussed the importance of the fact that the child hears his own kernel propositions transformed in the parent's subsequent turn. For example:

> CHILD: Put milk there.
> MOTHER: Put the milk where?
> CHILD: In cup.

A parental prompt like this is one kind of turnabout, a "contingent query" (Garvey, 1977). Corsaro (1977) describes another type, "clarification requests" (including, e.g., "Huh?"); Keenan and Schieffelin (1976) describe "incorporations"; and Ervin-Tripp (1977) lists a variety of other types. All are used mainly by adults in speaking to children. In Ervin-Tripp's words, they are a matter of "programming speech acts to build dialogue." What these authors have said about the specific types is true, I believe, of all or most turnabouts: They provide important information to the child about the meanings and usages of conventional expressions. This information comes from the back-and-forth flow of discourse, from protracted chains of mutual responses. Thanks to the fact that the mother's turns will combine mand and response, the child's turns do not have to; yet he still finds himself a participant in dialogue.

So the child does not have the problem, as was once thought, of constructing a knowledge of his parents' language from a corpus of overheard speech. Instead, he is plunged into ongoing discourse on topics very largely selected by his own interests. His meanings are interpreted, expressed, and expatiated upon almost before he really means anything at all.

Our observations of parent-child discourse in the third year will lead us into the question of socialization, to be treated in Chapter 11. For the broadest implications of the Kaye and Charney findings are that the social structure, the discourse itself, is not mastered by children before they go on to the specifics of their parents' syntax and semantics. Adults will create and maintain the discourse structure for them, thus teaching them how to participate in that structure and eventually take it over as their own.

This apprenticeship in the language community recapitulates the same process as we saw in the earlier incorporation of the child into the behavioral system. Rather than thinking of the apprentice period as a particular stage in infancy, I see apprentice membership in successively more sophisticated systems as one of the invariant functions of human development, extrinsic to the child but nonetheless a birthright of the species.

A Cross-cultural Replication. Although the study with Charney helped us pin down some facts about how mothers take leadership in dialogues with their 2-year-olds, it raised a number of unanswered questions about what factors bring that about. The conversational asymmetry we had found might have been due to the inadequacies of the 2-year-olds, or it might only have been due to the status difference between adult and child. Similarly, the mothers' behavior might have been a matter of maternal guidance as we supposed, but on the other hand it might only have been normal adult behavior.

A study by Martinez (1982), primarily designed to see whether the results would generalize to a different linguistic (Spanish), racial (Indian), cultural (Mexican) group, also succeeded in disentangling those unanswered questions. Martinez paired 20 Mexican[8] mothers with their children and with each other; then he paired the children with each other. Half the children were boys, half girls. Half were 30 months and half were 48 months old. He paired each 2-year-old with a 4-year-old of the same sex. In a second sample of eight families he observed each child with his or her own mother and then with one of the other mothers, a stranger to the child.

The results showed that, except for a higher proportion of non-verbal turns, these Spanish-speaking mothers and children behaved just as our Anglo sample had done. Furthermore, it made no difference whether mothers were with their own child or with another child. The children were not significantly more adept at turnabouts with each other than with their mothers, nor did the 4-year-olds take the leading role in this respect when playing with the 2-year-olds. When mothers were talking with each other (in a 5-minute discussion of the picture book and how their children had responded to it), there were far fewer turnabouts; instead there were long chains of responses that were not mands. (A mand is not necessary with a fellow adult. Merely pausing with appropriate floor-yielding cues is sufficient. In fact, at the level of frequency with which they occur in speech to children, mands would be impolite between adults.)

In summary, the asymmetry of mother-child conversations is due to more than just a status difference (in which the child would merely

8. Although the study was done in Chicago, the subjects were really Mexican, not Mexican-American. All were non-English-speaking recent arrivals from rural Mexico. Each pair of families came to a community center together to be videotaped; in all other respects Martinez replicated the Kaye and Charney procedures exactly.

be playing a subordinate role because of the mother's domination of the conversation). Two-year-olds and even, in a Mexican sample, 4-year-olds do not take it upon themselves to promote the flow of connected dialogue. Mothers do take that responsibility upon themselves (with any child, not just with their own) and, in doing so, they behave quite differently than in conversation with another adult.

Growth of Sophistication in Turnabouts. Still, the 2-year-old does produce some turnabouts, and we have to regard those as his first steps in taking a share of responsibility for the flow of the dialogue. An examination of children's turnabouts shows that the vast majority occur singly, that is, not in a continuing series like turns 3, 5, and 7 in the example on page 100. Even in that transcript, one knows at once that it is the mother whose turns are on the left. In the first place, the topic being maintained is the topic of the other person's (the child's) interest. Mothers do that, whereas our children produced almost no turnabouts designed to maintain the topic of their mothers' activities, interests, or opinions. Second, notice in that example how the mother's turns are directed toward a sustained question. This was rare among the children. Even when they took over the leadership to produce a substantial chain of responses, the nature of that chain was like Vygotsky's (1962) "chain complex" classifications, each item strung on to the end because of its relation to the previous item:

Mother		Child (girl, 26 months)	
		1. This is the family doll house.	(M)
2. Yeah, that's the family.	(R)		
		3. And they got a table. [Expectant tone]	(RM)
4. That's the table.	(R)		
		5. This is another table. [Points]	(RM)
6. Yeah. That's the barbecue.	(R)		
		7. And where's the chair?	(RM)
8. Well here, here's some. [Points]	(RM)		
		9. Oh, there's some.	(R)

This child was our most advanced, linguistically; the reader would have no way of knowing from individual utterances which was the child and which the mother. Furthermore, due to the connection between each turn and the previous one, the whole series of turns created by this child deals with a single superordinate theme. We know from studies like Vygotsky's that she would not have been able to explain why house, table, and chair belong together, yet she has put them together in sustained discourse. However, on closer examination these turnabouts are of a primitive structure: "And . . ." ". . . another . . ." "And . . . " This is characteristic of children when they begin taking the turnabout role.

The following example from the same child 4 months later was quite unique:

Mother	Child (girl, 30 months)
	1. Do they have a baby? (M)
2. No, they don't. This family doesn't have a baby. (R)	
	3. But this is a cradle. [Shows bunk bed] (RM)
4. No, it's a bunk bed. There's the other half. See? It's not a cradle. (RM)	
	5. [Plays] (U)

Here, although it involves only one turnabout, we do see an adult-like presuppositional logic: Cradle implies baby; when the mother denies that the set contains a baby, she is expected to answer to that inconsistency. The example stands out just because 2-year-olds rarely converse in that way.

How Conversation Becomes Rule-governed

We now take on a major question: How does turn-taking change from a tendency we can observe statistically, one that adults are largely responsible for, to something governed by rules, something not just statistically significant but, under the right conditions, virtually certain? This change is an important one, given the fact that human behavior is rule-governed in ways not seen in any other animal, and given the fact that this only comes to be true gradually. It is not true of the young infant. The question how it comes to be true, then, is one of the problems inherent in the general question, What is man?

What one means by "rule" and "rule-governed," however, is not so clear. It is a family of usages more than a definable class of things, much like Wittgenstein's famous example, the word *game*. Toulmin (1974) has listed seven different ways in which the word *rule* is used, just within the domain of describing regular sequences of human behavior. He pointed out, however, that these usages could be arranged in order from physiologically constrained regularity to purely intellectual exercises and that boundaries could be drawn between them for specific purposes. In that spirit, I shall try to define *rule* (and its synonym, *convention*) as it will be used in the present discussion. A rule or convention is a mutually recognized obligation to behave in a consistent but not inevitable way. By "mutually recognized" I mean that the behavior is expected by both the person responsible for it and the persons (if any) with whom he is interacting. By "obligation" I mean that when the behavior does not occur the rule is mutually understood to have been violated. By "consistent" I mean one of several alternatives listed below, all involving either zero likelihood or 100% likelihood of occurrence of a certain type of behavior under certain conditions. (This is quite different from a contingency, which means only that the likelihood of occurrence is statistically different from chance, not that it ever becomes 0% or 100%.) Finally, by "not inevitable" I mean to exclude all sequences of behavior that are due to the physics or physiology of organisms. If you prick a man and he bleeds, or if you sweep his legs out from under him and he falls, he is not following a rule. If you extend your right hand to him and he reaches out to shake it, he is following a rule; if he failed to do so, you and he would both be aware of it as a violation. In other words, it may have nothing to do with consciousness when it is being followed; but in order to be called a rule, as opposed to a typical pattern of behavior, it must at least enter consciousness when it is violated.

The rule need not be described the same way by the participants as by the psychologist/observer. The participants might notice that someone's behavior is deviant, rude, inappropriate, without being able to describe precisely the rule to which it failed to conform. The psychologist ought to be able to characterize it either as an obligatory response or an obligatory suppression of some response, and either in terms of a sequence of events or in terms of the simultaneity or nonoverlap of various categories of behavior. However, it is not a matter of stochastic parameters. All rules involve decisions of the "yes/no" type. There are only three different logical relations involved in rules.

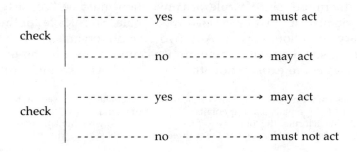

```
                    ----------- yes -----------→ must act
        check       |
                    |
                    ----------- no  -----------→ must not act
```

On the basis of a check against conditions (yes/no), there must be two possible outcomes, at least one of which has either a 0% or 100% probability of eliciting the act in question.[9] The two outcomes cannot both be stochastic (where the probability of response would change, e.g., from 35% to 80%). Nor can the decision itself be a stochastic function like *S* and *B* in Figure 6-1.

A closely related term is *role*, but this usually refers to a whole set of expectations about how one is supposed to behave with particular others and in particular situations. In playing a role, one obeys a number of rules, and one may do a number of additional characteristic things that are not rules. Both *rule* and *role* imply that the people involved actually refer mentally (though perhaps unconsciously) to some representation of the regularity in their behavior; it is more than just a statement that the regularity exists.

Now we can see how critical rules are to the notion of a social system. One cannot follow a rule unintentionally, for it is more than a regularity in behavior, it is a representation one refers to in behaving. One matches one's behavior against a representation of how one expects oneself to behave, and (in fact) expects to be expected to behave. There lies the purposiveness: The person intends his behavior to be determined by the rule. In addition, there is someone else who expects this person's behavior to conform to the rule. (This second person will not necessarily conform to it himself, for the rule need not be symmetrical.) When two or more people share a sense that their interaction is governed by rules, they must have a shared intention, which is part of the definition of a social system. They at least share the intention to interact, though it is a further question whether they share a purpose with respect to the outside world. They fulfill, in other words, a necessary condition for a social system.

Furthermore, since a rule or convention must be "consistent but not inevitable," it must be learned, not innate. So rules fulfill the other necessary condition as well. Any two or more organisms who follow rules are a social system. Therefore we cannot appeal to the notion of a social system to explain how the infant's behavior becomes rule-gov-

9. In logical terms, the first form corresponds to "p entails q," the second to "q entails p," the third to "p entails q and q entails p." If we substitute "not p" for p, by switching yes and no in each rule, the logic is essentially the same. Any relationship between p and q that cannot be reduced to one of these three entailments is not a rule.

erned. Rule-governed behavior is the basic condition of a social system. The infant has to learn to interact according to rules before he can become a member of a system.

The same TOTE units that are involved in rules—the "yes/no" checkpoints schematized above—can be built into innate behavior, complete with the "mutual expectation" criterion. The mutual expectations (not necessarily conscious) are inherent in the built-in programs for action and reaction. For example, the male black widow spider could be said to follow a "rule" in attempting to mount females. He always approaches from behind (and carefully!). (So far as the decision processes that must be included in a P-model, these kinds of behavior are simpler, not more complex than stochastic contingencies.) I do not call such procedures rules, because an organism follows them by necessity, not by choice. But we could, in principle, change the definition of "rule-governed" so as to include these. And we could also imagine a world in which human rule-following consisted of nothing but these wired-in contingencies. There would then be nothing like the flexibility or "opportunism" we know to be man's great resource. For our secret is not in the quantitative measure of our rule-governedness; it is in (1) the ability of individuals to adapt quickly to the rules expected by others, and in (2) the ability of social systems to adapt new sets of rules to suit their purposes. Those two abilities are, of course, inseparable.

So instead of being born with rules, the infant is born with a few consistent patterns of behavior that will look enough like the rules— necessarily, like just the universal features of interaction rules—of adult life so that adults will treat him as a person. And, of course, infants are also born with learning mechanisms that enable them to improve the fit between the way they are expected to behave and the way they do behave. Those mechanisms include two that are common to many species: reinforcement, or the shaping of behavior by its consequences; and anticipation, or the shaping of behavior by habitual associations. These are, in effect, instrumental and classical conditioning. (There is also a third mechanism of learning, imitation, that we shall treat in a separate chapter.) My point is that, while other species may have some of these powerful learning processes as well evolved as man has, the adults of other species do not present their young with the kinds of experiences man does. Rule-governed turn-taking is one of the products of those processes; parent-managed turn-taking during the apprenticeship period is one of the things that make those processes effective.

Rules versus Stochastic Contingencies. I did not describe the contingencies of early interaction as rules. I said that the behavior of one partner "significantly increased the likelihood of" a particular type of response by the other. The effect might be a digital one, that is, the parameter B might have one value when mother does nothing, another when she is jiggling, and a third just after she stops jiggling. Or it may be a more continuous, analogue function of some kind, like the "tonic" effects described by Schleidt (1973), where the response depends upon the stimulus's intensity and frequency of repetition. There is some reason to think the jiggle-burst contingency involves a continuous change of that kind, since the contingency function subsides gradually to the baseline level after several seconds (Figure 3-4). The technical problem in answering such questions is that smooth curves can result from pooling many observations of what are really dichotomous or threshold-type phenomena. In any case, whether the changes are discrete or continuous, the probability of a response to any of the contingencies we have studied never goes close to 100%. We would not want to say, therefore, that the turn-taking in sucking or the mutual greetings in face-to-face play are *rule-governed*.

Shaking hands is an example of rule-governed interpersonal behavior. There are times one does offer to shake hands and times one does not. The probability shifts from close to zero at certain times (stepping into an elevator with a stranger) to close to 100% at other times (when he says, "Hi, I'm So-and-so").

A convention (i.e, rule) of that kind might or might not originate in a contingency. If it did so, it would begin as a tendency to extend the hand just a little more frequently when someone introduces himself than at other times. The tendency would increase over time (one imagines this happening as a result of partial reinforcement) until it is nearly 100%, and at some point the person would become aware of it. Once he was aware of himself failing to perform correctly every time—that is, once he experienced the negative instances as violations of what he was expected to do—it would become a rule and the likelihood of following it would rapidly increase. A contingency does not become a rule until (1) under certain conditions the contingency is practically 100%, and (2) people are aware if it is violated. Neither of these conditions is true of infant behavior in the first year, though both are crucial to what we think of as the unique rule-governed character of human behavior, including language, by the second year. So an important question is whether any rules, and if so which ones, appear simply as the culmination of gradually increasing contingencies of interaction. To turn the question around, given a rule of social discourse, we want to know whether it is adopted suddenly or has its origins in a gradually increasing contingency. The rules for face-to-face turn-taking may originate that way, but we cannot really be sure yet because, though we know about contingencies from the present data and about rules from studies of adults

(Duncan & Fiske, 1977), the pieces in between are still missing. However, it is clear that at some point in its development turn-taking is no longer a matter of quantitative effects on stochastic parameters.

The question for future investigation is, then, where does the 100% contingency (or the feeling that a 100% contingency ought to be observed) come from? Is it just the inevitable end point of a gradually increasing stochastic contingency? After all, probabilities have a ceiling at 1.0 and a floor at 0. Any consistent trend could culminate at one or the other. There are some problems, however. Stochastic contingencies do not have to keep increasing or decreasing with development, they can stabilize at any level (see, e.g., Figure 3-5). Only some contingencies become rules. If those that do so are explained simply as ceiling or floor effects on gradually increasing contingencies, how shall we explain the appearance of the "mutually recognized obligation" which is part of the definition of a rule? How high does the contingent probability have to be before that recognition sets in? On the other hand, can there be a contingency of 1.0 without such recognition?

These problems disappear if we assume that the effect is the other way around, that the child learns what is expected but not necessarily because of an increasing contingency—and this knowledge then forces the contingency to the floor or ceiling. The developmental change would be in the nature of the infant's awareness, the sharing of what certain signals mean to adults; and this shared meaning would then be manifested by a high level of observance of certain rules.

As we shall see in the next chapter, the definition of *convention* that I have offered does not quite distinguish man from all other species. However, in the following chapters I shall have occasion to mention two extraordinary facts about how conventions are learned by those other animals that can learn them. They always learn them as increasing contingencies, and they nearly always learn them from man! Man himself, however, even as a young child, does not always or even usually acquire conventions via gradually increasing contingencies.

We took up the question of turn-taking because of its importance in the various frames within which parents facilitate the development of skills and introduce conventional meaning. As an example of the infant's learning to follow rules, turn-taking itself has turned out to be a revealing skill. It changes from a loose sort of shadow of adult conventions to a fairly well-defined set of rules at about the time the child begins to be engaged in symbolic discourse. Thus it gives us two reasons—the shared recognition of obligations and the shared symbolic representations thereby conveyed—for turning now to the problem of intersubjectivity.

Part Two

Construction of the Person

Students of children's language learning have frequently returned to a comment made by Augustine at the end of the fourth century:

> When my elders named some object, and accordingly moved towards something, I saw this and I grasped that the thing was called by the sound they uttered when they meant to point it out. Their intention was shown by their bodily movements, as it were the natural language of all peoples. . . . Thus, as I heard words repeatedly used in their proper places in various sentences, I gradually learned to understand what objects they signified. [Augustine, *Confessions*, I, 8]

This passage is at once sensible and troubling, for it raises the problem of how a child can ever know what aspects of things are being named. For example, does "milk" refer to food, liquid, bottle, nipple, hunger, things made of glass, things to be held, things to put in the mouth, white things, opaque things, cold things, or what? At issue, besides just how children learn word meanings, is the whole problem of how language is possible at all. It turns out that the meaning of a word or other conventional form of expression—any gesture at all—is not something that can be defined precisely. As Wittgenstein (1953) forcefully argued, knowing what something means is a matter of knowing its uses in social discourse. Learning various uses to which a form of expression may be put is the very process of coming to understand it.

One of the implications of this view is that the units of meaning in a language are not morphemes or words. Language does not consist of lexicon plus grammar, words plus rules for combining them. The language games that the child has to play involve predications upon whole configurations of objects and events in the world. What we commonly consider linguistic rules (the rules of grammar, transformational or otherwise) only describe optional variations upon sentence forms. That explains the interest 20th-century philosophers of language have taken in *propositions* rather than words. And propositions, in turn, owe their meaning to the social context of speaker and listener (or of author and reader). This realization came relatively recently to students of language acquisition: "The changes produced in sentences as they move between persons in discourse may be the richest data for the [child's] discovery of grammar" (Brown, 1968, p. 288). More recently, Garvey, Ervin-Tripp, and other authors mentioned in Chapter 6 have redefined the problem of language development in terms of discourse and communication rather than as acquisition of grammar.

This has led us to ask what it is that moves between adults and infants in discourse, prior to the acquisition of language. What kind of structure has evolved for these exchanges, and do the structures themselves—turn-taking, for example—have to be taught to the infant? The answer suggested in the previous chapters is that adults behave in systematic ways conducive to the development of an infant's skills, his learning conventional ways to express meaning, and even his learning the fact that there is such a thing as conventional meaning. These patterns of behavior have the character of "frames" constraining what the infant is able to do within them and what aspects of the surrounding world occupy his attention at particular moments. We now turn to some important functions of those frames. One function is to make it possible—in fact, inevitable—that when a symbol is introduced into the exchange its use will be obvious. Another function is to make the infant himself perform skilled actions, including the use of symbols, when he may have intended the result but lacked the means to accomplish it. Still another function—and they are often inseparable—is to set up the optimal spatiotemporal situation for imitation to occur.

The social matrix that provides for human developmental processes is as important to cognition as it is to language. Others have described the development of thought as an interiorization of symbols, but they have not always included in their account the internalization of the social skills through which those symbols are acquired and through which they work. Thought is not just internalized symbolic meaning, a construction of propositions using an acquired code. It is an internalized discourse, a matter of anticipating what the response of others might be to one's behavior and responding to those responses in advance. Thought is, in fact, verbally or nonverbally, a dialogue with oneself.

Once objects and events can be represented symbolically, the world acquires a stability and permanence it cannot have for a lower organism. Chapter 7 explores the concept of representation, the mental process by which we can use the perceptions previously encoded in memory. "Intersubjectivity" is then defined as access to one another's representations and as the process of sharing meaning. Different levels of shared meaning are involved in different kinds of signs, from the *index*, which signifies something but is neither an intentional gesture nor a conventional signal, to *symbols*, which are both intentional and conventional. These two critical parts of the definition of symbols emphasize their inherently social origins and make it clear why symbols are unique to man.

Chapter 8 analyzes the facial, vocal, and manual expressions of infants at different ages, from the point of view of the intentionality and conventionality criteria. We conclude that there is no intersubjectivity until the period of shared memory, no real communication until the end of the first year when language development proper has begun.

Chapter 9 presents a theory of imitation, rejecting some major assumptions that other authors have made about it. Imitation has nothing to do with a passive copying of others' behavior, nor does it mean that the child's productions are identical to anything he has seen or heard others do. It is an active process of selective assimilation and accommodation. Furthermore, there is no one simple imitation skill with its own course of development. What changes is the type of behavior imitated. An important agenda for infancy is the progressive imitation of higher levels of use of signs, until the ultimate achievement of symbols. The principal role played by parents in this process is their provision of salient models within the facilitating context of the frames discussed in Chapter 5, which channel the infant's attention and organize his imitative efforts.

Chapter 10 discusses mothers' speech to infants, from the point of view of its structural features as well as its content. We find no evidence that babies have much influence upon this speech, as the notion of a mother-infant system would have suggested. Instead, the speech reveals stable individual differences among mothers, particularly related to their fantasies about what kind of person the baby is and their expectations about babies in general. Our study of mothers' monologues to babies will clarify some issues about the sample of parents' language that infants hear in the first year. The monologues reveal the prevalence of certain key themes, prefiguring the way a personal self-concept will eventually be communicated from parent to child.

Chapter 11 deals with the earliest stages of socialization and self-consciousness, arguing that consciousness of rules, of the system, and of self are all interdependent and therefore all develop together. Some ideas about the constituents of the self are reviewed, particularly the idea that a self is composed of *I* and *me*, an agent in the world plus a mental process capable of anticipating others' perceptions and reactions to what the *I* does. It is suggested that infants are socialized through a process more like co-optation than like mutual cooperation; hence not much in the way of self-consciousness or other-consciousness is required of the infant initially. However, the apprenticeship gradually demands more and more of those kinds of consciousness.

Chapter 12 continues the discussion of socialization and self, from the point of view of attachment to significant others and individuation from them. Attachment is really an interpersonal component of skills, involving confidence in ourselves in particular contexts. Theories of attachment and individuation have helped make clear the inseparability of cognition from affect, and of mental from social life. The four periods of parent-infant interaction (shared rhythms and regulations, shared intentions, shared memory, and shared language) are reiterated in terms of stages in the development of self.

7

Representation,
Intersubjectivity, and Symbols

"What's the good of Mercator's North Poles and Equators,
Tropics, Zones, and Meridian Lines?"
So the Bellman would cry; and the crew would reply
"They are merely conventional signs!"

Lewis Carroll, *The Hunting of the Snark,* 1876

Hide a small toy under a cloth in front of an 8-month-old. After watching you, the baby may look away, then apparently forget about the object. But if you lay the cloth over the toy when he is already reaching for it, he is likely to grasp the cloth and, lifting it, discover the toy. Do this a few times in the same place, and the baby will soon learn to find the toy every time.

Now do an experiment. After the infant has found it five or six times under a cloth near his left hand, put the toy under a different cloth at his right. The usual result is astonishing. The baby looks immediately back to the place where the toy was on all the previous trials. It is not "out of mind," as might have been the case on the first trial; the baby shows that he has not forgotten the object, for he actually searches for it. This phenomenon has been known for a long time (Piaget, 1954) and thoroughly studied in many variations (e.g., Gratch, 1975; Butterworth, 1977; Willatts, 1979). In all our repertoire of Piagetian phenomena I know of no more graphic demonstration that the world of permanent objects in an orderly, mappable space, which we take for granted (during our waking hours), is something infants only construct slowly.

The most common way to describe that construction process is in Piaget's terms, as the growth of representation, which in turn encom-

117

passes symbol formation. The two tend to be confused, so that Representation (with the capital R usually implicit) means symbolic
representation, and the earlier stages are described as way stations en
route to that achievement. The purpose of this chapter is to distinguish
between representation and symbolization. The former is a mental process; the latter is a social process. This chapter will have nothing to say
about babies; it is concerned with these concepts that are at the root of
many of the questions developmental psychologists have been asking
babies. In the following chapter, we shall examine the empirical evidence
for intersubjectivity between young infants and adults; then in Chapter
9 I shall present a theory of how the infant comes to be able to imitate.
Those discussions will require us to share a clear understanding of the
concepts of representation, intersubjectivity, and symbols.

Those who conceive of the development of symbols as a matter of
representation are taking an inside-out position. They assume that the
theater of development is within the infant's mind. In contrast, once we
agree to view symbols as a social process, by the time we reach Chapter
9 we should be ready to tackle the question of what role social interaction
plays at different stages in the child's construction of reality.

What kinds of evidence would lead us to conclude that social relations were important in this construction process? First would be the
existence of cross-cultural differences, that is, cognitive differences produced by social differences. If cross-cultural cognitive differences were
found in infants, and if they could not be attributed to race or other
physical conditions such as climate, they would be evidence of social
effects. I do not think such evidence exists. The infant stages and schemas we know about are probably universal across all the races and
cultures of man.

A second potential argument for the importance of social life in
early cognitive growth would be any evidence that cognitive structures
are acquired in the social domain first. There might be a decalage, or
time gap, between knowing something about people or about human
actions and knowing essentially the same thing about nonhuman objects
and their movements. For instance, a study by Bower (1974) suggested
that infants expect their mothers to behave like permanent objects a few
weeks before they expect inanimate objects to do so. If object permanence and other basic cognitive achievements consistently appear first
in the interpersonal realm, it would suggest that social experience is at
the leading edge of sensorimotor gains. Such decalage, however, does
not consistently appear when familiarity and other basic features of the
tasks are controlled (Jackson, Campos, & Fischer, 1978).

More persuasive is a third kind of argument, derived from a combination of epistemological and empirical considerations. This argument

holds that cognitive structures are acquired through social processes. It does not necessarily imply cross-cultural differences, for those social processes may be universal. Nor does it imply that the cognitive gains will appear first with respect to knowledge about other people. Any piece of knowledge is social in origin if it comes from infants' and adults' joint apprehension of the world. The phase of apprentice system membership creates a certain kind of joint agency and mutual dependence, in discourse even of the most primitive kind, managed by the adult partner. We have already seen that the effect of that apprenticeship is to establish shared intentions. But shared intentions imply shared meaning or intersubjectivity, which requires some sort of vehicle with which the two partners can have access to one another's representations of the world. In this chapter and the next, I shall argue that the only adequate form of representation for those shared purposes is symbolization.

Representation as a Mental Process

Representation is the process by which knowledge becomes accessible to thought, becomes the images about which and by means of which we think. To discuss representation it is not necessary to know anything (fortunately) about the actual *engram* or *encoded* information in memory. What is encoded can be represented in different ways at different times, depending upon situation and purpose. What is represented will often, perhaps always, be substantially different from any event that was originally encoded, because the reconstruction process combines elements from many encodings. As schematized in Figure 7-1, *memory* is a name for the fact that acquired information is stored over time. Representation does not mean memory. It means the process of retrieving information from memory and restoring it to a format something like the original

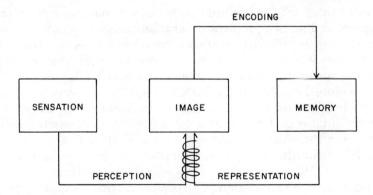

Figure 7-1. *Representation* in relation to other basic constructs of cognitive psychology.

experience of perception. (We commonly use the plural form, *represen-tations*, as a synonym for images.)[1]

A helpful metaphor for the distinction between memory and representation is a videotape. Examine the videotape in the minutest detail and you will find nothing to resemble the events that were occurring in front of the camera when the tape was recorded. Yet the information is there, stored in the tape's memory; it happens to be encoded magnetically, but it could be encoded in other ways on other kinds of devices. When the tape is played back on appropriate equipment, the original events are represented on the TV monitor: literally, they are presented again. This metaphor translates directly to Figure 7-1. "Sensations" are the camera, "image" the video monitor, and "memory" the videotape.

However, our perceptual and representational processes draw upon one another in creating images, whereas the video camera has no memory and the playback has no perception.

Representation is not necessarily veridical. Fantasies, hypotheses, illusions, all arise from representation. The succession of images is not bound by the physical laws that constrain sequentiality in external events. So the world of representation becomes a world unto itself, quite distinct from the external world. Yet it originates in that external world, and it employs some of the same mechanisms of reconstruction and of active scanning that are employed when we perceive external objects.

Perception, too, constantly draws upon encoded information. It reconstructs an image of what is probably there rather than making a faithful copy of actual events. For perception is something more useful than a faithful copy. It is an identification, an assimilation of the novel to the known. Perception is really representation's response to present stimuli, and representation is perception's reconstruction of previously encoded images.

The problem of the 7-month-old with the toy that has just disappeared in front of him is a problem of representation. (An older infant represents the toy as still present under the cover.) So is the problem of younger babies whose head and eye movements reveal whether they anticipate the movement of objects along a trajectory (Gardner, 1971; Bower & Paterson, 1973; Meicler & Gratch, 1980). Similarly, we can use habituation, discrimination learning, and visual fixation experiments to discover what infants of different ages learn from their experience with objects and with three-dimensional space (Bower, 1966; Caron, Caron, & Carlson, 1978) and what kinds of concepts they are capable of acquiring (Cohen & Strauss, 1979). Behind all of this work is the problem of equivalence: What shapes or sounds or natural objects are treated as belonging

1. But not just visual and auditory ones. There are motor images (what it feels like to be doing something), emotional images, touch, taste, and smell images.

to categories? And behind the notion of categories is representation: When the eye focuses upon a square tilted so that it casts a trapezoid upon the retina, does the eye's mind see a trapezoid or a square? What does the mind's eye remember having seen?

All three aspects of knowledge—the encoding process, the representation process, and the information stored in memory—develop. When we loosely speak of the development of representations of the world, we should be referring to all three aspects. An "inside-out" theory might hold that any one, two, or all three aspects have to develop first before communication with and about representations becomes possible. An "outside-in" theory might hold that the process of encoding perceptions, or perhaps the knowledge that is stored, or the process of representing that knowledge (or any combination of those) is an internalization of the way infants have learned to communicate about events. Hence we can see that "inside-out" and "outside-in" theories need not necessarily be mutually exclusive.

Ignoring the social context, experimental psychologists have constructed inside-out theories by focusing upon the progressive transformation of storage and retrieval processes. Terms like *recognition memory, constancies, permanence,* and *recall memory* all refer to the infant's expectations based upon stored knowledge about objects in the world. The newborn has built-in expectations in the selective attention mechanisms of his sensory apparatus (his preferences for faces, for edges, for moving objects), and these determine what categories he will habituate to and what simple associations he will learn. This learning creates "recognition memory." The perceptual "constancies" that are then recognized (as evidenced by surprise when we experimentally violate them) are expectations about what aspects of things usually remain invariant across variations in other aspects. These coalesce into "object permanence," the expectation that an object will always occupy one and only one sector of space (that the toy, which disappeared under one cloth, cannot transport itself underneath the other cloth), and finally to "recall memory," or Representation with a capital R, implying a new form of representation whereby the child can now conjure up the image of an object in its absence. The evidence for recall is merely the child's continued search for things that fail to appear in their most probable location.

Our knowledge of this series of stages in representation is largely due to Piaget (1952). Although the subsequent experimental evidence fits his observational descriptions at each stage, the evidence does not really justify calling the developmental change a change in the *processes* of memory storage and retrieval. It could be that the same processes are being used to encode and represent more complicated events (e.g., symbols), rather than that the apparatus itself changes. Furthermore, Piaget himself elsewhere (1951) described the same period from the point of view of semiotics, which focuses upon the available codes and what is encoded. Simple assimilation leads to accommodations in schemas. These in turn allow the infant to acquire significations, the learned relations between signs and events in the world. Gradually, those signs become symbols.

The two ways of describing the changes, "memory development" and "semiotic development," pretty much refer to the same set of observations, though in different terms. In both cases, Piaget and the many investigators whom he inspired have assumed that the critical developments took place inside the infant (perhaps "interiorizing" the object world) as prerequisites for communication with others. They write as though representation could develop in an infant whose biological needs were met by robots and who had to acquire all of his knowledge of the world autonomously. They fail to see that parents, as repositories of symbols, are crucial agents in the whole affair.

Symbols, which I shall try to define shortly, are (though purely conventional) the most permanent attributes of permanent objects. (I think that is what Gertrude Stein meant by "a rose is a rose is a rose.") In fact, symbols even give permanence to impermanent events, like Sunday, childbirth, the King. The teething ring disappears from the infant's mind even while it remains in his hand; we say it lacks permanence for him, or he lacks object permanence. But it does not disappear from the parent's mind. As seen in Chapter 5, the parent provides a spatial-temporal frame in which an object of intention keeps reappearing. The theater of development is not internal. It is an outdoor stage, and the parent is very much the director, cuing the entrances and exits of the participating audience's favorite characters. When those characters are referred to by name, it removes any confusion that might have resulted from changes of costume or posture.

The choice between "inside-out" and "outside-in" theories about the construction of reality becomes this: Did our ability to represent objects develop because we had symbols for them? Or is it the other way around: Does the infant learn symbols as a result of what he has learned about the behavior of objects in the world? Can both answers be yes? Can object permanence and symbols both be prerequisites for each other? Suppose the parent and infant happen to engage in a form of play in which the parent, just because of the way he or she conceives of and represents objects, guarantees their permanence for the infant: stores them, re-presents them to the infant, refers to them with conventional gestural signs. Within the parental frames, the apprentice might find himself sharing in the parent's representations of the world.

Piaget's Sensorimotor Theory

The process of representation can be modeled either formally (C-models) or functionally (P-models). The models of modern cognitive psychology are mostly P-models. They depict the flow of information through the nervous system, from sensory organs to short-term memory (STM) buffers of one kind or another, to recognition or decision trees, to long-term memory (LTM); and then, when retrieved, back to STM, etc.

The principal model of how representation develops over the first few years of life, however, is Piaget's sensorimotor theory. And that is not a P-model. Although Piaget and the many authors who have taken up the problem do occasionally describe real-time processes, for the most part the discussion of how representation develops is carried on at the level of C-models. Unfortunately, as pointed out in Chapter 2, a C-model may be the wrong kind of model from which to try to explain developmental changes.

In Piaget's view, symbol formation is an *orthogenetic* process, meaning that it has its own spontaneous genesis within the child's mind, and only after that inner development has progressed to an appropriate level is the child able to acquire the special conventional kind of symbols used in communication with others. To one who assumes that development is orthogenetic, the inadequacy of C-models may not be obvious. But if one seeks to explain the functional causes for development, C-models will not do. Vygotsky (1962) was one of the first to recognize this.

Vygotsky complained that Piaget's (1926) account of the socialization of egocentric speech, at ages 3-5, was an inside-out theory. It happens that Piaget's account of sensorimotor development and the learning of the first linguistic signs is equally inside-out. Only the books on nursery school children were known to Vygotsky, who seriously challenged the inside-out view. We shall return to his arguments against that particular view of socialization in a later chapter. At the moment we are addressing the inside-out theory Vygotsky did not have a chance to read, the one in *Play, Dreams, and Imitation in Childhood; The Construction of Reality in the Child*; and *The Origins of Intelligence in Children*. If he had known about it, he would not have liked it any better than the earlier work that dealt with the older child.[2]

2. Piaget himself was not able to read Vygotsky's work until 25 years later. He regretted that the great Russian psychologist, not having understood the whole Piaget, inferred from the part he knew that Piaget's views on education were very different from his own. For some reason, Piaget's comments were only included as an unbound insert in the first English edition of Vygotsky (1962). Since they have fallen out of most library copies and were omitted from the paperback edition, they travel through the Piagetian underground in *Samizdat* xeroxed form.

Specifically, Piaget saw the origins of representation in the infant's construction of a stable space containing permanent objects. The construction referred to is, in fact, representation in just the sense defined earlier: reconstruction of images based upon perception and upon what one knows of the world. The infant is also constructing a *stored* knowledge of the world, but the construction we are concerned with is the process of *re*construction of a world, by the mind,[3] based upon that stored information in the brain. When our retinas see a round lump in the surface of a blanket, we know there is a ball under it. So does a 12- to 15-month-old child, as he shows by pulling away the blanket with one hand while reaching with the other. This action "goes beyond the information given," as Bruner would say; a representation must be occurring based upon the shapes of objects previously covered by blankets. The 6-month-old does not behave in that way. He may see the lump, but he does not see it as a ball. He does not reach for it unless we uncover it.

Shall we merely say that the 6-month-old does not have enough experience of what balls under blankets look like? Then suppose that instead of a lump under a blanket, we let the two children see the ball being placed under a bowl. Once under the bowl, it is invisible; yet the older child, like an adult, easily finds it. This, too, must require representation. It is not a matter of knowing what balls look like under bowls, for there is nothing to see. It is a matter of knowing that objects still exist when they have disappeared under things. That is a property of the 15-month-old's representational schemes, that is, of the processes by which he reconstructs images that guide his actions. In this case it may well be a motor rather than a visual image. The point is that Piaget expresses the knowledge (object permanence) in formal terms, as competence. Ultimately, what psychologists really want to know is how such representational processes work. What is it that changes in the child over the first 18 months or so, and what causes the change? This is a more difficult question than Piaget's, What does the 18-month-old know that the 6-month-old does not know?[4]

3. Miller and Buckhout's authoritative psychology text (1973) defines mind as "a four-letter Anglo-Saxon word." I prefer McDougall's (1912) definition: "We may define the mind of any organism as the sum of the enduring conditions of its purposive activities. And, in order to mark our recognition of the fact that these conditions are not a mere aggregation, but form rather an organized system of which each part is functionally related to the rest in definite fashion, we may usefully speak of the 'structure' of the mind" (p. 69).

4. Questions like, "At what age does the infant possess knowledge of X?" (object permanence, size constancy, etc.) are initially posed in C-model terms, but sooner or later students of the epistemology of infancy ask their questions about competence in more and more detailed ways, inevitably pushing toward P-models of what the infant actually does over the milliseconds involved in perceiving. As has already happened in the study of the adult mind, epistemology will yield to cognitive psychology (see, e.g., Bower, 1975).

In adopting the concept of *schema* from Baldwin (1895) and from the early British students of skill (Head, 1920; Bartlett, 1932), Piaget did represent knowledge as process. The notion of a circular reaction, for example, in which a schema's result elicits its repetition, is very much a P-model. By taking that approach, Piaget emphasized that perception is action (and, for the young infant, always *overt* action, whereas covert action is representation), and he emphasized the importance of active encounter with objects for the child's gradual differentiation of schemas. In the sensorimotor period more than in any other, Piaget's theory at least hinted of the outlines of a theory of knowledge as process rather than as formal structure. (As an example of the latter, the "operations" involved in classification or in conservation are not cognitive operations in real time. They are components of the mathematical "grouping" that expresses those kinds of knowledge in a concise and logical form.)

However, beyond the notion of the schema, in theorizing about the significant changes over the first couple of years, Piaget abandoned P- for C-models. He described stages through which the child passes, and those six familiar stages are what many readers think of as Piaget's theory of sensorimotor development.

Although it has proved an accurate description, Piaget's list of stages reflects a failure to be clear about whether what develop are the processes of intelligence or merely its contents. This, I think, is at the heart of his ambivalence about which type of model, P- or C-, he was offering. Of course, a list of stages is not a theory of development, nor did Piaget claim it was. The theory was that each stage inevitably transforms itself into the next (orthogenesis) because of disequilibrium (imbalance) between the invariant functions of assimilation and accommodation, which all living systems constantly strive to equilibrate. The specific disequilibria that were supposed to account for stage transition were sometimes expressed as a conflict between schemas and the actual movement of objects in the world (e.g., the infant's surprise when a toy, consistently hidden in one place and then hidden in a different place, reappeared from that new place rather than from the place where it had always reappeared in the past). Sometimes they were expressed as a problem of coordinating competing schemas (e.g., at 9 months Jacqueline learned to bite her finger in imitation of Piaget, after separately producing the finger movement and the mouth movement). For the most part, however, the disequilibrium referred to was between assimilation and accommodation:

> As long as equilibrium has not been achieved, either there is primacy of accommodation, resulting in representative imitation, or there is primacy of assimilation, resulting in symbolic play. When equilibrium is first achieved, there is cognitive rep-

resentation, but thought only reaches the level of preconcepts or intuition, since both the assimilation and the accommodation are still incomplete, the former being direct, without hierarchies of nestings, and the latter still linked with particular images. When, however, with further development, the equilibrium becomes permanent, imitation and play are integrated in intelligence, the former becoming deliberate and the latter constructive, and cognitive representation then reaches the operational level, having acquired the reversibility characteristic of the equilibrium between generalized assimilation and accommodation. [Piaget, 1951, pp. 273–274]

In other words, Piaget's only explanation for stage transition was that disequilibria are intolerable to the organism itself. He paid no more than lip service to the fact that signifiers become available to the child primarily through the social institution of language. He completely ignored the fact that what the child imitates are other people; that disappearing and reappearing objects are moved around by other people, not just by the laws of physics; that other people interpret the infant's intentions, providing the instrumental frame, the memory frame, the feedback frame, the discourse frame. The infant's cognitive structures, Piaget was satisfied to say, like those of the older child, continually equilibrate because they *must* equilibrate. If we understand this *must* as an evolutionary explanation (organisms that do not adapt do not survive either as individuals or as species), then it is not circular. But it is a reduction to the status of universal law rather than a specific explanation. It tells us nothing, really, about how human intelligence develops except that we must remember human intelligence is a biological phenomenon and therefore subject to the laws of adaptation.

All explanation is a matter of reducing what is not understood to something else that is understood better. But a *reductionist* theory is one that only reduces a phenomenon to something else that is *not* understood any better. To take an example from a different domain, suppose a social psychologist were to say that the behavior of a crowd consists of the behavior of all the individuals plus cohesive social forces. That would be to say nothing at all. The question is what makes individuals behave as they do when assembled in crowds; how do those supposed forces act, and whence do they arise? To postulate "cohesive forces" would beg those questions. Piaget's theory of sensorimotor stage transition, the general theory, was reductionist in that way; though some of his accounts of how specific changes may take place were much more powerful proposals.

What was distinctive and important about Piaget's theory lay in the kinds of explanations it specifically rejected. It rejected, for example, the possibility that the infant is simply adapting to the environment in the simplest way, by having his schemas shaped through reinforcement. It rejected the notion of learning by association; that is, learning to antic-ipate what will happen next simply through the repeated presentation of contiguous events. In fact, it rejected any outside-in theory. It insisted instead upon the intrinsic organization accomplished by intelligence it-self, interacting with the environment but only under the direction of invariant intrinsic functions. Unfortunately, it did not seek the·expla-nation of that organization in unique properties of the mind or of any-thing else about the human organism qua human—only in those invariant functions said to be found in all structures, all genesis from a structure in disequilibrium to a more equilibrated one.

I am making three criticisms of Piaget's sensorimotor theory, all of which have been made by others. First, he arrived at an inside-out view only by virtue of ignoring the dynamics between infant and parent. Second, he begged the question of how to explain man's uniqueness. Third, because representation itself was not explained as a process, there was no chance of getting at the process of its development, inside-out or otherwise. The point that is being made here for the first time, I think, is that these three criticisms are closely related. To adhere to a C-model is in fact to pretend that the description of a developmental phenomenon were the same as its explanation, and thus that one could look to or-thogenetic transformation rather than any kind of interactive process. This criticism applies to all inside-out theories (e.g., Werner & Kaplan, 1963), not only to Piaget's.

It is possible (indeed, sensible) to agree about the inadequacy of conditioning theories and of associationist theories of mental develop-ment and yet remain dissatisfied with Piaget's explanation of how the mind organizes and reorganizes itself. It is possible to acknowledge the universals in human development and yet see the infant's environment as sharing the responsibility for those universals. For the environment itself, even the social environment provided by adults, may have uni-versal properties too. I believe that Piaget's minimization of the adult role in sensorimotor development was due to his equating "nurture" with environmental variation as opposed to invariant functions. But we have already (in Chapter 2) rejected that equation and opposition. Ex-trinsic functions of "nurture," such as the several parental frames I have discussed, are just as invariant and universal—just as much a part of "nature"—as the intrinsic functions like assimilation are.

"Intersubjectivity": Access to Others' Representations

A difficult but important concept has made its way recently into the psychology of infancy:

For infants to share mental control with other persons they must have two skills. First, they must be able to exhibit to others at least the rudiments of individual consciousness and intentionality. This attribute of acting agents I call *subjectivity*. In order to communicate, infants must also be able to adapt or fit this subjective control to the subjectivity of others: they must also demonstrate *intersubjectivity*. [Trevarthen, 1979, p. 322]

Although used in somewhat different ways by different writers, intersubjectivity means something like "shared meaning," two people having approximately the same representation of some object, event, or symbol. We shall not be concerned with sorting out the possible different usages of the word. The question is how infants come to share meaning with others.

How, in fact, can any two minds, experiencing the world separately, agree about particular objects and events? Until the end of the 19th century, there were two principal ways out of this dilemma: the empiricist route (two individuals have experienced the same objects and events, and their perceptual apparatus is identical) or the transcendentalist route (the mind consists of a priori categories). Neither philosophical position could help psychologists who regarded the developmental question as one that was open to empirical investigation. The problem became more complicated when scientists began to notice cultural and linguistic differences in how the world was categorized. It became clear that somehow one's community, not just one's physical environment, must have effects upon one's mental development.

This discovery led psychologists and linguists back to some basic issues in philosophy. How could the nature of reality be learned through interaction with others if there were not some prior agreement on the categorization of objects and events about which to interact? For example, how could the child learn what an adult means by "cup" without some prior understanding of which features of the object pointed to are likely to be the critical ones for the concept "cup"? In short, even if full-fledged intersubjectivity can only result from learning how members of a specific community view the world, this learning itself must act upon a mind already possessing some degree of intersubjectivity.

The greatest concern with intersubjectivity is found in phenomenology, for which it is a central concern. Unfortunately, phenomenologists and the sociologists whom they influenced have revealed no way out of the chicken-and-egg circularity of intersubjectivity and mind. Husserl (1960) made individual consciousness the starting point for an analysis of both physical reality and the intersubjective world. As a consequence, social interaction could not be involved in the creation of that consciousness. So Schutz (1962), Merleau-Ponty (1964), and Berger and Luckmann

(1966), despite their emphasis on the social construction of reality, were unable to generate a developmental theory dealing with the origins of intersubjectivity in infancy. They wound up, like Descartes and Kant, reasoning about knowledge as though it were not a developmental problem at all.

A more promising step was achieved by pragmatic philosophers such as Peirce (1877), James (1890), Baldwin (1906), Dewey (1917), Mead (1934), Langer (1942), Piaget (1952), Wittgenstein (1953), and Popper (1972). They dropped the question of *certainty* that had obsessed epistemologists since early Christian times. They defined knowledge of reality as knowledge adequate for action rather than as certain knowledge. This was a nontrivial idea in which the influence of Darwinism can be seen clearly. There was no reason to take reality as a constant. Verification of one's perception of the world could only consist in confirmation by others.

To the pragmatists, the method of theory confirmation by a scientific community offered a good analogy for ordinary intraindividual thought processes as well. For Mead and Wittgenstein in particular, intersubjective gesturing (the social use of categories of objects, events, intentions, etc.) was a precondition for their private use in reflective thought. Despite great differences in their approaches,[5] these two philosophers both recognized that there is no certainty in meaning; instead, they defined meaning as use. "How do I know that this colour is red?" Wittgenstein asked, and replied, "Because I have learned English!" (Wittgenstein, 1953, Pt. I, p. 381). Such a view neatly sidesteps the question that had obsessed earlier epistemologists up to Kant, of how we can be certain that our knowledge is veridical. What a word means, and therefore the very concept for which the word stands, is a question of social usage. Unfortunately, neither Mead nor Wittgenstein managed to spell out a noncircular theory of how those usages are learned.

To show the importance of breaking away from the idea of certainty in meaning, Wittgenstein criticized the inadequacy of Augustine's theory (quoted on page 114). Augustine was used as an illustration of a fairly widespread view of how word meanings are acquired: that the child already has categories and merely has to be shown which signs represent which categories. This presupposes intersubjectivity, both in assuming that the child sees the same "object" the adult names, and in the idea of a "natural language" of gestures. It is an unsatisfactory theory for several reasons. As Wittgenstein showed, if it applies at all, it can apply

5. Mead viewed sign-response relations behaviorally, refusing to treat denotation as a phenomenon apart from action. Wittgenstein certainly did the latter. On the other hand, Wittgenstein seems to have lacked Mead's appreciation of semiotics prior to the level of the word.

only to the relatively small class of words that name specific things. More important, it offers no explanation for how the child comes to categorize the world in terms of specific kinds of objects and actions in the first place.

Nonetheless, despite the unanswered question of how categorical knowledge originates, it must indeed exist in some form before language-learning can occur. Modern students of child language (e.g., Macnamara, 1977) have argued that young children must be able to extract much of the meaning of adult utterances *from the context*, because the meaning is simply not encoded in the utterances themselves. "Put that away" is an extreme example; a simple word like "milk" is a less obvious one, which I have already mentioned. What aspect of the situation does "milk" signify? Although the child cannot know precisely what categories are to be signified before learning their signifiers, at least some intelligent guesses about what is signified must be an integral part of that process; and so must the prior assumption that signification exists, that utterances and gestures have meaning. Therefore the 1970's saw language development research being pushed back into the preverbal period: into investigations of the first comprehended words, of pragmatics, of discourse, and of some fundamental structural features found in language but also found in earlier-developing patterns of social interaction. The Augustinian hypothesis remained alive, for example, in this dialogue between two imaginary epistemologists:

> A: What we call a language is a fairly elaborate and sophisti-
> cated symbol system. Don't you think, Jason, that before
> anyone acquires a language, he has had an abundance of
> practice in developing and using rudimentary prelinguistic
> symbolic systems in which gestures and sensory and per-
> ceptual occurrences of all kinds function as signs?
> J: Yes; but *language*-acquisition is what is at issue.
> A: You remember, though, that the real issue is over *initial* ac-
> quisition of languages, since once some language is avail-
> able, acquisition of others is relatively easy.
> J: True; but surely you do not call those rudimentary sys-
> tems languages.
> A: No; but I submit that our facility in going from one sym-
> bolic system to another is not much affected by whether
> each or either or neither is called a language; that *acquisi-*
> *tion of an initial language is acquisition of a secondary symbolic*
> *system*; and that as we find no interesting limitations upon
> what we can acquire as a secondary language, we have no
> ground for believing that there are such limitations upon
> what we can acquire as a secondary symbolic system.
> [Goodman, 1968, p. 105; italics added]

Psychologists, then, were asked whether any of the early social behavior of infants—for example, in feeding, in imitation, in play with and without objects—could be considered to constitute or to depend upon the "primary" symbolic system philosophers had been looking for.

It will be my thesis in Chapter 8 that those students of infancy were premature who eagerly agreed that they had found the philosopher's stone. Although there is representation, there is no symbolic system prior to language: no intersubjectivity, and no social system in the strict sense. So long as the infant is only apprenticed to the system, neither true intersubjectivity nor true communication exists. I shall argue that intersubjectivity arrives neither early nor as a discrete achievement. The intersubjectivity in the parent's mind keeps a stage ahead of that in the child's, and in this fact lies the secret of cognitive growth in our species. In the course of that argument I shall reject what might be called the Hypothesis of Presymbolic Communication, a view held by many psychologists and by all parents. Unconsciously if not consciously, parents behave as if there were shared meaning, as though infants not only understood but also produced "natural language" gestures that the parents understood. In a way, the parents are entertaining a fiction, but it is a fiction with a function. It is a necessary stage preparing the way for language development.

Symbols as a Social Process

The foregoing section reviewed some of the history of how psychologists came to be looking so closely at protocommunication in infants. Now we shall spell out some criterial definitions for communication, shared meaning, and symbols, and then we will be ready to look at the evidence.

The idea of "shared meaning" involves two distinct criteria, each of which is really a continuum. One is *intentional signification*: the external representation of some class of things or events or relations using a sign that remains distinguished from the thing signified. We shall call this kind of sign a *gesture*. A gesture might take the form of a manual or facial expression, but it might also take the form of words, drawings, familiar melodies, etc. Gestures designate something without being equivalent to it. They must not be equivalent in the producer's mind, since his intention is directed at a person, not at the thing designated. And they must not be equivalent from the point of view of anyone who interprets them as gestures, since one is interpreting the intention, not the thing designated.[6] So the intention of the sign is crucial to whether

6. This is what I take to be the nontrivial meaning of Grice's (1957, p. 383) definition of meaning, "*A* uttered *x* with the intention of inducing a belief by means of the recognition of this intention."

it is differentiated from what it signifies. Footprints are an example of signs that are not gestures. The animal does not intend to leave footprints; and a hunter following an animal's tracks is in fact following the animal itself, not distinguishing sign from signified as a driver does when following road signs.

The second criterion is that the meaning is by convention only. We shall use the term *signal* for any sign that is related to what it stands for only because the members of a community have arbitrarily assigned it that meaning. Footprints do not meet this criterion either, because they owe their utility as signs to being an inevitable product of the animal.

These distinctions have been stressed repeatedly, by Saussure (1959) and Peirce (1940) in the 19th century, then by Mead (1934), Piaget (1951), and Langer (1942) among others. Since their terminology is not uniform, Figure 7-2 clarifies how I shall use the various terms to preserve the important points. An *index* is a kind of sign, because it stands for something else, but it only does so to the observer (not by the intention of the producer), so it is not a gesture. Nor is it a signal, because its meaning does not depend upon the establishment of a social convention. We shall reserve the term *symbol* for a sign that is both a signal and a gesture. Note that a sign can be a gesture without being a signal (e.g., a posture that has universal, biological rather than conventional, meaning), or a signal without being a gesture (e.g., an involuntary utterance, or even a mechanical signal like the taillights that go on whenever a driver touches the brake pedal).

These are relative rather than absolute distinctions. There are signs that are conventional but iconic, hence not completely arbitrary, for example, the international highway "symbols" for a steep grade or a railroad crossing. And there are other signs that are almost but not quite

		(SYMBOL)
SIGNALS (conventional)	brake lights involuntary "ouch"	words hitchhiker's thumb
(parts, effects, or nonarbitrary associates of the thing signified)	(INDEX) footprints cry of pain	threatening fist seductive posture
	(not intentional, not differentiated signifiers; meaning merely derived by observer)	GESTURES (intentional signifiers, differentiated from what they signify)

Figure 7-2. Signs.

gestures. For instance, some cries of pain are partly voluntary: one might start to cry out purely because of the pain, yet modify the cry purposefully.

Signals versus Nonconventional Signs. All four cells of Figure 7-2 represent ways in which meaning can be shared, but the upper cells do so more than the lower and the right-hand cells more than the left. The distinction between the upper and lower rows has to do with conventionality. In the bottom row, where signs do not depend upon convention, two organisms might be said to share meaning to the extent they share an *Umwelt*, that is, live in the same stimulus world. Without going beyond indexical signs, we can think of many examples in which one animal's behavior is meaningful to another. This happens whenever the second animal perceives regularity in that behavior and learns to anticipate what the first is likely to do next. When a dominant animal menaces a less dominant one and thereby takes possession of some food or territory, there is intersubjectivity of a primitive sort: But we would not call the behavior of either animal a signal, as I am using the word.

When the ability to anticipate one another's behavior is due to an established signal—a sign that is only meaningful within a particular community—then meaning is shared in a higher sense. The producer and the interpreter of the sign share an aspect of their personal histories. The meaning is shared only with the initiated, not with just anyone. Obviously, the acquisition of signals is "outside-in."

Whether the use of signals occurs among other species is questionable. Many animals can be *trained* to use signs with purely conventional meaning. For example, an experimenter with chimpanzees decides that blue triangles will signify "apple." This may be an arbitrary decision, yet from the point of view of the animal learning the meaning of the sign, it is consistently associated with what it signifies. The fact that it has repeatedly been paired with apples makes it as nonarbitrary as a red circle. So the use of conventional signals by animals may in fact be a human phenomenon, due to the trainer's ability to construct an environment in which arbitrarily chosen symbols (from his own point of view) function as indexical from the animal's point of view. Children learn their first few words in this way—but only the first few. Another way of saying this refers to our discussion of contingencies versus rules in Chapter 6. The child's earliest conventional signs, including a few words, grow gradually from contingent expressions much as the laboratory chimp's signs do. Soon (15–18 months), however, words are added to the child's vocabulary in instantaneous fashion, as *rules,* and then his vocabulary increases from a dozen or so words to hundreds of words in a few weeks. This rapidity would not be possible if each word had to be learned as a contingent, greater-than-chance association of vocal patterns with particular events.

Gestures versus Nonintentional Signs. Two people can share meaning whenever one of them knows what the other means. They do not have to know one another or see one another; in fact, only one of them need be alive (e.g., if the other is on film). Person A can gesture to B, yet C can take the meaning of the gesture as well as B. On the other hand, this is not the same as C's understanding the meaning of something that was not a gesture at all, such as the brake lights of an automobile. This is what the distinction between the left and right columns of Figure 7-2 is about. When we refer to the shared meaning of a gesture, we are saying that the signer intends the meaning attributed to his sign by its receiver. An intentional sign may have many receivers, including some unintended ones; but it always has at least one intended receiver, real or imagined, and its meaning as a gesture is the meaning it is intended to have to that person.

An act can be intentional, and also a sign, without being an intentional sign. A bird's taking flight, which may be an index of danger to other animals, is intentional behavior; but we have no reason to say the bird is *signing* intentionally. This distinction between intentional acts that happen to be signs, and gestures, which are intentional signs, is an important one deserving a little more discussion. For we shall have to admit that there are some acts that are gestures if they are intentional at all: A smile or a cry is either involuntary, that is, not an intentional act (though it may still be a sign, an index of internal state); or else its intention is to communicate and therefore it is a gesture. But other kinds of action can be intentional without being gestures. We can identify other goals besides communication, for example, reaching for an object.

So there are two sets of criteria, one for intention itself and one for intentional signs, and we shall just have to live with the complication that all acts meet the first definition if they meet the second; and that some acts meet the second automatically when they meet the first, because they can have no other purpose than communication if they have any purpose at all.

Remember that the psychologist's ascription of intention is not a matter of certainty. We do not claim to *know* what our subject intends; we merely find it more useful to describe the behavior in terms of its systematic consequences than in terms of its quite varied antecedents.[7]

7. There will be many acts in which we cannot observe enough repetition or persistence by a particular organism to make the judgment of goal direction on any objective basis. Nonetheless, we call an act intentional if it appears to belong to a class of similar actions produced under similar circumstances by other members of the same species at about the same age. Again, it is a matter of presumption, not certainty. If we see an adult

We have to play the language game of "purposive behaviorism" (as Tolman [1925] called it) if we are to have a psychology of action, not reduce the behavior of organisms to mere motion.

Second, "intentional" does not necessarily mean creative, nor does it mean unlearned. A completely habitual action, resulting from the simplest conditioning, may be intentional so long as it is produced to achieve an effect rather than merely being elicited by a stimulus.

An intentional *sign* is an act whose goal includes a particular kind of effect on another organism's behavior. What kind of effect? Not a response to the act itself but a response to something signified. Moreover, we should not say the signer *intends* that effect unless there is reason to believe he anticipates it, which means being capable of experiencing it from the point of view of the receiver. In Figure 7-2, all four cells are types of signs, but the left-hand cells are not gestures. Only the right-hand cells are examples of signification intended by the producer of the sign. An intentional act can be a sign and can be intended to affect others, yet still not be an intentional sign: The dog's barking to go out, an example from Chapter 2, falls short of being a gesture because it is a one-way signal produced by the dog for an effect but not calling out a comparable response in the dog. (When I bark at her, she has no idea what I mean.) When the dog barks, she wants *to go out*; we should not say she wants me to know she wants to go out. If I yell loudly at you and keep doing so until I get you to move, my yelling is both intentional and social, yet not a gesture. I am trying to generate a response to the loud noise, which does not signify. If I say "jump," however, in order to get you to jump, that is a gesture as well as a signal. Conversely, I might shout "doggy" every time I see a picture of a doggy, and while that must be a learned signal it would not be an intentional signifier unless I care about someone's acknowledgment (or am at least imagining someone's acknowledgment) of the fact that indeed it is a picture of a doggy.

The "communication" between dog and man is a useful example to prepare us for discussing the intersubjectivity of infants. When I talk to my dog, I behave as if I meant her to understand exactly what a person would understand by my words. So it is a gesture in my mind, as a dog lover, but it does not meet my definition of gesture, as a

---

turn a doorknob, we presume he is either trying to open the door or testing to be sure it is locked, the best two inferences based on other adults' behavior with doorknobs. But we restrict the domain of these inferences. We would not extend them to a baby or a chimpanzee doing the same thing. We would need to know more about their characteristic sequence of acts in this situation; we would entertain the possibilities that they were merely trying to make a rattling noise or that the behavior was not intentional at all (they happened to shiver while touching the knob). Without some such restriction on our inference of intentionality, we would have no basis for any comparative or developmental studies.

psychologist. There is no intersubjectivity. By the same token, when the dog barks I behave *as if* her intention were to communicate, but there is really no intersubjectivity.

Only Humans Gesture. To say that an organism produces an intentional sign—a *gesture*—means that it anticipates how the sign will be interpreted by the other, and uses it with the intention of having that effect. As with intentional behavior in general, we are always *presuming* a gesture's intentions rather than identifying them with certainty. We make these presumptions by generalizing from comparable organisms under comparable conditions. We should not presume that the producer can have had expectations about the effect of his sign on the other, with respect to the idea signified, unless (as a minimum condition) we have reason to suppose he knows what his own sign signifies. It is perhaps surprising to realize that we cannot say that about a dog and her own barking. In fact, no nonhuman has ever been shown to have produced a sign with the *intention of signifying* an event remote in space or time, so that the sign designates an event without being equivalent to it. This is not to deny that animals can be trained in the use of signs to obtain things, nor to deny that in the natural course of predation, defense, and reproduction animals often make interpretations of other animals' behavior. Still, in Mead's (1934) terms, no other animal puts itself in the attitude of the receiver of its sign.

That was not a controversial claim in Mead's day, but, in view of recent successes in training apes in the use of sign systems, it is a controversial claim today. Before we can argue the matter, we had better have a behavioral criterion against which other species (as well as infants) can be compared.

Imagine that organism A emits a response X and keeps emitting it until organism B provides food Y, and that A then ceases to do X and eats Y. This satisfies the definition of intention. We say, "A intended to attain Y." It is important to note that there is no certainty here: We remain uncertain about the actual state of A's mind (A might have been trying to get Z and merely settled for Y). However, we say "A intends to attain Y" because we have learned the language game of cognitive psychology. We·also say, "A knows that X is a means to attain Y," and "B knows what A means by X." The question remains: Does A, in doing X, also interpret X from the perspective of B? In other words, does he put himself in the attitude of the recipient of the sign? If not, X is not a gesture.

It would be hard to prove that A does *not* imagine B's perspective. The burden of proof, however, is on anyone who claims that a nonhuman ever *does* so. A minimum condition for such a proof would be that when the situation is reversed so that B does X to A, A gives Y to B; in other words, that the sign with which we believe A intends to have a certain effect has that very effect on A. Second, the two sign-response relations must not both have been taught to A. For X to be called a symbol (a learned gesture), either A must have learned X as a means to obtain Y, and then spontaneously offered Y in response to sign X, or A must have learned to respond to X with Y and then spontaneously used X to obtain Y.[8] This restriction is the only way we as observers can distinguish between a truly reversible sign and two independent but similar-looking signs, one of which A has learned to produce and the other of which he has learned to comprehend.

I follow Huttenlocher and Higgins (1978) in using the term *designation* for the reversible relation between sign and signified. Designation is a property only of gestures that are also signals—only of symbols—because the reversibility of sign and signified entails that the sign also be conventional so as not to stand in a fixed relation to the signified. Others have expressed the same idea in somewhat different terms: for example, Piaget's (1951) discussion of how signifier and signified are "differentiated," and Nelson's (1979) view of words as becoming "detached" from concepts. Putting the accent on the reversibility of sign relations is the best way to operationalize this sometimes vague notion. The detachment is precisely what allows the mind to think. Other animals may have representation, producing images. But only an organism that can use symbols can think.

The acquired vocabularies of the erudite apes—Washoe, Sarah, Koko, Neam Chimpsky, et al.—lack the property of designation. (For an anthology of review articles, see Sebeok & Umiker-Sebeok, 1979.) The animals do generalize a signal so as to signify new objects that are similar in some way to those for which the signal originally stood when they learned it. But it is not clear that they ever spontaneously produce a signal to which they have been taught a particular response, or spontaneously respond in the way they have been taught others will respond to a particular signal. This is at the very heart of human language learning. It is precisely what human children begin to do profusely sometime after their first birthdays; there is no parallel among the best-educated apes for the exponential growth that occurs in children's vocabularies.

This is not to suggest that human *infants* possess the simultaneous understanding of sign-response relations from both sides, which I argue

8. This condition, even if met, provides no *certainty* that A is gesturing intentionally and intersubjectively. In fact, I can only be certain of this when I am A. I am the only one who knows when I am taking the perspective of another, just as I am really the only one who knows that I am a Self, not an automaton. And it is only by taking the role of the other or, more precisely, putting the other in the role of a Self that one convinces oneself the other is gesturing intentionally (Chapter 11).

is a condition for gestures. I agree with Piaget (1951) that the first true symbols are words. But the first words, though signals, are not yet symbols (not "linguistic signs," in Piaget's terminology). Studies of 1-year-olds indicate that the first words are learned either to produce or to comprehend: Putting the two roles together is a separate achievement.[9] In terms of the numbers of words known, comprehension leads production (Goldin-Meadow, Seligman, & Gelman, 1976). From that fact it is sometimes inferred that the first productions are spontaneous generalizations of previously comprehended words. This does not seem to me to be the case. Many of the first productions are learned directly as productions by imitating their use in the appropriate context. Meanwhile, other words continue to be learned as comprehended words without being produced. Over the next few months, the child comes more quickly to be able to produce the words he comprehends, and more quickly to comprehend as listener the words he can produce as speaker. So (in the period of shared language) the lexicons for production and for comprehension become essentially one lexicon, with symbols being accessible for either purpose no matter how they happen to have been acquired.

One might imagine that this achievement could have taken place earlier with respect to preverbal signs. Why should it have to wait for words? In effect, that is what is implied by those who use the words "intersubjectivity" and "communication" between very young infants and their mothers, as in the quotation from Trevarthen (1979) above. Our discussion so far provides a criterion against which to assess preverbal communication: Meaning is not truly shared, in the sense implied by "intersubjectivity," until A's gesture means to B what A intends it to mean, and thus not until the gesture has a double status in A's repertoire, producing an effect in him when others use it and also producing that effect in him when he uses it to produce the same effect in others. In the following two chapters, we shall see when that becomes true.

The Representation of Symbols

The phrase "symbolic process" is misleading when used to refer to something that goes on in the brain, as though it were a special way of storing or processing information. As I have described symbols, they are social processes. They may have a mental process accompanying them, but that process is a different one from the gesture itself, which is an interpersonal act. The mental process, in itself neither a gesture

9. Surprisingly few studies of very early comprehension and production exist; they have been reviewed by Huttenlocher (1974) and Bowerman (1976). A rationale for more extensive studies of comprehension in the early period appears in Nelson, Rescorla, Gruendel, and Benedict (1978).

nor a signal, is representation. The mind can represent a symbol, or any kind of sign, just as well as it can represent nonsignifying objects. In other words, signs, like acts, events, people, and objects, are things in the world. Any of those things can be represented in the mind.

Nor are engrams symbols. The nature of engrams (the form in which information is actually stored by the brain for minutes, days, and decades) is an unsolved problem of neurology. Symbols must be internalized in the same way that other experiences are internalized. We should not equate the semiotic codes of communication with the neurologic codes of the brain. It is reasonable to expect that man's brain works the same as those of other complex animals. The differences among species will be found to be quantitative, depending upon the number of cells given over to processing and storing information in various modalities, and architectural, depending upon the organization of the parts and the complexity of connections among them. But we have no reason to suppose that actual brain processes are different. When we say that man's thought is symbolic, we mean that what he thinks *about* is often symbolic. The mind works with representations *of* symbols (as well as of acts, objects, and so forth), rather than working *by* symbols. It is because of the way those symbols signify in the world that they produce a unique kind of thought in the mind.

By conceiving of representation as mental process and symbols as social process, and by not merging the two into a single idea as Piaget did, we have kept open the possibility that the mind may develop "outside-in."

8

Expressions, Signals, and Gestures

---

*At tea-time, when the dog, Jip, came in, the parrot said to the Doctor,
"See, he's talking to you."*

"Looks to me as though he were scratching his ear," said the Doctor.

*"But animals don't always speak with their mouths," said the parrot
in a high voice, raising her eyebrows. "They talk with their ears, with their
feet, with their tails—with everything. Sometimes they don't want to
make a noise. Do you see now the way he's twitching his nose?*

"What's that mean?" asked the Doctor.

*"That means, 'Can't you see that it has stopped raining?' " Polynesia
answered. "He is asking you a question. Dogs nearly always use their
noses for asking questions."*

Hugh Lofting, *The Story of Doctor Dolittle,* 1920

How much meaning should we attach to infants' expressions, and how
much meaning can we be sure they attach to the expressions of others?
Like the questions of language production and language comprehension,
these questions have to be considered together.

The Interpretation of Expressions

In order to interpret an expression we need either (*a*) independent evidence of its meaning or (*b*) similarity to expressions whose meaning is
known. The first of these may be impossible, at least so far as certainty
is concerned; and the second criterion, classing the expression with
similar-looking expressions whose meaning we think we know, leads
to a circular argument. Charles Darwin posed the problem more than
a century ago:

140

It is well known to those who have the charge of young infants, that it is difficult to feel sure when certain movements about their mouths are really expressive; that is, when they really smile. Hence I carefully watched my own infants. One of them at the age of forty-five days, and being at the time in a happy frame of mind, smiled; that is, the corners of the mouth were retracted, and simultaneously the eyes became decidedly bright. I observed the same thing on the following day; but on the third day the child was not quite well and there was no trace of a smile, and this renders it probable that the previous smiles were real. [1872, p. 211]

In this dispassionate account, Darwin brings up the same issues current investigators have to address in interpreting the young infant's facial expressions.

Evidence for the meaning of an expression hardly matters so far as parents' interpretations are concerned, a topic we shall return to in Chapter 10. But it does matter to us as psychologists, for our concern is when and how the character of infant expressions changes from indices to signals and/or gestures. It turns out that the word *expression* (as in "infant expressions," "facial expressions," and Darwin's title *The Expression of the Emotions in Man and Animals*) is an unfortunate word if one wants to avoid ambiguity regarding the meaning of these signs.

Consider the sentence "Expression X shows that person A feels Q," which is equivalent to "X expresses Q." These sentences might have three different meanings:

(Sense 1) "X is a manifestation of A's inner feeling"—that is, it is an *accurate* index;
(Sense 2) "X leads someone to infer that A feels Q"—that is, it is *interpreted* as an index;
(Sense 3) "A wants someone to believe that he feels Q"— that is, X is a *gesture*.

Either Sense 1 or Sense 3 might be the case without the other. However, if either Sense 1 or Sense 3 is true of a given expression, then Sense 2 is justified. On the other hand, we know that Sense 2 is often the case without any basis for confidence in Sense 1 or Sense 3. That is, we interpret an expression as a meaningful index of someone's feelings without any independent evidence either of his actual feelings or of his intention to convey feelings. "Even the early incomprehensible utterances of the infant can have the force of demands, protests, greetings, etc., as they are interpreted by adults" (Miller, 1970, p. 198).

Darwin (1872) used the word *expression* only in Sense 1. Although the phrase "frame of mind" seems an antiquated and philosophically unjustified usage, especially when Darwin referred to cats and dogs, he used the phrase in the passage quoted above just because of his concern to marshal some independent evidence of the emotion motivating the given expression. This was his concern throughout the book. By "expression of the emotions" Darwin never meant "expression to others" (i.e., gesture); he meant something like "manifestations on the surface of the body, of underlying emotion" (i.e., index). When he wrote of his dog, "He showed his pleasure by trotting gravely before me with high steps, head much raised, moderately erected ears, and tail carried aloft but not stiffly" (p. 57), he did not mean that the dog was purposely showing pleasure. He meant that a dog feeling pleasurable sensations automatically assumes some such posture—an inference he supported with numerous other examples. This distinction should be kept in mind when interpreting the meaning of infant expressions.

A face does not have to be a human face in order to appear expressive to us. Watch people imitating and interpreting the faces of fish in an aquarium. They simply respond to the configuration of eyes, mouth, and snout, even though it is a permanent configuration having nothing to do with the fish's mood or personality. They project onto such an expression the meaning it might have if a human being wore it. An analysis of these different expressions, then, would be an interesting study of intersubjectivity in human beings, but it would not be a study of fish.

Exactly the same caution applies to those who attach meaning to infant facial expressions or hand movements on the basis of similarity to adult gestures. It is not surprising that babies' faces and hands assume configurations resembling those of adults. Babies have eyes, brows, nose, cheeks, lips, fingers, with the same musculature operating them as we do. It is impossible not to project adult feelings and ideas into them. This is particularly true when an investigator presents us with still photographs or drawings as Darwin did and as Trevarthen has done recently (1977, 1979). In freezing momentary positions of the face or hands, these pictures lead us to make assumptions about the smoothness or directedness of the movements leading up to them, assumptions that are often erroneous. (The similarity to adult gestures, incidentally, is less compelling when we see the infants in motion.)

On the other hand, there is a big difference between an infant's expressions and those of a fish. The infant at some point becomes a person; then we must suspend our skepticism about the meaning of his expressions. The question is when to do so and on what basis. The contribution of Trevarthen's studies is their demonstration that if we are to distinguish early expressions from true gestures, it will have to be on some other basis than a featural analysis, for the expressions of infants and adults do have similar features. I argue that we have to distinguish them on the basis of behavioral context.

A popular way of expressing the distinction between Sense 2 and Sense 3 is to use Austin's (1962) terms: *perlocutionary* for acts that *may have* an effect on an observer, if only to convey information (the perlocutionary force of "It has stopped raining" is the fact that it has stopped raining); and *illocutionary* for acts that *intend* to affect the observer (the illocutionary force of "It has stopped raining" is the attempt to persuade someone to go outdoors). These terms have been applied in relation to vocalizations as primitive speech acts (e.g., Bates, Camaioni, & Volterra, 1975). It is possible to use behavioral criteria, for example, that a vocalization would not be considered an illocutionary speech act unless the infant made eye contact with someone first. Harding and Golinkoff (1979) found that this simple criterion did not occur at all in Stage IV infants (9–11 months). So illocutionary vocalizations do not appear until about the end of the first year, which means there is not much time lost between that milestone and the first words. Trevarthen, however, was not discussing vocalizations but "prespeech" movements, nonvocal expressions. At what point can they be said to be intentionally communicative?

Figure 8-1 shows how the conditional rates of smiling and of vocalizing change over the first six months of an infant's life during face-to-face play while being held in the mother's lap (Kaye & Fogel, 1980). This situation is comparable to the one in which Trevarthen filmed infants. Having the infant in a seat as he and others have done, rather than in the lap as we did, may make some difference but it is not clear which is really the more natural situation. A more important difference is the fact that Trevarthen devised techniques for tracing the precise forms of very fine movements. Our coding was in terms of gross categories; but the advantage of our assembly-line methods was that we could code a large enough corpus of sessions to be able to analyze objectively the relationship, if any, between the infants' expressiveness, their attention to the mothers, and the mothers' behavior.

The fact that infant facial expressions were coded independently of the direction of the infants' attention, that is, on a separate viewing of the tape, and then intercalated with the other categories in the computer, enabled us to test the contingent relationships between these behaviors. (It would not be legitimate to do so if the codings were not independent, because then contingencies could appear due to the biasing organization of the coder's own behavior.) As Figure 8-1 shows, there were significant differences between the rates of vocalization when attending to the mother (head toward her, eyes open and alert-looking rather than glazed or drowsy) versus when not attending. But these differences only ap-

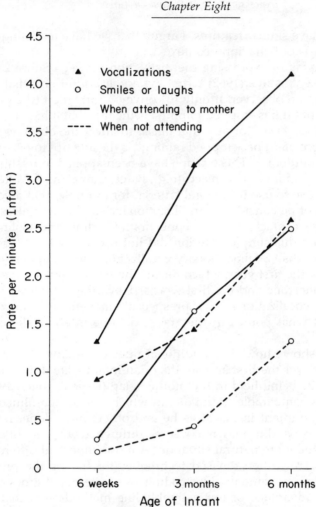

Figure 8-1. Infants' rates of expression in the face-to-face situation, as a function of attention to the mother's face. (Adapted from data of Kaye & Fogel, 1980.)

peared at the 3-month and 6-month sessions, not at 6 weeks. Exactly the same results are apparent for smiling.

These results severely weaken the claim that such expressions are, from their earliest appearance, attempts to communicate (Sense 3). We agree that mothers respond to those expressions *as if* they were communicative (Sense 2), but that is not the same thing. Mothers also reply to infants' startle movements. These are not adult-like, so no one calls them attempts to communicate. Nor would we call the infant's burping, spitting up or drooling, or the noises issuing from his other end, communications. Yet parents often pretend these are deliberate statements. This is a phenomenon we shall have much to say about later, but we should not confuse the adult's interpretation of an infant's behavior with the signification it may or may not have from the infant's point of view. In short, while I am prepared to make Sense 1 interpretations of babies' expressions with adequate contextual support, as Darwin did, I am not prepared to make Sense 3 interpretations in the first few months, as parents (and Trevarthen) sometimes do.

Figure 3-6 compared the likelihood of *spontaneous* infant expressions after attending to the mother with the likelihood of the same expressions as *responses* to the mother's greeting. Remember that we found the mothers' behavior necessary but not very effective in eliciting a greeting at 6 weeks, less necessary but more effective at 13 weeks, and neither necessary nor effective by 26 weeks. The infant expressions begin, in other words, as unintentional acts occurring rarely, only when elicited, and ambiguously even as indices of state; for they index internal state at best, with no objective justification for the social interpretation mothers place on them. Gradually they look more like intentional acts with the goal of eliciting a maternal response (recall from Chapter 5 Tronick et al.'s description [1979] of what happens when these behaviors fail to elicit the maternal response). But they still occur rarely. They clearly index socially inspired arousal (Sense 1), but there is no evidence of their being intentional signs. We can find no reason to agree with Trevarthen in attributing communicative intentions to the 2-month-old:

> The changes of communication throughout the first year appear to be principally due to differentiation of a highly complex, general intersubjectivity which is manifest very early in rudimentary form. . . . This function identifies persons, regulates motivation and intention toward them, and simultaneously forms rudimentary acts of speech and gesture in patterned combinations and sequences. It also provides internal images of face and hand movements for the identification and imitation of the expressions of others. Acts of adults that signify interest and understanding to other adults are selectively perceived by 2-month-olds, too, and taken as analogous to their own acts of like form. When the mother expresses excitement or pleasure it stimulates a function in the infant that is capable of generating a mirror or complementary act. Proof of these propositions is to be found in the communications of *primary intersubjectivity* that develop into elaborate form in the second and third months after birth. [Trevarthen & Hubley, 1978, p. 213; italics in original]

We agree on the transition to what these authors call "secondary" intersubjectivity around the sixth month. That is really the first level of
*inter*subjectivity, however. Its "primary" precursors are all in the parents'
interpretation.

Corroborating evidence to the effect that there is no reason to infer
intentionality in the infant's early smiling comes from Sroufe and Waters
(1976). They demonstrated that the earliest elicited smiles, in the second
and third months, are a direct outgrowth of the "endogenous" or spontaneous smiles of the newborn period. The smile can gradually be elicited
by more distal stimuli, and eventually (by 4 months or so) by stimuli
that the infant apparently recognizes as familiar. But the smile continues
to be an index of internal relaxation of tension (Spitz & Wolf, 1946; Wolff,
1963; Emde & Koenig, 1969; Kagan, 1971). In other words, to return to
our own data, the smile is a response to the mother and may tell the
mother something about the infant's state, eventually about the fact that
he recognizes her or a particular gesture of hers. But it is not a message;
not a gesture toward her.

The numerous studies of early interaction do not justify Trevarthen's
(1977) attribution of "mutual intentionality and sharing of mental state"
between baby and mother. Other investigators, citing the same infant
behavior and willing to join Trevarthen in calling it "protosocial" (Newson, 1977) or "proto-conversational" (Bateson, 1979), do not share his
view of the mutuality in mother-infant interactions:

> . . . we view mother-baby interaction as an attempt by the
> mother to enter into a *meaningful* set of exchanges with her
> infant, despite the fact that she herself will often be aware that
> the semantic element in any resulting communication lies more
> in her own imagination than in the mental experience of her
> baby. [Newson, 1977, p. 46; italics in original]

The evolutionary significance of this fiction on the part of parents is well
stated by Bateson (1979):

> Human infants, unlike ducklings, cannot walk away, are in fact
> extraordinarily helpless. Therefore, the immediate biological
> task is not to teach the infant to recognize the mother but to
> teach the mother to recognize, acknowledge and care for the
> infant—to mobilize a set of maternal behaviors or, alternatively,
> to set the stage so that she will learn these very fast. She must
> meet both the infant's physical needs and his emotional and
> communicational needs, thus structuring the environment so
> that the infant can learn. Thus, in addition to asking how the
> mother is triggered to nurture the infant and protect him (doc-
> umented by a whole library of material on how nursing is es-

tablished), we must ask how she is triggered to provide those stimuli that will allow the infant to learn according to his internal schedule. [P. 69]

Papoušek and Papoušek (1977) report that a baby's hand position alone is a good cue to his behavioral state (drowsy, distressed, alert) and that mothers use this cue without being aware of it. When trying to calm a fussy infant, for example, a mother will often try to open the tensed fists. In the Papoušeks' interviews, mothers were unaware of either the characteristic hand positions or their own responses to them.

One of the cues eliciting responses most reliably from adults is the baby's gaze direction. We follow an infant's gaze much as we follow an adult's gaze, and the resulting "co-orientation" (Collis, 1977) must play an important role, for example, in establishing the parent's instrumental frame. However, any intersubjectivity that results from co-orientation is only due to parental interpretation of infant intention. The converse never occurs in the first 6 months, and it is not clear at what age infants do follow the direction of an adult's gaze. Adopting a very lenient criterion—a head turn anywhere to the right or left when the experimenter turned 90 degrees in that direction—Scaife and Bruner (1975) failed to show that any infants younger than 11 months performed at better than a chance level. So the only "sharing of mental state" that can result from co-orientation in the early months is a one-way sharing. If I help myself to part of your sandwich, it is not the same as your sharing it with me. Parents help themselves to part of the infant's mental life—and only by guessing at that.

When infants younger than 6 months scan adults' faces with apparent interest, what evidence is there that they discriminate different adult gestures or different expressions in those faces? The experimental findings, based on habituation/dishabituation and visual preference techniques, are disappointing (Browne, Rosenfeld, & Horowitz, 1977; Nelson, Morse, & Leavitt, 1979). Although 4- to 7-month-olds demonstrate concept-learning for a number of different kinds of features that can be held invariant across different stimuli (e.g., a specific face regardless of orientation; Cohen & Strauss, 1979), facial expressions that we would label sad, happy, surprised, or afraid do not appear to be so easily learned as one would expect. It seems that facial expressions are just the kind of features that the infant is prepared to ignore when he searches for invariance. In other words, different kinds of exaggerated facial expressions may have different degrees of salience and affect infants' focusing versus gaze aversion, but there is no evidence that any concepts or meanings are associated with them.

Even when an infant recognizes the faces of particular others, we have no reason to suppose that he attaches significance to those faces beyond simply their relative familiarity. Visual preferences in the early months, as observed in Fantz (1961) choice procedures or in films of eye movements during scanning (Kessen, Salapatek, & Haith, 1972) are now understood to be guided by built-in brain functions rather than by any "subjective" preferences in the baby for particular objects. The organism seeks stimulation, seeks to fire neurons, and hence it fixates longer on stimuli such as saturated colors and vertical or horizontal lines, which elicit a higher rate of cortical firing (Bornstein, 1978; Haith, 1977). Similarly, when the infant's proportion of time looking at the mother declines in favor of other objects (Carpenter, 1974; Kaye & Fogel, 1980), we should not think of that as a declining interest in the mother. It is merely a shift from "captive" fixation on her face to active exploration of the environment (Stechler & Latz, 1966; Gibson, 1969). If a mother's exaggerated smile or frown is more successful in competing with that environment than a passive face is, it need not be because any meaning has been conveyed by the expression.

In sum, we should be skeptical about the "communication" involved in facial expressions by either partner. When infant expressions first begin to be treated as signs by adults, there is no reason for us to consider those expressions intentional acts, let alone intentional signs. By 6 months, expressions similar in appearance to those that have been produced earlier are used in consistent situations, so that mothers' interpretation of their meaning as indices of the infants' states is justified. Still, however, the behavior does not always meet a criterion of intentionality, and even when it does so there is no evidence that it is intentional signing, that is, that the infant anticipates the effect of the behavior on the adult. Nor is there any evidence that young infants attach meaning to the different facial expressions of adults. We have thus reached conclusions about intersubjectivity that are quite consistent with our conclusions in Chapter 3 about the "system": In the early months, there is neither intersubjectivity nor system.

Social Foundations for Symbolic Processes

Let me summarize up to this point and give a preview of the remaining chapters.

According to Piaget's inside-out theory, the establishment of conventional linguistic symbols (those signs that are gestures as well as signals) has to wait until representation has advanced to an adequate stage. The progress of representation does involve imitation of other people's behavior as well as response to the transformations of objects and space produced by others. However, according to the inside-out view, the infant interacts with those people as objects, as physical causes of interesting events. The actual business of socialization—establishing relations as a member of a social system—cannot begin, in Piaget's view, until there is at least a preconceptual mind to be socialized. That process begins when symbolic representation has already been achieved, so that it can be used as the instrument to establish the basic concepts of all cultures and the specific ones of a specific culture, largely through language-learning.

We also find this assumption in Parsons and Bales (1954) and in cultural anthropologists like Levi-Strauss (1966), where symbols are the means of inculcating patterns of thought particular to a culture. Some authors, such as Whorf (1956), argue that, from the time the culture's socialization process begins, the development of thought is outside-in; but because they presuppose a prior intrinsic development of the symbolic function, unexplained by any social processes, such theories implicitly assume that the direction of infancy is inside-out.

One alternative to the inside-out theory is the infant-as-innately-social view, which I have already criticized. That view, partly a reaction against Piaget's, held that socialization is not imposed upon the infant's autonomously developing mind; instead, social relations (in the form of intentional expressions) and thinking (in the form of certain representational capacities) are already present at birth. Rejecting those claims, I have concluded that in the first 5 or 6 months of life infants' expressions are indices of internal states, so that any meaningful communication resulting from them is only due to the parents' propensity for hyper-interpretation.

In the months that follow, most systematic interaction is still due to the parents' ability to half-perform the infant's role while also performing their own: to complete his actions, fulfill his intentions, interpret his grunts as gestures and his learned signals as full-fledged words. The account I am giving is, while opposed to the innately social, still very different from the inside-out account. Far from believing that conventional symbol development waits until an orthogenetic process has been completed, I argue that there is no orthogenesis of the mind. The conventional symbols inserted by adults into their systematic exchanges with infants during the first year are directly responsible for the dawning of human intelligence.

We have now rejected two hypotheses with wide currency among students of parent-infant interaction in recent years: in Chapter 3 the Hypothesis of Critical Dyad-Formation in the First Few Months of Life, and in this chapter the Hypothesis of Presymbolic Communication. Indeed, the question of when the infant truly becomes a system member is closely tied to the question of when true intersubjectivity develops.

We have rejected the idea that the precursor of symbolic communication is just a more basic form of communication using indexical signs and gestures instead of abstract and arbitrary conventional symbols. The precursor of communication is not really communication at all but an asymmetrical process of interpretation. Initially, the parent makes use of practically any aspect of infant behavior that resembles mature dialogue in any way, and fills in the other half of a dialogue so as to enhance that resemblance. At first, the infant sends out undifferentiated signs but receives differentiated responses. This in turn provides the predictable routines or temporal frames within which the infant begins to explore the object-world and receives repeated models for imitation. Through imitation as well as the contingent responses of adults, his own schemas differentiate, his intentions become less and less ambiguous, and adults' interpretations become more accurate. The parents complete or facilitate the infant's intentional actions toward them and toward the world. They do so at first with instrumental acts and partly instrumental gestures, which the infant imitates. With repeated use, these gestures become conventionalized signals within their shared experience. Gradually, the parents introduce the appropriate conventional symbols of the linguistic community. From that time on, the signals the infant learns to produce are the same signals he comprehends when produced by others, and therefore in using these symbols he anticipates how they will be interpreted. Only then is the infant communicating.

These conclusions about intersubjectivity exactly parallel our conclusions with respect to the dyad (Chapter 3). The infant is not really a member of a system (much less a member of the community) until his behavior is organized in service of the goals of that system. In our studies of early feeding, play, and instruction, mothers established the semblance of systems by anticipating what their infants were going to do next. They used the built-in cycles of attention and arousal to establish a turn-taking of which the infants were not conscious and for which the infants were not responsible. By this I mean that, while the _nature_ of infants is responsible for their systematic turn-taking with adults, they are not responsible for it as individuals. They are not "partners" or "members" of a social system.

The creation of a system will create intersubjectivity because parts of a system can only be coordinated in the service of the whole if they are communicating parts. So shared meaning is essential to the definition of a social system. Intersubjectivity involves being able to assume (correctly) that the meaning an object or event has to you will be the meaning it has to your partner. Without that, there can be no real dialogue. Its rudiments can be achieved, however, by either partner making a correct inference from the other's behavior. If the mother correctly interprets the infant's intention, or correctly assumes that the infant remembers the function or meaning some object had in a previous interaction, then there is shared meaning. If the infant categorizes objects by their similarity of use by the adult, there is that same primitive variety of shared meaning.

Only where there is shared meaning can there be shared purpose. So shared meaning is essential to the definition of a social system. On the other hand, the converse is also true: The meaning of individual signs is understood because they are introduced in the context of shared goals, for example, the instrumental and modeling frames, when the tutor makes a correct inference about the learner's intention. The development of the symbolic level of intersubjectivity—where the use of signs is reciprocal—depends upon the prior establishment of regular interactive routines. Those routines, in which the infant is an apprentice to the system, depend upon an asymmetrical type of "mono-" subjectivity, where the parent at least understands many of the infant's intentions and treats them as if they were communications.

Thus the four levels of parent-infant interaction outlined in Chapter 4 comprise a causal developmental sequence. In the first two periods the infant's role is provided by inborn rhythms and regulations, intentional schemas and the assimilation function. Interaction with adults is intersubjective only in the sense that the adults project their own subjectivity onto the infant's behavior. In doing so, however, they create regular dyadic routines, systematic exchanges that do not depend upon the infant's understanding but capitalize upon the adults' ability to interpret the infant's intentions, complete or facilitate his actions, and anticipate his reactions.

Through these dyadic routines the infant has an opportunity in the second half of the first year, the period of shared memory, to do two things with the adult interventions. He "comprehends" adult signals, by which we mean that he learns to respond appropriately to them. And he "produces" the signals by imitation. In both cases, he assimilates aspects of the signals to his own behavioral schemas and thereby accommodates his schemas to the conventional parental gestures. At first the infant has to assimilate comprehensions to corresponding productions, catch as catch can, but after doing so for a while the relation somehow becomes automatically reciprocal. Only then do the conventional signals satisfy our final criterion for true symbols, that a symbol understood when used by another is also a symbol available for use to another, and vice versa.

If we define intersubjectivity as the reciprocal use of equivalent signs, we will not see it before the period I have called "shared language." There may be dyad-conventional signs, but there are no dyad-conventional symbols. It seems that when the time comes to introduce arbitrary and differentiated symbols, parents just naturally use words. It may be that the child needs the arbitrariness of the word in order to grasp the differentiated character of symbols.

If, however, we ask what degree of shared meaning we do find in the early months, the answer lies primarily in the mother's interpretation of indices as signs. What parents and some psychologists interpret as meaningful messages are in fact rather primitive responses preadapted so as to fool the parents into treating the infant as an intelligent partner.

Intersubjectivity begins when the infant and parent first begin truly to comprise a system. From birth to 5 or 6 months, despite his having been produced by the parents' system, the infant is one open system and they are another. They use him as an external instrument toward their own goals and serve (when they can) as instruments toward his goals. It is true that the parents are indispensable for the infant's survival, and there is a sense in which he instinctively shares that goal, but there is no mutual anticipation in a joint effort to achieve it. That is, we do not see each partner playing a role and expecting the other to play a role. In the first half-year they are a system in the evolutionary sense only: preadapted for one another, as Any Mother and Any Baby rather than as individuals. After 6 months the infant is an apprentice, which means that at least some of the time the parent-infant interaction takes on the character of a single system, with the parent providing most of the planning, guidance, and memory. There are then some expectations on both sides about the roles to be played. But the infant is not fully a system member until those roles demand the reciprocal use of equivalent signs.

The months of apprenticeship lead to symbol formation. As Bruner (1975) has pointed out, once the infant turns to objects and the mother becomes a partner in his outer-directed exploration instead of just an object of it, their joint focus and their natural turn-taking allow the infant to begin differentiating gestures with which to communicate about those objects and about shared intentions toward them. A class of adult gestures becomes a signal for the infant when he knows either how it is used by others to signify or how to use it himself to signify. Finally it becomes a symbol when the signal comprehended and the signal produced are represented as one and the same. The achievement of this level of representation, in symbols, is a direct result of the communication already established within the parental frames. In the period of shared language, social interaction begins to be internalized, so every symbol produced is a symbol comprehended and every symbol comprehended is potentially producible.

Predication. Before we become carried away with the achievement of symbols, it must be pointed out that the essence of language is not symbols, it is the use of symbols to communicate. Similarly, the essence of symbolic thought is not the symbol itself but the predicative use of symbols. "A fish" is a symbol, and "to swim" is a symbol, and either symbol alone can convey a certain amount of meaning in appropriate contexts. But there are well over 100 ways the verb "to swim" can be predicated upon "a fish" (counting the various tenses, conditional forms, negative and interrogative transformations: "A fish will swim," "Would a fish not have swum?" and so forth). With the option of using "big" or "little" to describe the fish, "quickly" or "slowly" to describe the swimming, I can construct more than 1000 different English sentences.

The child's first predicated word comes several months before his first two-word sentence. Why? Because a fully predicative utterance (e.g., "Fish swim") involves both creating a topic and commenting upon it. At first the child depends upon established topics. For example, the parent says, "What's this?"; all the child has to do is comment. Even when the child produces what looks like a topic, it is usually a comment predicated upon some present stimulus. For example, he sees a car, says "Car," and the parent says, "The car is going fast, isn't it?" "Car" is a comment predicated upon what the child has seen, and the parent then makes that comment the topic of a new utterance (the type of utterance I called a "turnabout" in Chapter 6), to which the child may reply, "Fast."

There is intersubjectivity even in the one-word gesture, but there will be a higher form of intersubjectivity in the fully predicative utterance. In commenting on an *assumed* topic, on the context that he shares with whomever he is addressing, the child does not have to differentiate his own position from the other's. He relies upon a frame established by the other ("What does the cow say?" *"Moo!"*) or upon the other's ability to share his intention (*"Car!"*). Even though he employs conventional signs as gestures (for he intends to represent to the other something like what those signs represent to him), he does not himself create the whole message. But when the older child tells me "Fish swim," he requires nothing of me except that I share his language. Of course, both utterances—"Car!" and "Fish swim"—rely on shared presuppositions. But the latter is able to do so only when the child can fully anticipate what is required in order to bring me into the situation in which his predication is meaningful; whereas the former succeeds as soon as the child learns to supply predicates for topics supplied by others or by the passing stream of events, and his intersubjective gesturing must therefore rest upon the assumption that the person addressed will take the active role in sharing his intention and (often) his memory of past events. The child under 2 trying to show a toy to someone over the telephone reveals the extent to which he is used to relying on adults' ability to divine his meaning. Later, when he can create subject and predicate at once (and can use the richness of the language to do so unambiguously), all that his listeners need to share is the language, for the utterance can convey its own intention and a good part of its own context.

The adult's role in this transition from one-word utterances to fully predicative sentences is much the same as in the earlier achievement. Missing parts of the sentence are supplied. This expansion of the utterance involves both the instrumental and modeling frames. Even when the child does not immediately imitate an expansion, he at least has the opportunity to inform adults whether their interpretation is correct. If not, they try again.

Immediate imitation is not so important now that the child has a single lexicon available for both production and comprehension. Learning to comprehend a word now usually makes it available later for an attempt to produce it in an appropriate situation. The occasion may not arise for weeks, perhaps not until there is a long enough sentence frame to insert it into. In the preceding period, there were some words the infant learned to produce for an effect, like a well-trained circus animal, that he could not comprehend if they were spoken to him. He could say "Milk" and stretch out his hands for his bottle, but would not hand his bottle to someone who said "Milk" in the same tone of voice to him. Now, however, there are few if any sentences the child can say correctly (i.e., grammatical sentences, like "Give me milk") that he fails to comprehend; yet there are many he can comprehend but does not produce. This raises the topic of deferred imitation, upon which I shall defer my comments to the next chapter.

Imitation

All our lives long, every day and every hour, we are engaged in the process of accommodating our changed and unchanged selves to our changed and unchanged surroundings; living, in fact, is nothing else than this process of accommodation; when we fail in it a little we are stupid, when we fail flagrantly we are mad. . . . A life will be successful or not according as the power of accommodation is equal to or unequal to the strain of fusing and adjusting internal and external changes.

Samuel Butler, *The Way of all Flesh*, 1903

As mentioned in previous chapters, adults often act as though they expect infants to be able to imitate them. This latent assumption can be seen in the exaggerated facial expressions, smiles, and vocalizations to very young infants as well as in the more systematic tutoring that begins at about 6 months. Once one notices this aspect of parental behavior and becomes intrigued with it, one begins to see that it underlies the most common exchanges. Nor is it restricted to parent-child interaction:

> Hold it like this.
>> Like this?
> No, like this. That's right.
>> Oh. I get it.

What one "gets" is the way the pair of chopsticks, the paintbrush, or the scissors one is holding feels when it is being operated correctly. That sensorimotor knowledge is successfully transmitted from one person to the other. However, in between Person A "having" the skill and Person B "getting" the skill, what is actually communicated is a visual image, a demonstration, which only works because the learner can translate it

155

into specific hand and finger movements. The teacher relies upon that ability in the learner.

Most theories of imitation have treated it as a mental process, perhaps socially motivated, but essentially a process within the individual who does the imitating. This makes sense if one is imitating a bird call or a steam engine, but when the thing imitated is another person's action, imitation is really an interpersonal event: The ability to copy the model may depend as much upon the way it is presented as upon the skill of the imitator. The ways parents play with infants—particularly the modeling frame—may be as important a part of the innate human endowment as the abilities involved in imitation itself. That will be a recurring theme of this chapter.

Until quite recently, the history of social psychology had been marked by a steady trend away from concepts of social processes as inherent in groups, toward social behavior as inherent in individuals (Pepitone, 1981). Although Tarde (1903), McDougall (1908), and other early theorists began with the assumption that the group, family, or society as a whole was their subject, an increasing pressure for objectified scientific analysis frightened psychologists away from entities larger, vaguer, and less intact than the individual organism. So despite the name "social" psychology, the individual had become the unit of analysis. However, the advent of General Systems thinking (von Bertalanffy, 1968) has renewed the quest for modes of analysis adequate to phenomena that are inherently due to more than one person. Imitation clearly is such a phenomenon. We must understand the infant's cognitive capacity and the parent's structuring activity as having evolved simultaneously in the species. Both kinds of behavior—by demonstrator as well as by learner—are equally important prerequisites for man's learning to talk, to hunt, to cook, to weave; to operate a plow, a lathe, or a computer; to play the piano, to ski, or to do research.

Definition and Assumptions

Virtually all definitions of imitation, in common usage as well as in psychology, involve resemblance not attributable to coincidence. Behaviorally, any action is defined as an imitation if it resembles something that the actor has observed, the resemblance being so great or following within such a short period of time that it could not have occurred by chance.

There is less agreement about the actual processes involved in producing imitative actions. Two of the assumptions that have often been made by other authors will be specifically rejected here. First is the assumption that imitation is uncreative and passive. We shall assume instead that every act of imitation is a novel act; its resemblance to the model will never be perfect. Furthermore, every creative act probably incorporates some imitation, though the imitated features and the model from which they were drawn may be unknown or unrecorded.

Second, we shall not assume that all imitation is achieved by a single process. Behavior that meets the definition above could occur through relatively complex or through relatively simple cognitive processes (even in adults), depending upon the nature of what is imitated. There is not necessarily an imitation skill per se. (If there were, one should expect to find consistent individual differences in imitation ability, across all domains: sports, speech, music, mime, etc. There is no evidence that people who are more talented at imitating certain kinds of actions are consistently talented at others.) A theory of imitation in relation to the course of infancy should be more concerned with the role of imitation in the growth of other skills, and with the effect of those skills upon the kinds of action the child is able to imitate, than with the development of imitation itself.

Each of these assumptions needs to be examined briefly in order to set the stage for the present treatment.

Imitation and Creativity. Although the scientific literature on imitation is not one hundredth so voluminous as has been devoted to the symbolic processes, it is nonetheless an ancient and honorable tradition. How and why we imitate (also whether it is good or bad to imitate) have been debated by epistemologists, aestheticians, social philosophers, even theologians, for centuries.

To Socrates, Plato, and Aristotle, imitation was good. It was an accommodation to the natural laws of the universe, *physis*. In contrast, the attempt to invent personal truths or arbitrary social laws (the relativist law, *nomos*, which Protagoras and the Sophists had contrasted with *physis*) was at best a futile exercise and at worst a pernicious one. True creativity, the Socratics argued, lies in selecting from nature rather than in pretending to invent from scratch or to have a corner in objectivity. Imitation is never passive; it involves selection. Since there could never be a perfect imitation of nature, Plato and Aristotle understood that every act of imitation is also a creative act, and furthermore that every creative act involves imitation both of nature itself and of one's fellowman's representations of nature. Whether one uses the word *imitation* or not, creation emerges from the individual's grasp of nature, and even the most creative individual never escapes nature's grasp.

In the modern era, the corresponding issue turned on *society's* grasp. Marx (1964), Tarde (1903), Durkheim (1956), Dewey (1916), Mead (1934), and others wrote about imitation as either the source or the scourge of man's identity, sometimes both. Kuhn (1970) has discussed the problem of learning from exemplars, as a fundamental part of the sociology of all transmitted knowledge.

Such a grand perspective may seem remote from infancy and from the psychological analysis of imitation that concerns us here. But the critical issue in identifying the relation between an imitation and its model is the same with respect to poetry and social conformity as it is with respect to sensorimotor development and language-learning. No two things are identical, no two things are wholly dissimilar, so it is not easy to say what is or is not imitation. "The analysis only takes enough from the model to understand it; even as it imitates, it simplifies" (Delacroix, 1921, p. 108). Many investigators—particularly those concerned with language development (e.g., McNeill, 1970; Slobin & Welsh, 1973)— have insisted that creative or "generative" skills cannot be acquired through imitation because there is not an exact correspondence between children's productions and the models they have seen or heard. The issue of passive copying versus generativity, inherited from classical philosophy, has long been identified by linguists (Chomsky, 1959; Jakobson, 1968). However, *all* skills are generative; and no skills acquired by children fit the definition of imitation better than language, whose rules conform phonemically, semantically, syntactically, and pragmatically to the parents' and community's language. (To say that the resemblance between the children's language and their linguistic models is greater than chance would be quite an understatement!)

The "Development" of Imitation. Generally speaking, the process of imitation involves selective attention, assimilation to one's own schemas, and then production of some action resembling the model. But this merely reiterates the definition: It is not a model of any specific process. In fact, it may be that there is no special process for imitation; that it is merely an outcome of many different human cognitive processes under certain social conditions.

Piaget (1951), who used "deferred imitation" along with object permanence as a principal criterion for symbolic representation, listed these stages: "Sporadic imitation"; "Systematic imitation of sounds already belonging to the phonation of the child and of movements he has already made and seen"; "Imitation of movements already made by the child but which are not visible to him"; "Beginning of imitation of new auditory and visual models"; "Systematic imitation of new models including those involving movements invisible to the child"; "Deferred imitation." This list of changes in the context and contents of imitation, which Piaget inherited from Baldwin (1895) and Delacroix (1921), is often taken to be a theory of development in the process of imitation itself, but it is equally compatible with the idea that the child's ability to imitate different kinds of action at different ages is due to the development of many other, ancillary skills. Imitation at any stage might occur by several alternative processes having little to do with one another (Uzgiris, 1979); we shall not try to explain imitation as a single process with its own development. We shall be concerned instead with the changes in what is imitated and how they in turn affect the infant's repertoire of schemas.

At the heart of imitation is assimilation, or the classification of new events as equivalent to known objects or events. No author has ventured to explain assimilation as a process. It is a formal property of all organisms. We cannot imagine, let alone find in the real world, an organism that does not assimilate. Assimilation is involved in all categorical knowledge. I assimilate the object in my hand to the category "pen": Even without labeling the category with a symbol, I assimilate the object to sensorimotor schemas that know what to do with pens. When infants perceive modeled action X as an occasion for performing their own version of X, the fundamental ability involved is no different from the fundamental ability of any organism to recognize novel events as instances of known categories, despite their novelties. The process is hardly unique to man but is, as Piaget (1952) argued, the biological essence of intelligence. A P-model of assimilation would have to be an extremely abstract P-model indeed, like Figure 7-1. As soon as we begin to put some flesh on that bone (e.g., initial scanning buffers on the perceptual side, with arrows back to the sense organs), we have P-models of perception in the different sensory modalities, no longer a model of assimilation itself. In short, assimilation itself cannot be P-modeled so long as it remains in the reductionist status of a property of all organisms.

Instead of delving into assimilation, a theory of infancy can build out from it. We can trace the elaboration of more processes on top of assimilation. In this chapter, four increasingly sophisticated levels of imitation will provide a convenient trellis on which to hang the principal studies by Piaget and more recent investigators. We shall view these levels primarily as an elaboration in the kinds of behavior that can be imitated rather than as any change in the process of imitation or in assimilation itself. I shall also make two general points. First, the higher levels can be understood as an outgrowth of the lower ones, ultimately of simple assimilation. This begins to sound like an orthogenetic stage theory. But the second point is that the progression, which culminates in the achievement of symbolic representation, is only possible because of the ways adults organize the infant's world and selectively present imitable models to him.

The four levels can almost be called stages. I shall avoid that word because I wish to avoid the suggestion of discontinuities and of "equilibration" from one level to the next. But the levels are indeed developmentally ordered: They require progressively more complex cognition on the infant's part, they define progressive steps toward symbolic representation, and they correspond to progressively more systematic communication with adults. Furthermore, they correspond to the onsets of the four periods of parent-infant relations I listed in Chapter 4.[1] This correspondence is sketched in Figure 9-1, along with approximate ages of transition to each period. Advances in the "semiotic levels" to be described in this chapter change the nature of parent-infant interaction, and vice versa. The infant's ability to assimilate events to his schemas allows adults to anticipate his actions, and thus enables the sharing of *intentions*. When events can be represented in accommodated schemas and when many such accommodations have been made in situations that the parents have observed or created, they share *memory* with the infant. The use of learned signals, and soon words, give them the beginnings of a shared *language*; with true symbols, the child becomes a partner in the social system.

Conversely, even in the period of shared rhythms when parents insert themselves into the infant's activity, they alter its consequences. The earliest schemas therefore adapt in an environment that has already been partly structured in accord with adults' expectations about normal interaction. These expectations are internalized, in a sense, in the first *representations*, which are merely accommodations of schemas in response to the infant's experience. A representation of that kind does not require intersubjectivity; that is, sharing the meaning of signs. Shared intentions begin in the parents' projections, a unilateral kind of subjectivity that nonetheless associates signs with consequences and facilitates the infant's eventual intentional use of *signals*. Only then can we be confident that the shared meaning is truly intersubjective rather than merely an adult projection onto the infant's actions. Consistently interpretable signs on the part of both partners are evidence of a shared memory. That in turn is a prerequisite for the parents to provide and correctly interpret the first *words*, which are soon used as both signal and gesture, that is, *symbols*. With this achievement, of course (but not before it), human children surpass the adults of every other species.

The sequence of semiotic levels shown in Figure 9-1 shows signs as a subset of representations and symbols as a subset of signs. Together with the classification in Figure 7-2, this suggests that our theory of imitation should focus upon what kinds of signs are imitated: at first

1. Other authors who have divided infancy at roughly these same points, noting many of the same milestones that are relevant to the present treatment, include Emde, Gaensbauer, and Harmon (1976), Fischer (1980), Kagan (1979), McCall, Eichorn, and Hogarty (1977), Sroufe (1979), and Uzgiris (1976).

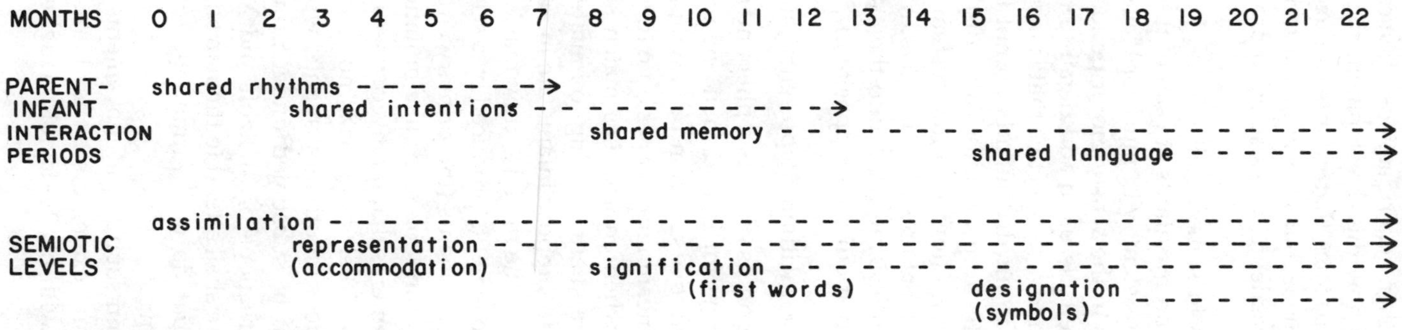

Figure 9-1. Attainment of the four semiotic levels in relation to the four principal periods of early interaction with adults. Ages are approximate, and the diagram intentionally shows the periods as overlapping.

only isolated movements, then generic actions, then conventional signs, then symbols. A theory of how this development can come about must deal with the cognitive capacities that infants can use to represent the world of events around them, but also with the factors that organize that world in certain propaedeutic ways so as to provide the materials for imitation.

We shall now discuss in some detail what is known and what is disputed regarding imitation by infants at each of these four levels. We shall reach conclusions consistent with much of Piaget's (1951) account of how imitation develops in the sensorimotor period. We shall review a number of studies that enable us to add detail to that theory. In addition, however, we shall add a perspective that is missing from Piaget's account. For we shall point out that infants do not have to select just what and when to imitate from an unbroken, disordered stream of events. We shall emphasize how parents systematically introduce models for imitation, at optimal times and in ways that facilitate infants assimilating them and synthesizing them into their own actions. Consequently, we shall end up at quite the opposite of Piaget's theory.

Assimilation without Representations

Imitation in the first few months of life is a phenomenon one tends not to see unless one is watching for it, and then one wonders whether it really occurred by any objective criterion or only appeared as a result of one's having projected meaningful shapes onto the kaleidoscopic flux of infant behavior. Even when an act does match some criterion, we cannot be sure whether the infant is trying to imitate or is merely confused. There is no reason to suppose infants are in any way aware that their own action is similar to the model's; they may simply mistake the model's movements for movements produced by a schema of their own. A continuation of those movements (the primary circular reactions described by Baldwin [1895]) can look to us like imitation. However, this should only apply to movements that infants can see or hear themselves doing: for example, waving their arms. It is not immediately obvious that the imitation of a model's mouth movements, which infants cannot see themselves doing, can be subsumed under primary circular reactions. So the recent observations of Meltzoff and Moore (1977) have received wide attention. We shall attend to them in some detail, for they are valid and important but do not warrant the interpretation those authors chose to give them.

The mirroring of certain sounds and movements in the first month is a phenomenon that many examiners of newborns have noted. Valentine (1930) described it with his 28-day-old daughter:

After half a minute, in response to her nurse's talking, Y. always responded by "talking" back, a slight "ah" coming softly and always in the intervals of the nurse's talk; an obvious reply. [The mother] tried to get the same response but was too hurried. I said, "Leave intervals for Y. to reply;" and then the response came. [P. 109]

Meltzoff and Moore (1977) were the first to provide statistical evidence that mirroring really occurs beyond a chance level. They reported several experiments; the most important one involved 12 2-week-old infants. They compared the rates of mouth opening and of tongue protrusions during three 150-second time periods. One was a baseline period, during which the experimenter merely stared at the infant with an impassive face. During the other two periods the experimenter's face was also at rest, but just before them he had demonstrated either 15 seconds of opening his mouth wide, over and over, or 15 seconds of sticking his tongue out. The infants' faces were videotaped during all three segments, and a coder who did not know which stimulus had preceded a particular segment recorded the numbers of tongue protrusions and of wide mouth openings by each infant. The 12 infants opened their 12 mouths a total of eight times (on the average, once every 225 seconds) after the experimenter did so; but they only opened their mouths a total of two times (once every 15 minutes) in each of the other two conditions. Tongue protrusions were a little more frequent, and they too were significantly more frequent after they had been modeled: The 12 tongues were protruded 39 times during the segments following the tongue-protrusion demonstration, 15 times after each of the other conditions. A problem with this study was that Meltzoff and Moore, by reporting the total numbers of occurrences instead of the actual rates or the numbers of babies producing any responses at all, accentuated the (statistically significant) differences between experimental conditions and played down the fact that the rates of responding were extremely low. Very few of the 12 babies produced any imitative responses at all; but a few of them did so, at a sufficient rate to make the total numbers significantly different under each of the conditions. In a similar experiment, modeled mouth movements were distinguished from hand movements.

Attempts to replicate these results have led to a number of failures (e.g., Hamm, Russell, & Koepke, 1979; Hayes & Watson, 1981), but also to at least one successful replication (Field, Woodson, Greenberg, & Cohen, 1982). More important, perhaps, the original results supported the observations of many of us who have examined hundreds of newborns: Some babies appear to imitate some of the time. Furthermore, the claims were in the spirit of the decade. As Hayes and Watson (1981) put it, "Judging from the alacrity of its dissemination by both lay and professional writers, evidence of neonatal imitation seems to provide exemplary support for the exciting new notion that infants possess heretofore unexpected cognitive perceptual competence" (p. 659). However, the flurry of attempts to corroborate or refute the results obscured the fact that even if replicated they would not support Meltzoff and Moore's interpretation regarding the cognitive powers of newborns.

Meltzoff and Moore regard such imitation as indicating that neonates are capable of representation because they have to represent the visual display in a nonvisual modality or represent their motor schema in a visual modality, if they are to match the two. Such reasoning is based on the dissimilarity between the feedback infants get from their own facial muscles and the visual stimulation produced by the examiner's face. Meltzoff and Moore argue that the connection between the visual display and the motor schema must therefore be of a higher order than assimilation. However, a more plausible assumption is that the connection is of a *lower* order than would be the case in assimilating one visual experience to another. This is especially plausible in view of the fact that the phenomenon disappears after the first month or two, being replaced by quite a different way of imitating mouth movements, to be described shortly.

There is no clear distinction between neonatal reflexes and the beginnings of schemas. The grasp reflex, for example, is elicited by tactile stimulation of the palms. Later a similar-looking grasp is elicited by visual stimuli of certain size and distance; yet we call that a schema, not a reflex. In both cases, a generic response is activated by a generic stimulus, that is, by a class of stimuli somehow treated as equivalent. This is assimilation. We cannot specify exactly how an adult's mouth movements tend to trigger mouth movements in the newborn, but neither can we say exactly what it is about the tactile stimulus that tends to stimulate grasping. In both cases, a series of experiments could define more and more precisely what stimulus properties elicit the response; but we would still have to take the assimilation function itself as a given.

The connection Meltzoff and Moore observed can be wired in, as what ethologists call a sign-release mechanism. Support for such an interpretation is found in a study by Jacobson (1979). She elicited as much tongue protrusion in response to a black pen moved toward and away from the baby's face as in response to her own tongue protrusions.[2]

2. Although the Jacobson study itself was not definitive, Burd, Milewski, and Camras (1981) also elicited some tongue protrusions to a moving pen and to mouth opening and closing. However, the adult's tongue protrusion was the most effective stimulus. The sign-release hypothesis explains Burd et al.'s results just as well as it does Jacobson's, Meltzoff and Moore's, and Field et al.'s. None of these authors has found any accommodation to the stimulus over trials.

Trevarthen (1979) aptly calls this "magnetic" imitation. It leads us to pose the question squarely in terms of stimulus properties: What features do and what features do not elicit a given class of responses? We use the word *imitation*, as defined earlier, because the stimulus and response happen to share certain features (i.e., the in-and-out motion); we have no reason to think the response actually involves any cognitive matching of those features, as Meltzoff and Moore assume.

Assimilation and Accommodation. Baldwin (1895) long ago noted the important difference between "simple imitation," which covers the phenomenon just described, and "persistent imitation," which involves successively greater resemblance to the model over trials. What we see in the first few months involves no selection of features and no improvement over trials. It is merely a statistical probability of a certain class of stimuli eliciting a certain class of responses. Visual detectors for certain kinds of movement may be linked to certain efferent nerves so as to produce a relationship somewhat greater than chance between seeing a movement of a certain type and performing a similar movement. An organism born with a few linkages of this kind, especially concerning facial, vocal, and manual expressions, obviously has a significant head start toward the differentiation of those expressions into conventional forms. The head start is due to the fact that adults are bound to react selectively to behavior that resembles communicative reciprocal facial expressions. We shall have more to say about that in Chapter 10.

The distinction between simple imitation and the persistent matching over trials is merely a special case of the basic development from assimilation to accommodation. At the level of simple assimilation, we do not see lasting accommodation of schemas. There may be momentary adjustments that fit a schema to the requirements of a situation (e.g., adjusting sucking to the shape and stiffness of a rubber nipple), but we reserve the word *accommodation* for adaptations that actually change the schema. Only when the sucking response changes as a result of experience, so that it becomes suited to either a narrower or a wider range of nipples than was the case at first, would we say that it has accommodated. An accommodation is therefore a representation of the world. (Notice that the first occurrences of this kind of accommodation are not by means of imitation; they are simply the adaptation of schemas to objects.)

What leads the infant from simple assimilation to the second level of imitation with accommodation? This involves an even more basic question: How can an organism equipped only with the assimilation function and a few built-in schemas develop any new schemas? Why does it not go on all its life perceiving the world in terms of the categories entailed by its initial set of schemas? Piaget (1952) proposed a neat solution, showing that accommodation could be explained as a direct result of assimilation. As the author understands Piaget's argument, we need only assume that a given event is likely to be assimilated to more than one schema. "It is not a question of associations imposed by the environment, but rather of relationships discovered and even created in the course of the child's own searchings" (p. 55). As there are many such relationships, alternative schemas in a sense compete with one another to assimilate the event. But each one of those assimilating schemas is itself an event and can therefore be assimilated by the competing schema. This process of "reciprocal assimilation" of competing schemas, according to Piaget, is the origin of change in schemas, that is, of accommodation.

In seeking to explain accommodation by reducing it to reciprocal assimilation, Piaget was avoiding the idea of reinforcement (or "training" as it was then conceived). He saw that imitative accommodation often occurs without external reinforcement. Guillaume (1971), doubting this, had argued for a training explanation of specific early imitative achievements and thus of the imitative ability itself.[3] Piaget (1951) agreed that imitation is learned, but he considered the learning to be a matter of practice, not training. "Learning" to Piaget meant coordination of schemas, assimilation of new models, and equilibration: internal functions as compared with reinforcement. Our own account will distinguish between the role of assimilation in the imitation of selected features of models, and the role of reinforcement, or success, in shaping the form of schemas that the infant constructs out of those imitations. In other words, accommodation can be reinforced by the improvement in skills themselves; it need not be reinforced externally. Unlike either Guillaume or Piaget, however, we do not see the process as depending upon the happenstance appearance of assimilable models. By the beginning of the period of shared intentions, parents are busy providing the most readily assimilated models in contiguity with the infant's own intentional actions, within the framework of turn-taking games (Fogel, 1977; Stern, 1974; Trevarthen, 1979).

Note that the infant is, in a certain sense, incited to imitate by the adult who plays with the infant by imitating him. Grown-

3. Guillaume's comprehensive monograph defies summarization and should be read more for its treatment of all the philosophical issues raised by imitation from the point of view of behaviorism, Gestalt, social and comparative psychology when all of these were young schools, than for any important findings. In this it is the opposite of *Play, Dreams, and Imitation* (Piaget, 1951), which infuriates most readers with the opacity of its theoretical argument but contains some of the most lucid, remarkable, and replicable observations of infants ever published.

ups concentrate on imitating babies perhaps more than the reverse, to such an extent that the child becomes familiar with the copy of his movement or his voice returning to him via another. This stimulates him to copy in turn. Then everyone reinforces his attempts with their approval and encouragement. [Delacroix, 1921, p. 133]

Delacroix's point has been reiterated by recent observers such as Pawlby (1977). However, they tend to ascribe importance to adult imitation of the infant only during Piaget's stages II and III when the adult is considered a kind of mirror, eliciting the secondary circular reaction. We shall hypothesize instead that the kind of behavior described by Delacroix goes on at all ages, though different actions are imitated and different degrees of intersubjectivity, or shared meaning between adult and infant, are required.

Representations without Signification

When schemas accommodate in a lasting way to some class of stimulating events, we can say that a schema *represents* that class of equivalent events in terms of a class of appropriate intentional actions. The 3-month-old has a representation of bottles in the form of the ability to recognize them visually and orient them correctly with hand and mouth.[4] That is the dawn of representation. Still, it is not the kind of representation that uses one kind of act to stand for another. In other words, it does not *signify*. Young infants' actions are undifferentiated from the process of perception, and both together constitute the schema (Piaget, 1952). We cannot distinguish between the infant's perception of events and his overt action toward them. In the third period, we can make that distinction because there begins to be more than one alternative action for a given perception: The infant has to make a choice prior to overt action. Only then will we call the representations (or the stimuli that evoke them) *signals*. Signals are a subset of signs, and symbols will be a subset of signals (Figure 9-2).

In the period of "representations without signification," when infants are about 3–8 months old, they do not yet *produce* signs intentionally. They do, of course, produce indices of hunger, pain, etc., which are signs from the parents' point of view. Furthermore, the first step in infants' learning to *comprehend* signs also takes place in this period at the level of indices, as contingent relations between events rather than as the conventional signs adults know them to be. Piaget uses the word *interiorization* in connection with the development from ordinary rep-

---

4. Both in this period and the next, we are referring to overt representations, which Piaget (1951) called "representative imitation" (see quotation in Chapter 7, page 125), rather than to covert Representation.

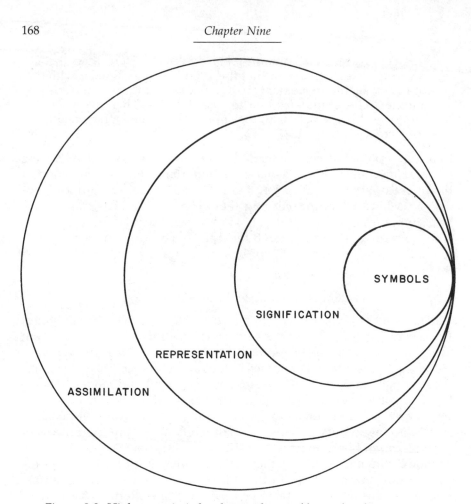

Figure 9-2. Higher semiotic levels as subsets of lower levels.

resentations to signs. Interiorization emphasizes (as Piaget's theories typically do) the part of the process for which infants themselves are responsible. But the various studies of parent-infant interaction show that this change does not occur in a vacuum. I shall argue that it occurs because of the parent's tendency to carry out the infant's apparent intentions. Babies learn what certain kinds of events signify in the world when they learn how other people respond to those events.

Accommodation and imitation, having begun independently, come together for the first time in this period. The first accommodations had nothing to do with imitation, and the first imitations involved no accommodation. Now, however, every imitation is a potential step in the accommodation and differentiation of instrumental or "means-ends" schemas. (This "means-ends" differentiation in turn will later be a necessary part of the process of differentiation between sign and signified.) The literature on imitation frequently distinguishes between imitating a means (e.g., the solution to a puzzle box or the path to a goal) and imitating an end not necessarily by the same means (e.g., one hears a melody on a piano and then hums or whistles it). The two kinds of imitation might not involve the same cognitive mechanisms (Bandura, 1971; Uzgiris, 1979). What is clear, however, is that by about 4 months infants are capable of both kinds.

Imitation of a Means to an End. When adults infer an infant's intention and then fulfill it with an instrumental act, they also provide a model for imitation. Dewey (1916) considered the ability to make use of models for the child's own ends the only intelligent form of imitation:

> Imitation of ends, as distinct from imitation of means which help to reach ends, is a superficial and transitory affair which leaves little effect upon disposition. Idiots are especially apt at this kind of imitation; it affects outward acts but not the means of their performance. When we find children engaging in this sort of mimicry, instead of encouraging them (as we would do if it were an important means of social control) we are more likely to rebuke them as apes, monkeys, parrots, or copy cats. Imitation of means of accomplishment is, on the other hand, an intelligent act. It involves close observation, and judicious selection of what will enable one to do better something which he already is trying to do. [P. 43]

Consider the paradigm in which 6-month-old infants were taught how to reach around a Plexiglas barrier for a small cube containing a bell (Kaye, 1977a). Recall that the infants were seated in their mothers' laps, facing a table on which the toy was clearly visible within a few inches of one hand; but the direct reach was blocked by the Plexiglas on that side, and the solution was to reach in a wide arc with the other hand. In the original experiment, 41 (55%) of 74 mothers whose infants failed the pretest were successful in getting the infants to reach around the barrier. The mothers' principal strategy was simply to reach for the toy slowly, making sure the infant was watching, take out the toy and then (sometimes after letting the baby play with it) put it back. Some mothers tended to combine this strategy with another we called the shaping strategy, in which they set the toy partly outside the barrier and then moved it gradually behind on successive trials. Others tended to push the baby's arm or body around the barrier on some trials. But every mother included some simple demonstration trials, in effect relying on the infants' ability to imitate. The mothers alternated their demonstrations with the infants' own attempts; as shown in Figure 3-7, they used the infants' gaze direction as an index of when to take their turn (the infants always looked away from the task after an unsuccessful attempt). This turn-taking often continued for as many as 20 or 30 trials.

Since repeated demonstration appeared to be the most popular maternal frame for a situation of this kind, we tried an experiment relying upon that frame exclusively. We exaggerated the "showing" strategy and omitted the "shaping" and "shoving" that many of the mothers had combined with it. The author served as instructor with seven fresh 6-month-olds, strictly applying three rules: (1) wait for the infants to avert their gaze from the task or to withdraw their hands from the barrier before demonstrating how to reach around it; (2) provide nothing but the demonstration, regardless of what the infants do on their turn (e.g., do not reinforce them in any way for what might look like an approximate imitation); and (3) continue for many trials even when an infant seems to be making no progress. With this method, all seven infants (after failing the pretest) learned to retrieve the toy within a few minutes (Kaye, 1970).

An important feature of this experiment was that we established the infants' intention to obtain the toy prior to showing them how. Their repeated attempts to reach through the Plexiglas, ceasing whenever the toy was removed, left no doubt as to their intention. The model provided a means toward the infants' ends. Furthermore, since the form of the modeled action was determined in advance, there was no possibility that the experimenter had really been imitating the infants (as is often the case in real life). The question remains, however, how the babies could know that what the adult did was a means to achieve their own goal, and, particularly, how they could know which features of the adult's act were really instrumental.

The answer is that the infants did not know which features were instrumental. This was shown in the first study by the fact that some features irrelevant to getting the toy, such as a mother bobbing her hand up and down in an effort to hold the infant's attention, were just as likely to be imitated as those features that were instrumental. Only gradually, after some successful trials, would we see the irrelevant features drop out. This suggests that two somewhat independent processes are involved: the imitation of salient features and the selection of those relevant to the goal. Imitation of features did not necessarily relate to any goal. In fact, the infants need not even have realized that the adult's behavior contained a means toward the goal.[5] This suggests that the difference between modeling means versus ends may not really be so

5. For a pertinent discussion focusing on older children's imitation of adults, see Sonnenschein and Whitehurst (1980).

important for the act of imitation itself. After imitating various features, however, the intention to get the toy must have been involved in the accommodation over trials, that is, in dropping the irrelevant features and retaining the ones that were instrumental.

In a third experiment (Kaye, 1979a) we tested the effect of the goal object (the preestablished intention) upon imitation of the model's hand movements. We compared two groups of 15 infants each, all 6 months old. In this experiment the teaching was done by the mothers, but each trial was under the experimenter's direction so that the same three rules were followed as in the previous experiment. The control group was to go through the same procedure of pretest, training, and posttest with the cube behind the barrier. The experimental group first received prior training with the Plexiglas but without the attractive cube to reach for. When the mothers demonstrated the detour-reaching act without any toy behind the barrier, their infants often assimilated particular features. In this case, all such features must be considered "irrelevant" to any intention of the infant of which we could be aware; yet they were imitated. What we did not see were infants systematically selecting an efficient final form of reaching, as we had seen in the previous experiments and as we saw on the later trials with the goal object. So that process of accommodating the skill must be due to its efficacy in leading the infant to the intended goal, though the imitation of particular features of the model in the first place occurred without a goal.

It is easy to explain the refinement of the skill—the selection of *relevant* features—by a process of reinforcement and extinction. But the features that are tried, the candidates for reinforcement or extinction, are not randomly emitted operants. They are assimilated features of the models presented by adults, just those components of the action that adults happen to do in a salient way and that also happen to be available in the infant's repertoire of schemas. Because these features are assimilated in the very act of perception, and perception is not yet differentiated from covert action, the infant is practically compelled to imitate them.

The second result of the experiment was that in the prior training without a goal, which constituted a kind of orientation tour of the apparatus before being given a problem involving it, those infants who happened to reach around the barrier learned nothing that in any way helped them later get the toy more easily than the control group did. In other words, there was no transfer. Infants who learned to get the toy out could transfer the skill to the other hand (not immediately, but after a few trials with no further instruction), and could use it to retrieve different toys (Kaye, 1970). This illustrates the importance of intention in the lasting accommodation of schemas as opposed to mere assimilation (Kaye, 1979a).

The detour paradigm is a laboratory version of what we have called the instrumental frame. Whenever the instrumental solution is something the infant can imitate, the exchange of turns can also be seen as a modeling frame. Another common situation in which models are presented is in the discourse frame. Often mothers, in mimicking a particular noise or expression the infant has just produced, will also exaggerate it, then wait for a moment in hopes of getting a game started. Or they may introduce a modification of the original expression that changes its implication, as from a fussy cry to a song on the same pitch (Kaye, 1979b). Those are the situations in which parents expect to get a response. In other words, they do not present models at random times or in random fashion. The only adults who present infants with arbitrary actions out of context and say, "Can you do this?" are experimental psychologists. That is the best way to be sure that the infant's baseline probability of spontaneously producing the act is virtually zero (Guillaume, 1971). In normal play, however, adults rarely suggest actions unless they think the infant either already can do them or is trying to do them.

Imitation of Meaningless Acts. Despite what has just been said, the experimental group's performance when there was no toy behind the barrier shows that infants need not have any understanding of the relation between the demonstrated means and their own ends, in order to imitate some of what they see the model do. Indeed, they would be poorly designed organisms if they did operate under that constraint. Much of the time infants' limited grasp of space, objects, and causality must make it absolutely impossible for them to know which features of the adult's act are instrumental and which are irrelevant. Besides, the adult will often misread an infant's intention, so there is not necessarily *anything* in the adult's behavior that is a means toward the infant's own ends. The same applies when a mother imitates her infant's own expression, which occurs about four times as frequently as the infant's imitation of the mother at this age (Pawlby, 1977). Whenever that expression happens to have been unintentional on the infant's part, there is no end for the adult's response to be a means toward. In other words, it will appear to the infant as a meaningless act; yet it is an act that the adult knows to be within the infant's capacity.

In either of these two cases—when the adult misreads the infant's intention or when the adult imitates the infant—the action offered is a kind of tentative gloss on the infant's behavior. It is an interpretation of what the latter's intention might have been, with the implicit question

"Is this what you mean?" Regardless of the answer to that question, the infant may then imitate the action. This kind of exchange has three social consequences. First, it creates the opposite kind of asymmetrically shared meaning: Now the infant interprets the adult's behavior, "understands" it by trying to assimilate it. Each participant is assimilating the other's act to his or her own schemas, resulting in a semblance of dialogue that still falls short of genuine intersubjectivity.

A second consequence of mutual imitation is that so far as the adult is concerned the infant has answered the question "Is this what you mean?" in the affirmative. The parent feels that a meaningful exchange has taken place. This is comparable to the impression engendered in the mother in feeding her newborn, that her jiggling is an effective response to the infant's pause: that she has thereby elicited the next burst of sucks. It is comparable to the pretend conversations that go on in face-to-face play between mother and infant. It is also comparable to what takes place later in verbal dialogues, when the 2-year-old mainly just responds perfunctorily but the mother responds each time with a question or request so as to elicit another response on the same topic and thus create a chain of connected discourse.

A third consequence of these interchanges occurs when an adult happens to be correct in attributing a particular intention to the infant. Then, and only then, the two assimilations correspond to each other. Shared meaning is born in the form of what might be called *correspondent assimilation*.

For all the foregoing reasons, it is important that infants can imitate acts having no apparent instrumental value. Our experimental studies of this kind of imitation used the method derived from what we had seen mothers do in the detour-reaching study; but we now used arbitrarily selected models. As reported above, the detour reaching experiment was not very successful without a toy visible through the barrier: The experimental group matched the "meaningless" act of reaching around the barrier only half as well as the controls did when the same act was a means toward an end. In a subsequent series of studies, however, we did get systematic accommodation to arbitrarily selected modeled actions. The secret was to give the infants plenty of time to respond and to leave the timing of the model's presentations strictly under the infants' control. Kaye and Marcus (1978, 1981) tried this method with a variety of tasks between 6 and 12 months, using eye contact as the trigger with which the subjects elicited a repetition of the model. The tasks included open-and-close mouth movements, hand-clapping, toy-shaking, ear-touching, and a vocalization "gi-gi-gi."

It is important that the tasks were selected a priori, not in response to the baby's behavior. Furthermore, although the moment at which we presented the model was contingent upon a signal from the infant, neither the form of the model nor anything else about the experimenter's behavior was contingent upon what the infant did on any trial. The features that were to be assimilated, in other words, depended only upon their salience and accessibility to an infant's own repertoire of schemas at that particular age. This experiment shows what babies can do with the benefit of the modeling frame, even when it is not also an instrumental frame.

For each task, we found a consistent order in which relevant features of the task were produced and then combined by the infants. First, they assimilated the tasks to single features of schemas in their repertoire. For example, the rhythmic series of four hand claps led the babies to touch the experimenter's hands, touch their own hands, or beat a rhythmic series with their arms or legs. Later, those features were combined as separate acts on the same trial: touching their two hands together, pausing, and then kicking a few times in an echo of the experimenter's clapping. Finally, by combining the various features in a continuous act (e.g., clapping the hands), the infants gradually constructed approximations to the model. Over months 6–12 they added features of the modeled actions in a regular order of progressive approximations for each task, and this same order was recapitulated within those single sessions in which they "worked up" to a better approximation (Kaye & Marcus, 1981).

An intriguing result of this experiment was that our subjects refused to restrict themselves to practicing each task only within the block of trials when we were modeling that task. Instead, the first successful hand-clapping, for example, was produced by three of the nine infants not on hand-clapping trials but on trials when the experimenter had been touching her ear. These infants apparently interpreted the task by assimilating a feature—touching one part of the body to another—that we could not have defined a priori as a criterion for "correct" imitation. (We were still able to prove the statistical significance of such results by comparison with baseline periods.)

A number of observers have noted that the earliest assimilations of adults' actions to the infant's own schemas are cross-modal assimilations. By 4 months and probably earlier, infants are quite good at detecting synchronies between sounds and movements (Spelke, 1979). For example, an auditory stimulus may elicit an excited waving of legs or arms in the same rhythm as the stimulus (Gardner & Gardner, 1970). A movement of the mouth is "imitated" by a similar movement of the baby's hand, or vice versa (Piaget, 1951). If one imposes an absolute criterion for resemblance between movements, insisting that they involve the same body parts, one may not consider such events imitation.

The problem disappears when imitation is defined as any resemblance beyond what could have occurred by chance within the given time interval, compared with baseline observations.

A majority of the infants succeeded in the mouth opening task at 6 months. Since the infants could only visually observe the model doing this, yet could not see their own mouths, this accomplishment was superior to what Piaget (1951) and others had reported. However, that is due to our improvement upon the traditional method: Piaget presented each task only two or three times in a given session, then went on to something else when his children did not immediately imitate. Parents do something similar in one way to our method and in another way to Piaget's. Infants normally experience at least as many trials as we gave them, but the trials are spread over many hours or days and interspersed with other activities, like this:

> At 0;6(25) [6 months, 25 days] J. invented a new sound by putting her tongue between her teeth. It was something like *pfs*. Her mother then made the same sound. J. was delighted and laughed as she repeated it in her turn. Then came a long period of mutual imitation. J. said *pfs*, her mother imitated her, and J. watched her without moving her lips. Then when her mother stopped, J. began again, and so it went on. . . .
> At 0;6(26) J. frequently made, during the day, the sounds *bva, bve* and also *va, ve* without anyone imitating her. On the next day, however, at 0;6(27), when I said *"bva, bve,"* etc., to her, she looked at me, smiled, and said: *"pfs, pfs . . . bva."* Thus instead of at once imitating the model given to her, J. began by reproducing the sound she had become used to imitating two days earlier. . . . The evening of the same day, every time I said *bva*, J. said *pfs*, without any attempt at imitation. Afterwards I heard her saying *"abou, abou"* (a new sound derived from *bva* which she was trying out on that day). I thereupon said *pfs* a number of times, she smiled, and each time said *abou*. . . .
> At 0;7(15) she was in her cot saying *mam, mam*, etc., and could not see me. When I said *bva*, she was silent for a moment, and then, although she still could not see me, softly said *bva, bva*, as though she were trying it out. When I again said it, she said *bva mam, bva mam*, etc. [Piaget, 1951, pp. 19–20]

In these cases the model presented was an imitation of something the baby had previously produced, but adults also try the same kind of thing with new models or with variations on what they think the infant is capable of:

> At 0;8(26) Jacqueline watches her mother who is swinging the flounce on the bassinet. As soon as she stops, Jacqueline

pushes her hand to make her continue. Then she herself grasps
the flounce and imitates the movement. That evening Jacqueline swings a hanging doll in the same way, with great delicacy.
[Piaget, 1952, p. 256]

This brief sketch in Piaget's diary records in the fewest possible lines a
process of great moment and universal experience. The mother may
have been swinging the ruffle of the bassinet idly at first, but continued
because it attracted the baby's attention. She stopped, perhaps in order
to see what would happen. Thus she could test her inference that this
movement was what Jacqueline was interested in; and Jacqueline's imitation of her was undoubtedly reinforcing.

Our method works with younger babies, too. Roth (1980) studied
infants as young as 4 months, succeeding in eliciting imitation from
most of them in a vocalization task and a hand-clapping task. She also
trained the mothers to administer both tasks, and they had even more
success than she. In a similar study, Kessen, Levine, and Wendrich
(1979) found that infants were able to match vocal pitches (D, F, and A
above middle C) significantly often.

The first thing one sees when using this procedure, within two or
three trials, is clear evidence that the infants know the model is under
their control. For example, when eye contact is used as the trigger, they
will keep their eyes averted, then meet the experimenter's eyes and
immediately look to his or her mouth (or hands) in anticipation of the
movement. They have learned, then, even before any actual imitation,
to produce a *signal*. It is not a *gesture*, for there is no reason to think
they experience it from the point of view of the other. But it is an agreed-
upon contingency between a particular type of action on their part (eye
contact) and a particular type of response by the adult. An interesting
fact about these signals is that they can be established without any prior
intention on the infant's part, merely by the adult's choosing to respond
in a consistent way to some class of infant acts.[6] So the earliest signals
are just a matter of learning from experience what goes with what.

Unfortunately, using the word *signal* in this way blurs the distinction
between *conventional* signs (signals) and *indices*. The contingency between trigger and model is indeed an arbitrary convention from the
adult's point of view; but so far as the infant knows, it is merely a
contingent *index* of an interesting event. The fact that the signs used by
adults are neither universal nor inevitable is really irrelevant to the infant

6. Whereas the signal itself may be a quickly established operant, the immediate
looking to the experimenter's mouth probably involves classical conditioning. The US is
the experimenter's behavior, such as mouth-opening, to which the infant orients (UR) on
the first trial or two. The CS is eye contact, if that is used as the signal; and the CR is the
orienting response when it comes to anticipate the US.

learning to comprehend their meaning. For example, the adult says "No!" in a frightening tone. It makes no difference that *no* is a word in a particular language: To the infant it may simply be an index of adult anger. In the same limited sense, we can say that a bottle signifies the feeding situation, or that my dog's leash signifies to her that we are going outside.[7] The same can be said about the sign languages that have been learned by apes (Chapter 7). In the next period, however, signals take on a very different role.

Signification without Designation

The continuum from representation to signification to designation can be thought of most simply as a progression toward greater differentiation between signs and the things they signify. Undifferentiated indices elicit representations without signification, in the sense that they do not really stand for something completely separate from themselves. (A footprint does not exactly *signify* that someone has been in the garden; it is a *part* of their having been there.)

The distinction can also be expressed in another way. Signification is interpersonal representation, since both gestures and signals owe their meaning to intercourse with other people. In the previous period, the infant learned to interpret certain signs used consistently by others, without it mattering whether those were indices or signals. Comprehending or producing signals that had been paired arbitrarily with certain events, and hence were conventional from the adult's point of view, was the transition to differentiated signs. By 6 months or so, the infant began to produce certain signs in order to affect the behavior of others. This is still not the same as using acts spontaneously to signify one's own intentions. The present period begins at around 8 months, when the infant moves from indices to gestures as well as from indices to signals. It will take another 6 months or so, however, before signal and gesture are combined in one completely differentiated *designation* (Huttenlocher & Higgins, 1978), or *symbol*.

Signifying is a form of representation more complex than what is involved in simply accommodating schemas to the nature of the world. The infant takes a giant step in the construction of reality specific to a cultural group by entering the group's world of conventional signs.

Those signs the infant learns to produce are learned almost exclusively by imitation. But the process is not one in which the child has to

7. The dog helps to illustrate that we are talking about the infant's guesses rather than certainty as to the meaning of adult words and gestures. The dog does not *know* you are going to take her out. She only guesses you are, and that excites her. Furthermore, her excitement signals something to you that makes you almost certain to take her, even if you were not already intending to do so. So that makes her guess an even better one, but *certainty* still has nothing to do with it.

analyze the passing parade of conversation, figure out what signs are conventionally used for what referents, imitate them and remember them in case he needs them later. Instead, it is a recapitulation of the same form of interaction as earlier: The adult sees what the child wants, or understands what the child is trying to express. In completing the utterance, the adult provides the appropriate conventional sign in just the context that facilitates imitation.

C: [reaching toward bear] Unh.
M: You want your bear.
C: Beh.

Signification, then, is a natural outcome of the same accommodation process we have already seen. But now adults suggest conventional signs as verbal or gestural means toward ends, in place of providing the instrumental, direct motor solutions such as we found in the detour situation.

In order to see how the transition occurs, we need to go back to the earlier phase of shared intentions, when adults characteristically complete many of the infant's instrumental acts. Through correspondent assimilation, they interpret the latter's intentions and either fulfill them or make it easier for the infant to fulfill them. For example, they see the baby's arm move hesitatingly toward a toy duck, and they push the duck closer. This is not only a facilitation of what the infant is trying to do (the instrumental frame) but also a model for imitation (the modeling frame). The detour situation is a good example. When our mothers reached around the barrier to bring the toy out to the open area where it was easier for the infant to get, they were also modeling the detour reach. In fact, this will usually be the case: Completing the infant's instrumental actions will provide a model that, once imitated, teaches him to complete the action on his own. Now suppose that, instead of moving a toy closer, the parent simply asks, "Duck?" (For in this period, as soon as the infant is actually capable of producing gestures, adults stop pretending—as they have done since the third trimester of pregnancy—that the infant's noises and wiggles are gestures, and they start demanding confirmation.) The question both interprets the child's intention ("Does that extended arm mean you want the duck?") and provides the conventional sign for the object the child seems to want. It also models a means toward the child's goal (if the duck is indeed the goal), for if the infant imitates the word *duck* the parent will happily fetch the duck.

What has happened? In the earlier period, the kinds of models provided were actions that would, if imitated, allow infants to complete their own intended actions upon objects. But in the example just given, the model provided (the word *duck*) is only an instrument toward goal attainment if, when an infant imitates it, other people are present who know what it means. From birth, babies hear such verbal models spoken in their presence and even directly to them. But it is only toward the end of the first year, after age 8–10 months or so, that parents place these gestures in the modeling frame, the same temporal frame that was previously established to help the infant imitate instrumental solutions.

Another example will show that the modeling of gestural means need not always involve words. It may begin, in fact, with gestures that are not conventional: with pointing. The child reaches for something that is beyond arm's length; the parent, guessing that the infant wants the object, tests that assumption by pointing to it with the index finger extended and the other fingers curled under, then looks back at the child (Murphy & Messer, 1977). In pointing to an object in which the infant seems to be interested, the parent may only be asking for verification of the intention he or she attributes to the infant. Any time this attribution is correct, however, the parent will in effect have modeled a pointing gesture. After many such demonstrations, the infant will imitate. The mechanism of imitation is the same as at the previous level, demonstrated by the Kaye and Marcus studies. In the preceding section we discussed the gradual accommodation of schemas by assimilation of selected features of a model, combined through reciprocal assimilation. Now a more abstract and convention-dependent action gets modeled in the same turn-taking frame. The infant learns a means of obtaining things, but one that only works when there are others present who will respond to the gesture (Bruner, 1977; Clark, 1978).

An adult action does not have to be presented deliberately as a model—in fact, it seldom is—for the infant to imitate it. It does, however, have to be presented in a suitable context. The same selective factors that affect what kinds of acts parents think the infant might now be able to imitate also affect what kinds of gestures they think the infant might be able to understand. Thus there will be a tendency for those acts presented in the modeling frame to be increasingly complex and symbolic as the infant gets older. And as parents begin to do certain kinds of things within that frame, they expect more from the infant. Instead of asking, "Do you want that?" they ask, "What do you want?" As they expect the infant to name certain objects, they tend not to name them for him. They stop narrating a play-by-play account of what the infant is doing (Chapter 10). Most important, they stop pretending that all squeaks, grunts, and grimaces are communicative expressions. Now some really are, and the parent has to distinguish which ones are meaningful and what they mean.

The Modeling Frame and the Apprentice Theory. The apprentice metaphor is more than a compromise between extrinsic explanations (e.g.,
that child development is largely a matter of conditioning) and intrinsic
explanations (such as maturation or orthogenesis). It proposes something that is not necessarily entailed even by a combination of those
views. Parents do much more than reinforce hand movements that look
like pointing, reinforce babbling that sounds like words, and so forth.
A parent also *models* pointing, sometimes with the intention to model
but more often just in the natural course of trying to understand what
the infant's behavior might signify. Furthermore, the whole situation
involving child, parent, and objects has been structured by the parent
in the first place. As pointed out earlier, reinforcement of correct solutions is only involved in the lasting accommodation of schemas, and is
accomplished at least as much by the contingencies of objects and space
as by anything adults say or do. Imitation itself occurs without extrinsic
reinforcement. The principal contribution of adults is the model; the
feedback is secondary.

Cognitive versus Social Reasons for Imitating. There are at least two different
kinds of motivation for infants to imitate, corresponding to two different
functions that imitation seems to serve in development (McCall, Parke,
& Kavanaugh, 1977; Uzgiris, 1981). The cognitive motivation involves
the accommodation of skills, as illustrated in the imitation of means
toward ends, discussed above. Several studies at various ages have
found that moderately difficult models are imitated more than extremely
familiar or extremely novel or difficult ones (e.g., Harnick, 1978; Shipley,
Smith, & Gleitman, 1969; Sibulkin & Uzgiris, 1978). It is clearly adaptive
for children to attempt to imitate models just beyond their levels of
competence rather than wasting time on actions they have already mastered or cannot yet hope to master.

   On the other hand, imitating and being imitated have important
effects upon interpersonal relationships (Fouts, Waldner, & Watson,
1976; McCall et al., 1977; Mueller & Lucas, 1975; Thelen, Dollinger, &
Roberts, 1975) as well as being evidence of prior positive relationships
(Bandura & Huston, 1961; Matsuda, 1973). Therefore the child has a
motive for continuing to imitate some very familiar or very silly kinds
of actions, when doing so will create or maintain a mutual attraction
with a parent, interesting adult, sibling, or peer. These social relationships involve both "attachment" in the sense of proximity and mutual
interest, and the repeated turn-taking games whose frames and rules
are shared with specific adults.

   These two motives are closely related, once infant and parent move
into the period of shared memory where the parent possesses special

knowledge about the infant's interests and experience with particular toys, games, and expressions. This knowledge makes them for the first time a dyad, sharing jointly managed skills not available to the infant in interaction with strangers. An infant's ability to make optimal use of imitation for cognitive development, by being presented with salient models on the frontier of his existing repertoire of skills, is facilitated by greater dyadic experience with adults who know where his frontier is.

As infants develop their own memory, in this period, of the significance of actions with particular objects in particular contexts, this knowledge affects their interest in imitating different sorts of models. Actions performed upon appropriate objects (e.g., pushing a toy car or drinking from a cup) are more readily imitated than the same actions upon inappropriate objects (Killen & Uzgiris, 1981) or the same actions performed as empty movements in space (Abravanel, Levan-Gold-schmidt, & Stevenson, 1976; Rodgon & Kurdek, 1977). A year later, that difference disappears. So there is a particular period when the imitating infant attaches great importance to what actions go with what objects, and it is probably no coincidence that this happens also to be the period of attachment to particular others.

To summarize the period of signification without designation: The transition from primitive representations to more and more differentiated signification is a gradual affair, unmarked by any clear boundary. It advances on two fronts. Those adult actions that the infant understands—that is, assimilates to schemas involving an anticipation of what the adult is going to do next—increasingly include *signals*, conventions of the dyad and of the wider community. The infant, like the chimpanzee discussed in Chapter 7, has no way of knowing which of the adult's actions are signals (as defined in Figure 7-2) and which are merely indices. The important point is that he is in the role of interpreter of what those actions signify. Similarly, he does not necessarily know that those same signifiers will work just as well when he himself uses them as *gestures* to others, and that the gestures he has learned by imitation of others, as means toward his own ends, have that same meaning when used by others toward him. In other words, I am proposing the very opposite of the inside-out theory: Infants have to be involved in interpersonal communication before they begin to acquire a mental understanding of it.

What this level lacks is *designation* (Huttenlocher & Higgins, 1978). The infant produces some signs and comprehends some signs, but the signs and what they signify do not stand in a reversible simultaneous relation to one another. That seems to come only after the child has had time to assimilate the comprehended signs together with the identical produced signs. As discussed in Chapter 8, through "reciprocal assimilation" this connection soon becomes relatively automatic. The acquisition of a lexicon then accelerates tremendously. For then every word is learned as a true symbol, and immediate imitation is unnecessary for subsequent production. That is the fourth level, when symbols finally have been achieved.

The Achievement of Symbols

Designation is achieved around the middle of the second year, after the child already knows some words. The first words do not really designate, for each word is either produced or comprehended, not automatically both. But as their vocabularies grow beyond a dozen or two dozen words, one begins to see children generalizing immediately from their comprehended lexicons to their productive lexicons and vice versa. The criterion for designation is a unified lexicon. We cannot say that children intend to produce an effect in a listener's mind until we know that the gesture they use would indeed produce that effect in their own minds when produced by another.

It turns out that this "unified lexicon" criterion entails what Piaget called "deferred imitation," his own criterion for symbolic representation. When a symbol enters the lexicon through the comprehension route and is available later for spontaneous production, we can use the term "deferred imitation" if we like. However, symbols can just as well enter through the production route, with their addition to the lexicon being manifested in later comprehension. Although this has never been called deferred imitation, it is the obverse side of the same process.

To illustrate this, suppose a child has not previously understood the meaning of "juice" but learns it in the following way. The mother, holding a glass of juice, asks, "Do you want some juice?" and the child replies, "Juice." This imitation need not imply comprehension of the word as a symbol. But the mother treats it as if it did, and gives the child some juice. The word thus enters the child's productive vocabulary through immediate use in a signifying context. The child has learned to say the word in order to obtain juice, but need not necessarily know what it means when others use it. However, suppose the next day someone says, "Where's your juice?" and the child points or looks toward the juice. This indicates *comprehension* of the word. So it turns out that the word was indeed acquired as a symbol, not just an instrumental means. It really designates juice.

Now suppose another child first comprehends the significance of "juice" when the mother says it, associating it with juice but not producing the word. The next day, seeing his mother pour some juice, the child says "juice." This is what has traditionally been called deferred imitation. But in the previous example, we did not call the child's behavior deferred imitation of the way the mother had decoded what that word signified. By the same reasoning, in the present case we should not call this behavior deferred imitation of the mother's production of the word. Because symbols *designate* bidirectionally, the word was available for production in the appropriate situation even though the child was only taught to comprehend it. Deferred imitation of arbitrary gestures, when the child is in an appropriate situation to make the gesture to another, is really the deferred production of representations that were comprehended symbolically in the first place.

When children achieve this level of representation—the symbolic one—their linguistic knowledge may still be quite limited, but it is unlike the representation of any other species including the best trained circus animals. By virtue of its bidirectionality, the child's lexicon belongs to a shared language between parent and child. The importance of this cannot be overestimated. The child then belongs to the community as much as to the family system, for the conventional gestures are, in fact, words in the community's language. Parents and older siblings, in beginning to expect and require those gestures in appropriate situations, act as socialization agents for the community. I shall argue in Chapters 11 and 12 that this is a socialization that creates a mind, not one that subverts it. Before children share our language they are not fully persons (not full members of the system), and they have no symbolic processes.

Imitation seems to change when the child reaches this level. The boundaries become completely blurred between (1) actions produced by the child's own repertoire of schemas, (2) creative accommodations, and (3) imitations. We know that the meaning of a word in the child's lexicon continually changes. The child never loses the capacity to imitate others' usages of words. Inherent in the nature of language, this process continues throughout life. Words like *system* enter our lexicons as easily as *juice* once did. It becomes impossible to decide to what extent the act of using a symbol is imitative and to what extent it is a creative generalization. But this impossibility is not just restricted to symbols. It is true of all behavior. When I ski with my body bent in a certain way, how can I measure how much of that posture is due to what feels comfortable and coordinates easily with everything else my body is doing at that moment, and how much I am imitating ski instructors, ski movies, and other skiers I have seen over the years?

With respect to the mechanisms of imitation itself, the changes may be more apparent than real. The imitation of symbols is simply a new use of assimilation, a new form of representation, and a reversible signification. But the processes of imitation are not dependent on symbolic processes. In fact, imitation itself does not presuppose representation.

Just the opposite: Representation, signification, and designation all pre-suppose the cognitive and interpersonal processes involved in imitation.

The Modeling Frame and Designation. While granting that human infants' abilities to imitate are sophisticated and far more flexible than in other species, we have emphasized in this discussion that infants are not left to their own devices when it comes to imitation. At each level, they are helped by the kinds of models adults present to them and by the fact that those models tend to be presented at optimal times. So the achieve-ment of symbols is not to be explained by the autonomous development of the imitation processes themselves any more than it is to be explained by the maturation of brain functions or by a culmination of interaction with objects. It is the culmination of social routines, specifically due to the fit between (1) the cycles built into the infant's neurophysiology, which the parent cannot help noticing, adjusting to, and anticipating; and (2) the natural tendency of adults to complete what they perceive as the infant's intentions.

In those perceptions of intention, those initial one-sided accom-plishments of "shared meaning," we can see that there is no more cer-tainty on the adult's part than on the child's. The mother does not *know* what her infant's gropings mean. Nor is there a point in development at which her attributions become perfectly correct, for even two adults never mean exactly the same thing (including every presupposition and connotation) when they understand each other. Nonetheless, a parent's interpretations of the infant's intentions are bound to come closer to what those intentions really are, the more parent and infant live in the same social context.

How is designation achieved? I have said that so-called deferred imitation is a necessary component. But it is not sufficient. For apes often defer their imitations, they imitate conventional signals, they com-prehend signals produced by others. What they do not do is put all three abilities together, acquiring true symbols that they can utilize later in the opposite role from that in which they were acquired. Why do humans so reliably do what apes never do, even when the apes have been laboriously trained by humans?

An obvious part of the answer is that man has a bigger and better brain; but brains alone are not enough. We know of no structural feature that could explain the chasm between *homo* and other hominids, with respect to signs. We should assume, however, that a brain has to have the right kind of experiences. What is there about parent-infant relations that makes them a plausible causal factor in the transition from intelligent learning at the level of signification-without-designation, which is not unique to man, to symbolic representation, which is?

The answer to that question is to be found in the facts we have established in previous chapters. Human parents (and other adults as well) do two things practically simultaneously. They (1) treat infants as though the latter were making gestures to them long before that is really true; and (2) take infants' turns for them in dialogues, speaking for them and thus providing a model. The parent switches between these two roles of interpreter and gesturer, just as the child will eventually be expected to do. This has the effect of providing both the culturally correct signals and the appropriate responses to those signals in association with salient objects and events. The infant cannot help but eventually assimilate those signals to the schemas for the events themselves. Because there is a double assimilation going on in very close temporal proximity (assimilation of signals to events and of events to imitated signals), there is bound to be assimilation of the two to one another. We can rely upon the explanation Piaget (1952) offered for the origins of accommodation: "reciprocal assimilation."

I do not claim that an ape treated constantly in the normal human parental way would achieve symbols. Brains must have something to do with it as well. However, as argued in earlier chapters, the nervous system's contribution to the symbol development process is more than just the effect of its capacity and architecture upon cognition. In other words, it may be a mistake to look at the human nervous system for specific cognitive and linguistic capacities. It may be more fruitful to look for mechanisms that facilitate the kinds of social relations within which human infants find themselves. Their behavior from birth onward is a very large factor in the way their parents interact with them. It is *not possible* to treat an ape as if it were a human baby, with respect to the most important aspects of parent-infant interaction. Infants are biologically endowed with specific patterns of behavior, such as the burst-pause patterns in neonatal sucking, the visual tracking of objects, and the predispositions to imitate selected features of human models, all of which conspire to elicit the kinds of parental behavior that gradually transform the infant human organism into a person.

We know very little about how these processes between adults and infants vary across cultures. However, the observations in the literature indicate that any culturally or racially varying dimensions are superimposed upon a matrix of universal features of infant behavior that promote certain kinds of universal adult responses (Freedman, 1974). This still leaves a great deal of room for cultural expectations about children's roles and capacities, and about the nature of dialogue itself, to affect the processes I have described. Precisely because so much of the infant's early apprenticeship in the system depends upon parents' acting *as if* the infant were already behaving as a person (Chapter 10), our culture-specific notions about what a person is can alter the frequency, contents, contexts, and consequences of interaction in the various frames that evolution has made available to us.

Summary

We began with certain assumptions about what imitation is and how it develops in the human species.

In the first place, imitation is active and creative. An imitative act is never a perfect copy, always a novel act. Hence the construction of novel utterances, for example—for which the child has never been presented with an identical model—still has imitative learning as its basis.

Another assumption was that we should not regard imitation itself as a single process. The criteria we use for applying the term imitation—action resembling a model, produced after observation of the model within a time span and under conditions in which it would not have been likely to have been produced in the absence of the model—give us no reason for thinking that there is a common mechanism underlying all instances of the category. "Imitation" is another word like Wittgenstein's (1953) "game": It is a family of diverse sorts of things. What makes the different kinds, degrees, circumstances, and uses of imitation interesting to us is the fact that they are all involved in the social transmission of knowledge. But this does not make them one phenomenon, much less one process to be explained with a single model, even a model that addresses the "development" of imitation. I do not think imitation is the kind of thing that has a development. It is rather a set of phenomena, all of which must be of interest to anyone interested in human development.

The most important assumption was that imitation is often achieved by the joint action of children and their models. Although it clearly involves cognitive processes within the child, the progressive development of symbols is a social process whose evolution in our species must have involved the behavior of parents and other adults, as well as the behavior of their imitators. No symbolic system could have survived from one generation to the next if it could not have been easily acquired by young children under their normal conditions of social life.

The theory that emerged has several distinctive points. First is the link between each major step in the progression toward symbolic representation—assimilation, representation, signification, and designation—and a series of developments in the parent-infant relationship: the sharing of rhythms and regulations, then intentions, then memories, and finally language. The final step in the two progressions is, in fact, the same: Designation, as a criterion for true symbols, means shared language. The earlier levels, however, are more than just alternative sets of terms for the same achievements. Progress up the semiotic ladder makes possible and inevitable each advance in adults' abilities to participate in the infant's cognitive world, and each of those advances in turn presents a new agenda for imitation.

Second, we cannot reduce symbolic representation to "deferred imitation" or to any other extension of the ability to imitate, as though it were due to some orthogenetic developmental principle within the child. This objection to Piaget's formula follows from the fact that animals capable of deferred imitation (i.e., capable of imitating an action long after they have observed it) still do not achieve symbolic processes. The objection also follows, of course, from our insistence that imitation is not a process undergoing transformation at all.

A third point is that imitation does not entail representation. On this point we are in agreement with Piaget. The most primitive kinds of imitation, seen in newborns and continuing throughout the life span, are simple assimilations. When a tap dancer demonstrates a combination of steps to her partner, the partner can imitate without making an accommodation of his lasting schemas. Representation may or may not be involved, but even when it is involved it is an additional fact not inherent in the act of imitation. The ability to assimilate another's act to one's own schemas is as evident in the built-in imitations and circular reactions of the pre-representational infant as it is in the immediate imitations of the skilled performer. However, it is accurate to say that representations are both product and cause of the fact that the developing child imitates more and more complex actions. They are a cause in the sense that the repertoire of differentiated schemas widens the range of actions that can be assimilated. And they are a product in the sense that imitation creates new skills and makes the infant more and more a participating member of the social system. The infant's experiences thus widen. At the same time, adults' expectations increase so that they play the infant's role less and demand that the infant accommodate more.

Fourth, our own experiments especially have shown that infants even at the second level, when accommodations first appear, do a great deal of their own task analysis during imitation, breaking down the model's actions systematically into components they can add to their own attempts. Sensorimotor development, fortunately, does not depend upon the exact content of a parental curriculum, for an infant's existing repertoire of schemas, along with the ability to assimilate any of a large number of alternative features of an observed action, result in a kind of self-structured curriculum.

Finally, however, we have seen that older human beings (not exclusively adults, and certainly not exclusively mothers, though some of our investigations focused upon them) play a large role in setting up the modeling frame, in deciding that more complex actions are ready to be put on the infant's agenda, and in alternating trial for trial in the way that the Kaye and Marcus studies merely exemplified. The parental frames are not a matter of conscious instruction. They are a matter of play for the joy of it, pretend conversation, showing off the infant's genius, and eventually behavior control for reasons of safety as well as of cultural norms. Even on those rare occasions when a parent or any elder is engaged in "teaching" a baby some trick, the object of instruction is merely the trick itself, never any of the grander accomplishments like object permanence, the concept of a gesture, or symbols. Yet those are the determined outcomes of ordinary playing with babies.

10

Pretty Words That Make No Sense

Women know
The way to rear up children, (to be just)
They know a simple, merry, tender knack
Of tying sashes, fitting baby-shoes,
And stringing pretty words that make no sense,
And kissing full sense into empty words,
Which things are corals to cut life upon,
Although such trifles . . .

Elizabeth Browning, *Aurora Leigh*, 1857

Genuine poetry can communicate before it is understood.

T. S. Eliot (on Dante), *Selected Essays 1917–1932*

The many studies of face-to-face play between mothers and babies have been motivated primarily by an interest in the developing infant. None-theless, a number of investigators have noted that the behavior of mothers in that situation bears study in itself. We come to this conclusion all the more strongly, having said that the baby's expressions in face-to-face play situations at first have no intentional meaning. What meaning should we attach to the meanings mothers attach to those expressions?

Among the students who gathered the data in our project, the conversation in the car on the way back from visits to the subjects' homes often centered upon the differing goals, anxieties, and fantasies revealed in the mothers' monologues to the babies. Other students who had the job of coding the videotapes never actually met the mothers, yet they felt they had come to know many of them by the form and

189

content of the repeated verbalizations on the tapes. The intensity of these verbalizations (about one discrete utterance every 3 seconds) must have been partly a result of the videotaping situation. Mothers were asked to "try to get his/her attention and play with him/her as you normally do." So they surely felt under a constraint to do something; long periods of silence or of not paying attention to the baby would have seemed awkward or uncooperative under our camera's gaze (in this culture). However, whatever pressure existed to talk more than usual, it was still the case that all of our mothers were filmed under the same conditions, so that the differences among them cannot be attributed to the procedure. Nor do we believe the basic characteristics of their speech to the babies, to be described below, were unrepresentative of how mothers behave when alone with their babies. For psychologists are not the only ones who have described this behavior, as the poem quoted above indicates.

Browning goes on to be gratuitously insulting to fathers. I do not share her observation that

> Fathers love as well
> . . . but still with heavier brains,
> And wills more consciously responsible,
> And not as wisely, since less foolishly.

Although interesting differences have been observed (Lamb, 1977), the principal conclusion from a large number of studies is that fathers interact with babies pretty much the same way mothers do (Belsky, 1979; Parke, 1979). The only differences are quantitative rather than qualitative and may have a lot to do with the conditions under which fathers are observed. Golinkoff and Ames (1979) found no differences on a variety of measures, except that when fathers and mothers were both being observed together fathers took fewer turns than mothers.

Our study happened to focus upon mothers because we had a representative sample of families, not a "liberated" upper-middle-class one. Despite many changes in the attitudes toward sex roles in our society, at least 90% of young infants still spend at least 90% of their waking hours with their mothers, and the rest are with grandmothers, aunts, or female neighbors more than they are with fathers.

Let us look at what some of our mothers said. My purpose in summarizing these results is merely to set the stage for a discussion of how the development of the infant's own mental life is accompanied by parallel changes in the mother's image of him. I want to suggest also that the latter—the imagined infant—differs greatly among mothers in some ways that are stable, over and above any developmental changes, and that are only partially a reflection of the actual infant. Eventually

I shall argue that these differences among mothers are bound to affect an infant's development once he becomes a member of the system.

Structural Parameters of Mothers' Speech

Here is a mother of a boy at 13 weeks:

Are you going to give me a smile?
Or going to be a bastard.
Come on Alan.
Come on.
You can give Mommy a smile.
Come on.
You give Mommy a smile.
Come on.
Come on.
Come on.
Can you give me a smile?
Can you give me a smile, sweetheart?
Come on.
ARRRRRRRR.
ARRRRRRRR.
Can you give me a smile?
Can you give me a smile?
Yeah.
Come on.
You can give me a smile.
Come on.
Come on.
Oh, what you going to do, Al?
What you going to do?
Come on.
Come here.
Come on.
Give me a smile.
Give me a smile.
Hey, Alan.
Hey.
Come on.
Ally.
Alan.
Come on.
Come on.
Give me a smile.
Give me a smile.
Come on.
Come on.
[etc.]

The mother kept repeating short, insistent imperatives to her baby throughout the session; she had done the same thing at 6 weeks, and did so again at 26 weeks.

Now listen to Mother II, talking to her daughter at 6 weeks. This monologue is just as repetitious as the previous example, but the proportion of indirect requests and simple questions is about four times as high:

> What you doing?
> Huh?
> What you doing?
> Look at all the people.
> You want to look at all the people?
> Huh?
> You want to look at the sun?
> Huh?
> You don't want to look at the sun?
> You want puppy dog to give you a kiss?
> Give me a kiss.
> See.
> Oh, what was that?
> Puppy dog give you a kiss?
> Puppy dog gave you a kiss?
> Yeah.
> Yeah.
> Yeah.
> You don't want to look nowhere else.
> Huh?
> No.
> You just want to take a shit.
> And then you'll be fine this afternoon, if you can just go.
> Huh?
> Yeah.
> You'll just be fine.
> Yeah.
> You going to smile again?
> Is Jennifer going to smile?
> Is Jennifer going to smile again?
> Huh?
> No?
> You're not going to smile?
> You're not going to smile?
> You're not going to smile?
> Why?
> [etc.]

Mother III, whose daughter was also aged 6 weeks in the session from which the following excerpt is taken, gives no imperatives at all, only running comments about what the baby is doing, seeing, thinking, and "saying":

What?
What's over there?
Do you want to see something over there?
[Laugh]
Oh you do like to look, don't you?
You really do.
You like to see what's out there.
What's over there?
Something over there?
What you doing?
Huh?
You know your trouble?
You are just not satisfied looking at Mommy.
That's your trouble.
I mean there's a whole wide world out there.
But I'm out here too.
Yes I am.
Now you say, "Who cares?"
"Who cares about that?"
Huh?
You say, "There's color out here."
Right?
"There's color."
"Things that I don't get to see in my crib."
"I can always see you, Mommy."
"But I can't see all those colors."
Huh?
Is that what you see?
[etc.]

These three samples are very different from one another (and each is representative of the kind of utterances produced by that mother through all three sessions). On closer analysis, however, they also have much in common. They are similar to the monologues that other investigators have recorded (Stern et al., 1977; Sherrod, Crawley, Petersen, & Bennett, 1978; Sylvester-Bradley & Trevarthen, 1978). Unlike those other investigators, we had the opportunity to analyze a relatively large corpus of 13,574 utterances, all from the same group of mothers at three different ages. We restricted our analysis to those 36 mothers (37 infants, because the sample included a set of male fraternal twins) from whom we had clear tapes at all three ages. We also had other data on this same group: We videotaped and transcribed the speech of a stranger to the

same babies at the same ages, in the identical situation; we had transcribed audiotapes of the mothers' speech to a female interviewer, a
comparable face-to-face situation in which, because of the nature of the
topic (motherhood), they did 80%–90% of the talking; and, for most of
the subjects, we had mother-child dialogues recorded in a play situation
2 years later (Chapter 6).

Along with the large corpus of speech, we also had another resource
not available to previous investigators: the computer language, CRES-
CAT, which we had developed in order to do the sequential analysis of
behavior in our more microanalytic studies (Kaye, 1977c). It allowed us
to compute words per utterance, rates of exact and partial repetition,
and frequencies of utterances of certain categorical types without the
exhaustive process of hand-coding that slows down most research involving language. All the utterances were typed into the computer,
checked, and then the coding and counting was done by CRESCAT—
without the benefit of human judgment, of course (there are no "borderline cases" for a computer), but with perfect reliability. Analysis of
the thematic content did require a human coder. We shall discuss the
structural characteristics of the mothers' speech first (Kaye, 1980c).

As mentioned already, the utterance rate to the infants averaged 21
utterances per minute. To the 2-year-olds, the mothers said only 14.5
utterances per minute; but the children themselves produced about six
utterances per minute, so the total rate of utterances was about the same
at the two age periods: one every 3 seconds or so. The similarity in
combined speech rate suggests that with the infants the mothers were
essentially doing the speaking for both partners, as the examples above
illustrate.[1]

The second finding was that 16% of the mothers' utterances were
exact repetitions of the immediately preceding utterance. This, too, is
exemplified above. (By contrast, their speech to the 2-year-olds included
only 3.8% exact immediate self-repetitions. In their speech to the adult
interviewer, mothers never repeated a whole utterance.)

The utterances most likely to be repeated, not surprisingly, were
the short ones; and those mothers with the fewest words per utterance
(WPU) were the ones who repeated the most. This refers to exact repetition of a whole utterance. Partial repetition, with the addition or dele-
tion of at least one word, was another story. Even mothers whose
sentences were rather varied used a relatively small set of words, over
and over. The extreme case was a mother who produced 188 utterances,
of which more than two-thirds (129) consisted of nothing but "Tommy,"
"Hey," "Come on," and "Goo." But even in transcripts containing long

1. On the other hand, the mothers' own rate of *words* per minute was about the same
in both situations (Table 10-1).

and varied sentences, there was a lot of repetition of words. For example, in the excerpt from Mother III above, more than one-third of the words are *I, you, what, see,* or *there.*

A third finding was that we noticed a class of one-word greetings, consisting of utterances like "Hi," "Hello," "Yeah," "Oh," and 16 other types (but not, e.g., "Hey" or "Come on," which are usually said when the baby is not looking at mother). The greetings, which we called *phatics* because they seemed to serve more or less the function Malinowski (1923) described as the phatic function of language—to keep the channel open—were nearly always confined to the times when the mothers had succeeded in catching the infants' eyes. They therefore declined significantly over the three sessions: 25%, 22%, 17% of all utterances at 6, 13, and 26 weeks, respectively. The Kaye and Fogel (1980) analysis of these same videotapes showed the reason for the decline: Mothers occupy a declining share of their infants' attention over this period, as other objects begin to attract the infants more. The babies were looking at the mothers' faces 55% of the time at 6 weeks, 36% at 13 weeks, and only 29% at 26 weeks. So if the phatic utterances were "greetings" responding to the infant's attentive expression, we should expect them to decline over the three sessions as they did.

All of the variables mentioned here, though independent of one another, correlated positively across the three sessions. In other words, we found strong individual differences in these characteristics of mothers' speech (details in Kaye, 1980c). This was true after controlling statistically for infants' sex and mothers' education. However, those two variables also contributed additional stability to the measures across time. In fact, with the exception of utterance rate, more variance in the maternal speech measures was accounted for by educational level than by individual differences per se.

What evidence do we have that these differences were really characteristic of the mothers themselves rather than due to differences among their infants that might have brought out different kinds of maternal speech? That was the reason for analyzing the speech of a stranger to all the same babies. The stranger (who did not know that we would later decide to analyze her utterances) turned out to have a consistent style of her own rather than behaving differently with individual babies. Nor was there any correlation between the characteristics of her speech to the babies and the corresponding characteristics of the mothers' speech to the same babies, which would be expected if these aspects of adult speech were due to qualities of the babies. In addition, we had the individual differences in the actual gaze and greeting behavior of the infants themselves from our earlier analysis (see Figures 3-6 and 8-1); these infant variables were completely uncorrelated with any of the

variables in the mothers' speech. On the other hand, our maternal variables (repetition, length of utterances, and rate of utterances per minute)
predicted the corresponding variables 2 years later in the mother-child
dialogue (Kaye & Charney, 1981).

All of these results are consistent with those reported in Chapter
3. Mothers' speech reveals no evidence of an interaction system affected,
in any way that we were able to detect, by characteristics of the baby.

The fact that the maternal differences were stable over time only
means that they must reflect characteristics of individual mothers' approach toward the task of speaking to their children. The *differences*
among mothers endured over the 2 years, but this does not mean that
the speech itself was the same over time. Indeed it changed: WPU increased, phatics and exact repetitions drastically declined (Table 10-1).
The big change in mothers' speech takes place around the first birthday
when the infant begins to be an active partner in the dialogue. Our
research put this transition in a somewhat different light than the previous literature had suggested.

Table 10-1
Parameters of Mothers' Speech to Infants (Averaged across Three Sessions)
and to the Same Children 2 Years Later

	To Infants	To 2-Year-Olds
Utterances per minute	21.0	14.5
Words per utterance	2.76	3.68
Phatics	21.1%	2%–3%
Exact repetition	16.0%	3.8%
Partial repetition	33.4%	31.0%

Others had noted that speech to language-learning children was
repetitive, restricted to certain syntactic forms, and consistently reduced
in WPU. To contrast it with ordinary adult speech, this form of speech
had been called "Baby Talk" or BT for short (Snow & Ferguson, 1977).
Some authors (e.g., Roger Brown in his preface to Snow & Ferguson)
had suggested that BT might be a simplification, a matter of coming
down to the child's level in order to facilitate his understanding and/or
his language learning.[2] When we compare BT with adult-directed
speech, this is plausible, but when we compare BT with the speech
directed to very young infants, we find that mothers *increase* the complexity of their speech rather than simplifying it when their babies begin

2. However, there is no evidence that children of mothers whose speech is largely BT
learn language any faster than those whose mothers stick to more adult speech (Newport,
Gleitman, & Gleitman, 1977).

to talk. The shortest and most repetitive maternal utterances are produced to the youngest infants. I have called this mode of speech BT-1,
and the speech to language-learning children BT-2 (Kaye, 1980c).

The unique characteristics of BT-1 lead us back to the question of
whether face-to-face interactions with infants are communication. Our
evidence once again suggests that the baby is not really a partner in
these conversations at all. The mothers' monologues are, indeed, a reflection of certain aspects of the infants' behavior. But the reflection, in
the early months, is a unilateral performance by the mothers, and it is
not particularly responsive to differences among the babies. They adjust
to the general structure and timing of infant behavior, which comes in
brief repetitive expressions. It would be much odder to respond to such
expressions with long involved sentences than with short greetings,
exhortations, and simple comments. Mothers mirror their infants' behavior back to them, and besides using facial expressions, head nodding,
and the like, they also use speech.[3]

This realistic adjustment to the structure and timing of infant behavior accounts for the universal properties of BT-1. We have still to
account for the reliable individual differences in the several parameters
we measured. To account for them, we must look at the content of the
utterances and see whether it could produce differences in the structural
parameters. Recall that we were unable to relate these parameters to
any differences among the babies. So there must be an unrealistic element, an element of fantasy in each mother's attributions and interpretations of her baby's expressions, and these fantasies are enduring
aspects of individual mothers. This pretending has been accurately described by Snow (1977) as making up for the deficiencies of the conversational partner. It is also, I think, a matter of the mother's active
construction of a theory about who her baby is. We perceive others as
persons by making ourselves feel we understand their intentions, motives, sentiments, and beliefs as well as their perceptions of us (Heider,
1958; Tagiuri, 1969). What each mother does in different ways is make
the baby into a person and herself into his best friend. This fantasy
endures into the language-learning years. Even as the discourse changes
from one-sided to two-sided with the child taking real turns, as the topic
changes from here-and-now-and-you to a shared perspective on an outside world, still the dialogue will be much less symmetrical than the
mother pretends. As we reported in Chapter 6, the mother only slowly
relinquishes her role as manager of both sides of the dialogue over the
course of the third year.

3. For similar findings at age 12 months, see West and Rheingold (1978).

In order to see how the content of mothers' fantasies may be responsible for some of the structural characteristics of their speech, let us look at two more excerpts. The actual behavior of these infants was very similar, but their mothers' response to it was not. Mother IV's baby was a boy, aged 6 weeks:

> Come on.
> Talk.
> Talk to me.
> Can you talk to me?
> [Laugh] Say something.
> Come on.
> Talk.
> Can you talk?
> Can you say something?
> Well, talk.
> Well, say something.
> Can you say Mama?
> Well, come on.
> Come on.
> Come on.
> Come on.

Mother V had a girl, also aged 6 weeks:

> Is that a burp?
> Huh?
> Or are you going to get the hiccups?
> You going to get the hiccups?
> Huh?
> Yeah.
> Hi, there.
> You look like you're just concentrating so hard.
> Roseann.
> Hello.
> What?
> What?
> Hey, you follow me, don't you?
> You follow my voice.
> You follow my voice more than you follow me.
> Yes.

Mother IV kept up the series of imperatives, requests, and exhortations throughout the session and at the later sessions as well. Mother V continued her narrative discussion of the baby's appearance and behavior, making no demands or requests of the baby at all. Thus her utterances were longer, more varied, but also contained more phatic greetings than Mother IV. These and other parameters of their speech are compared in Table 10-2 (based on the whole sessions from which the examples above were taken). Clearly their speech was similar in some respects—all grammatical, all referring to the infant, no direct deixis of the kind that one would use when actually expecting the infant to learn the name of something. Instead, the mothers used indirect deixis, pretending that they and the baby already shared references to the world, that they already shared meaning.

Table 10-2
Comparison of Two Mothers' Speech to Babies

	Mother IV	Mother V
Words per utterance	2.81	3.22
Phatics	14.6%	28.6%
Exact-immediate repetition	14.9%	6.3%
Partial repetition	57.5%	42.2%
Exhortations ("Come on")	18.8%	12.2%
Specific requests ("Talk")	43.8%	0
Utterances without verbs	18.8%	53.1%
Direct deixis ("That's a doggie")	0	0
Indirect deixis ("Use those legs")	8.3%	14.3%
Fragments ("Huh?" "Once more")	24.0%	56.0%
Deleted auxiliary (% of questions)	20.0%	50.0%
Ungrammatical utterances	0	0
Pertaining to child	95.8%	93.9%

Although there are clearly differences among mothers in the nature and extent of their beliefs about the young infant's capacity to interact as a person, I do not believe there are many mothers from whom this kind of pretending is entirely absent. Some studies have found that mothers differ when interviewed as to their beliefs in the infant's capacities, and particularly that lower-class mothers are not so ready to attribute communication skills to babies as middle-class mothers are (Tulkin & Cohler, 1973; Tulkin & Kagan, 1972; Ninio, 1979). But this is only a matter of what they say; what they do, at all socioeconomic levels and probably in all cultures, is treat the baby as a person. When cross-cultural studies like Callaghan's (1981) find Navajo mothers, for example, vocalizing much less to their babies than our mothers did, it is just because they are indeed treating the baby as they treat a person: quietly. In this connection, Tronick, Ricks, and Cohn (1982) in a study of face-to-face interaction between Gusii mothers and infants in Kenya made an important observation. In that culture, where displays of emotion between adults are rare and subdued, face-to-face play with 3-month-old babies is also rare (as compared with object play a few months later). When the Western investigators set up the face-to-face situation, mothers typically were concerned to keep their babies calm. By averting her own gaze whenever the infant began to be excited, a mother would produce the same still-faced profile that Tronick et al. (1979) had used as a violation of Western mothers' normal behavior. This undoubtedly produced a very different pattern of mutual gazing and facial expressions than we saw in our own study (Figure 6-3). Yet in both cultures the mothers' expectations for the baby correspond to their culturally determined expectations of persons in general. And in both cultures, as Tronick et al. (1982) point out, the mother's management of infant arousal is also a process that socializes the infant's internal affect along with his external displays (see Chapter 12).

Themes

The foregoing observations led me to look more closely at the thematic content of what the mothers were saying. To my surprise, I found that I could categorize everything the mothers said into only 10 different themes (Table 10-3). Each theme was really an oppositional pair, because it was impossible to distinguish "You are smart," for example, from "You are dumb." Many utterances seemed to have both meanings: "Can't you talk?" seems to mean both "You are smart enough to be able to talk" and "You are dumb not to be talking." It raises the issue of the baby's mental capability without reaching a conclusion. In fact, even a direct statement such as "You are smart" or "You love Mommy" or "Mommy loves you" cannot be taken at face value, but one can count the fact that the mother chose to raise the issue at all.

Again the reader is referred to the original journal article for details as to method, reliability of coding, and suggestions for future work with these themes (Kaye, 1980b). The relative frequency of each of the 10 issues is shown in Table 10-3. Three of the issues accounted for 71% of what the mothers said to their babies. The four least frequent issues together accounted for less than 10% of what the mothers said, but there was still a considerable number of sessions in which they were raised at least once.

The principal result was that all 10 variables (the proportions of a mother's utterances that were given over to each of the issues) were stable over the three sessions; like the speech parameters, they measured significant individual differences among the mothers.

Analysis of variance showed that the *allies-opponents* issue increased with the infant's age, at the expense of the *strong-weak baby* and *cute-ugly*

Table 10-3
Relative Frequency of Issues ($N = 37$)

	% of Each Session (Infant Age in Weeks)			% of Sessions (All Ages)
	6	13	26	
Dyad vs. World "Can I get your eye?" "See your puppy?"	27.3	29.4	32.4	95.5
Strong vs. Weak Baby "Can you sit up?" "You're so tired."	26.2	20.4	18.3	91.9
Happy vs. Sad Baby "What's the matter?" "Give us a smile."	21.0	19.7	18.5	84.7
Smart vs. Dumb Baby "Not going to talk no more?" "Wave bye-bye."	7.9	8.9	7.2	55.9
Allies vs. Opponents "We're on camera." "Don't bite my finger."	2.9	5.2	9.0	52.3
Good vs. Bad Baby "Such a good boy." "You stinker."	5.0	5.6	4.9	40.5
Cute vs. Ugly Baby "You little muffin." "Fat like your father."	5.3	2.8	2.8	36.9
Loving vs. Rejecting Baby "Now you love Mama again." "Making raspberries at me?"	2.0	2.4	2.5	26.1
Loving vs. Rejecting Mom "Who's Mama's favorite?" "You're going back to the stork."	0.8	2.8	2.7	22.5
Good vs. Bad Mom "Mommy understands you." "I'm not doing too well, eh?"	1.5	2.8	1.6	28.8
Total	100.0	100.0	100.0	

baby themes. Notice that as the mothers had greater reason to be concerned about their alliance with the infants (because of increasing attention to other people and objects, as mentioned above), the *allies-opponents* theme increased; and as they had less reason for concern about the baby's viability and attractiveness (he had survived so far, grown hair, etc.), those themes declined. The implication is that even though themes might be expressed in either a positive or a negative form, what they primarily reveal to us is the mother's anxiety about the issue. This probably also accounts for the only effect of mothers' education on these variables: The *smart-dumb baby* issue was raised by more than twice as many mothers in the high school or college graduate groups as among those who had less than a high school education.

Considering the small sample of "pretty words that make no sense" obtained from each of our subjects—5 minutes (an average of about 100 utterances) at each of three occasions—the existence of individual differences in the prevalence of particular themes is surprising. On the average, more than 25% of the variance in any issue's frequency at 26 weeks was predictable from the extent to which mothers had raised the issue at previous sessions. The effects of infant's age and of mother's education were few in comparison with these individual differences.

What are we to conclude from the foregoing observations of mothers' speech to their infants? There are individual differences in both the content and the form of mothers' utterances. Since these differences persist over several months, even when we assess them from a tiny sample of the mothers' speech at each age, they must be very robust. This means that whatever effects they may have upon the developing infant, they have many opportunities to work those effects. By a reasonable estimate, the baby will have heard more than half a million of his mother's utterances before his first birthday. They will have been based, especially in the first 6 months, upon the mother's *interpretation* of what her baby might be saying, perceiving, feeling, and thinking; not upon any intersubjective communication or gesturing on the baby's part. In a sense, the mother is not really talking to the baby. She is talking *for* the baby, to herself.

11

Socialization and Self-Consciousness

My mother . . . had merely lifted a glass to her lips and drained it of some strawberry punch. But my daughter was watching her. And when my daughter, who was herself being trained then by my wife and me to drink from a glass and faithfully rewarded with handclaps of delight and cries of "Good girl!" whenever she succeeded, saw my mother drink from a glass, she banged her own hands down with delight and approval and called out:
*   "Good girl, grandma!"*

Joseph Heller, Something Happened, 1974

The observations presented in the preceding chapter show that individual mothers' monologues to their infants are consistent, and that mothers' reactions to their infants seem to originate in fantasies related to their own self-concepts. Surely a lot of what mothers say to their babies contains information that, if understood, would affect the babies' notions about themselves. Furthermore, there are plenty of nonverbal events—weaning, for example—that are charged with emotion and would seem to contain messages that the infant could interpret in a self-evaluative way.

In fact, that is precisely what Klein (1963) argued. As a revision of Freud's emphasis upon Oedipal conflict, she assigned a larger role in later neuroses to early infantile anxieties and conflicts with the mother. This argument assumes a greater understanding about persons than I am willing to attribute to the young infant.[1] The fact that mother-infant

---

1. There is a methodological problem with Klein's argument. So long as styles of interaction are perpetuated by the mother or by the parental system, much of what an infant experiences in the first year of life (the ways in which one infant's experiences differ from another's) will continue to be experienced later. Hence parents' continuity of behavior may make it impossible to gauge their effects in particular age periods.

interaction is complex and full of affect, and even the discovery that it has great importance for the infant's growth into the system, do not necessarily mean that the parents transmit any particular self-concepts to their infant prior to the time they share a language. In this chapter and the next, we shall be concerned with aspects of self-consciousness that are probably universal, produced by the growth from apprenticeship to personhood. A general self-consciousness is a prerequisite for the formation of specific concepts about the self as an individual; hence individual self-concept cannot begin to develop until around the end of the second year.

We shall consider the origins of that concept from the point of view of the infant's consciousness of his place in a social system. But first we had better consider the political implications of such a question.

The Ideology of Socialization

One needs to read only a few sentences of any psychological work on socialization of the child to get a pretty good idea of the author's deeply rooted attitudes about the nature of man. In the first place, the very assumption that children have to be socialized implies a conflict between what they are in their original nature and what they are to become as members of society. To be socialized can be seen as a triumph of good over evil (reality principle over pleasure principle) or the opposite, as when Rousseau's Civilized Man prevails over Natural Man. To be socialized can be a restriction of freedom, as it appeared for a time to my own "counterculture" generation; or it can be the essential step toward freedom through citizenship, as it was to the Greeks.

Soviet psychology, for example, has had a problem with the idea of socialization. The Soviet state was to be a disciplined state. The citizen was to prosper through cooperation, not competition; through joint ownership of the materials and products of labor, not through exploitation of laborers. The creation of a socialist state sounded as though it must involve socialization. But it was fundamental to Marxism (and to its political success) to hold that the social form of life was the natural state of man; he did not need to be socia*lized*. It was not to be an enslavement of the individual by the state; on the contrary, the Revolution freed the masses from enslavement by capitalists. Socialism was historically inevitable; it was, in a sense, innate.

The necessity of this view explains a good deal of the broadest level of theorizing to be found in Soviet psychology (in much the same way that a fundamental tenet of our own political system, the inheritance of private property, explains our interest in the inheritance of abilities). For example, there was the emphasis on Pavlov's "second signal system" rejecting the view of man as mere animal.[2] And there was Vygotsky's insistence that "the true direction of the development of thinking is not from the individual to the socialized, but from the social to the individual" (1962, p. 20).

We also find in Western authors taking a Marxist or "dialectical" approach to human development (see, e.g., Riegel & Rosenwald, 1975) the firm conviction that the infant is innately social, that the social contract is arrived at through mutual accommodation rather than through any suppression of antisocial or entrepreneurial tendencies in individuals. An individual's identity only emerges in the first place through membership in a larger system.

As will have been clear in the foregoing chapters, I find much in that rhetoric with which to agree. I certainly agree with Colwyn Trevarthen's (1978) comment that a child is no more "socialized" than a plant is "photosynthesized"; the process is in the nature of the species. However, the compatibility of this viewpoint with any particular political philosophy is irrelevant to its adequacy as a scientific theory. There is no logical reason that a theory of human development has to run parallel to, justify, or be justified by one's views about economics, government, or the law. Furthermore, reducing the issues involved in understanding how a child becomes a member of a community to dichotomies like whether the infant is or is not an asocial beast, and whether mind precedes or follows social processes, vastly oversimplifies what happens in the first couple of years of human life.

The human infant has to acquire a special kind of consciousness about the relation between self and others. The direction of development is neither from the individual to the socialized nor from the social to the individual. It is from an organism to a person. The infant human organism elicits social responses and responds to social stimuli, yet is not truly social and for the same reasons is not truly a person. It becomes one when it becomes an individual member of a social system. That change is located as much in the infant's consciousness as in his interactions with others.

Is it the mind, then, that gets socialized? If so, one must have a mind in the first place. On the other hand, if the mind only comes into existence through the socialization process, what does it come *from?* What is it that becomes socialized? Is an infant asocial, antisocial, presocial, or unsocialized prior to joining the system? In what way is he then "socialized"? I shall argue that the process is not primarily one of

2. "Darwin did not know what a bitter satire he wrote on mankind, and especially on his countrymen, when he showed that free competition, the struggle for existence, which the economists celebrate as the highest historical achievement, is the normal state of the *animal kingdom*" (Engels, *Dialectics of Nature* [1895], p. 19; italics in original).

mutual accommodation. Accommodation does occur on both sides, the infant's and the parents', but to call it mutual is to imply that the accommodation is equal on both sides. It is not. The infant is socialized not just to make him social, which he is in some ways already programmed to be, but to make him a member of a particular system. That system, the family, exists before he does. It makes some accommodation to him, but his accommodation to it is a hundred times greater.

Ideas of the Self

There is a large literature on the concept of self in philosophy. There is another large literature on the self in the fields of personality and social psychology. Tied to both of those, there is a third literature in clinical psychology, where questions about the self are different for students of different phases of development. Self-esteem is the central problem during the school years and young adulthood. Identification of the self with parents and other role models is an important part of the study of the preschool child, the adolescent, and the adult couple giving birth to their own first child. For a student of infancy, the crucial question is how the basic consciousness of self emerges; a consciousness upon which all the later acquisitions depend.

The self is often explained as consisting of dichotomous relations, for example, between *I* and *thou*, *I* and *we*, *we* and *they*, *I* and *me*. From the point of view of the beginnings of self-consciousness, there are two basic kinds of distinctions involved. The first is *I/other*, and the second is *I/me*.

I and not-I. The discovery of boundaries between what one experiences as *I* or *self* and what one experiences as *not-I*, *other*, or *they*, is involved in several developmental achievements. One achievement has to do with sensing and controlling one's own body; then there is the realization that other bodies are comparable to our own; then the ascription of minds to those other bodies; and finally the ability to imagine the world from points of view other than one's own.

The earliest sensorimotor achievements differentiate particular schemas for the control of body parts, especially hand and mouth, and for the use of those body parts in exploratory play. As for the second achievement—the realization that other bodies are comparable to one's own—the 5- or 6-month-old has accomplished that when he distinguishes between his own hand and another hand in the visual field, yet can accommodatively imitate an action performed by the other hand. Ascribing minds to other bodies is a further developmental achievement, which we have already discussed in terms of the end of the period of shared intentions. At around 9 months, after months of pseudo-intersubjectivity due only to the subjectivity of adults, the infant first begins to infer others' intentions. (As was indicated in Figure 9-1, by then the next period has already begun. Reciprocally shared intentions are based on shared memory.)

Strawson (1959) describes the universal assumption about others in the following way:

> Among the things that we observe, as opposed to the things we know about without observation [he means our own actions], are the movements of bodies similar to [our own body,] about which we have knowledge not based on observation. It is important that we should understand such movements, for they bear on and condition our own; and in fact we understand them, we interpret them, only by seeing them as elements in just such plans or schemes of action as those of which we know the present course and future development without observation of the relevant present movements. But this is to say that we see such movements as *actions*, that we interpret them in terms of intention, that we see them as movements of individuals of a type to which also belongs that individual whose present and future movements we know about without observation; it is to say that we see others as self-ascribers, not on the basis of observation, of what we ascribe to them on this basis. [P. 112]

Strawson's point is that we associate our own mind and body automatically, without any deduction from experience; and then we ascribe minds to other moving bodies through observation of their similarities to our own movements. I think it is an error to conceive of that observation process as depending upon conscious, passive interpretation of what other people do. The important thing about other bodies' movements is that "they bear on and condition our own." The fact that we attribute intention to others does not depend upon observation. It comes from participation in interactive routines that rely upon the regularity in other bodies' movements, that is, upon actions the infant cannot directly control but can either anticipate or elicit. His own skills fit into higher-order routines that rely upon the expectable behavior of others, and the intention is mutually not just unidirectionally shared. The attribution of intention to other people (of minds to other bodies) is still not a matter of consciousness, but it is implicit in sensorimotor interaction.

However, I have said that consciousness is inherent in rules, and we shall see shortly that for the interpersonal contingencies to become rules there must be consciousness of self and system.

So far as the consciousness of self is concerned, the component of it that has to do with boundaries between *I* and *other* is firmly established by the end of the second year. This must include attributing intentions to others. The next step, imagining the world from other perspectives and from the point of view of those other intentions, takes another 10 years or so.

I and me. Simultaneous with the developing *I/other* dichotomy, and closely related to it, are the two aspects of experiencing the self, which Mead (1934) called the *I* and the *me.* James (1890) had distinguished between the "pure ego," one's consciousness of being a unitary agent and experiencer, and the "empirical me," one's interpretation of the responses one gets from others. Whereas James had equated this *me* with the self, to Mead the self consisted of a developmental integration of both aspects, the *I* and the *me.*

The *I* is the actor, while the *me* is a simultaneous anticipation of how the action will be seen and reacted to. Mead emphasized the idea of reversibility between gesturers, which has been discussed throughout this book as an essential aspect of symbols. The child's *I* communicates with the adult's *me,* and vice versa. But Mead also saw something that his predecessors Cooley (1902) and James had missed: that the *I* and *me* within each personality are in constant communication with each other. The *me* anticipates the reaction to what the *I* is about to do; the *I* acts upon what the *me* has just felt.

> There would not be an "I" in the sense in which we use that term if there were not a "me"; there would not be a "me" without a response in the form of the "I." These two, as they appear in our experience, constitute the personality. . . . The self is not something that exists first and then enters into re-lationship with others, but it is, so to speak, an eddy in the social current and so still a part of the current. It is a process in which the individual is continually adjusting himself in advance to the situation to which he belongs, and reacting back on it. So that the "I" and the "me," this thinking, this conscious adjustment, becomes then a part of the whole social process and makes a much more highly organized society possible. [Mead, 1934, p. 182]

Mead's point can also be expressed in terms of the basic definition of action, an organism trying to bring about alterations in the situation in which it finds itself. The *me* is the situation, the *I* the inalienable ability of the organism to alter it. What then is the self? Where does consciousness come into that open-system model of the organism? Perhaps not so much in the combination of those two components (for each entails the other by definition) as in the discovery that the world consists of other organisms whose *me*'s are affected by my *I* and whose *I*'s affect my *me*.

The Self as Process. If, in defining the self, we use a phrase like "the discovery that . . ." (as I just did), we are settling for a C-model type of label. Can we instead attempt a P-model of the self? If it is to be conceived of as a process or set of processes in the course of action, what are those processes? In what domain of actions do they come into play? For the self is not involved in all action. The self is involved, in fact, only in social actions: actions with potential or imagined social consequences. The *me* situation is essentially the impression one believes oneself to be making on other people; it consists in "stepping outside oneself" and anticipating how someone else will or would react to one's actions.

For example, riding my bicycle to the library, I attend to the potholes in the street, planning a few yards ahead so as to avoid them: no consciousness of self involved. Seeing a pothole, I might even fantasize what it would feel like if I were to descend into it: how hard would the bump be, would I fall off the bicycle, etc. These imaginings with respect to my own bodily sensations are not what we mean by my consciousness of self. But when a thought crosses my mind about how I would look sprawled out in the street, or how the bystanders would react, that is self-consciousness. Or suppose that, still riding along, I hear a car coming up behind me. I move over to the right, near the cars parked along the curb. I think the driver can see that there is enough room to pass me and that I am aware of his intention to do so. That awareness includes a consciousness of myself: And what is it really but a consciousness of another person looking at me, a consciousness, in short, that there are other selves? I do not know with certainty that they exist or that their awareness is what I think it is, but I assume so thousands of times each day.

The self, thus defined, is a special kind of loop or detour taken by consciousness in the course of action, whenever our attention falls upon some aspect of our situation to which we anticipate a social response. If we have to choose a moment when the infant first has self-consciousness, it is the moment when he first looks around to see if anyone is watching. For example, he falls when taking his first steps, and he looks around to see how others react. He would not do this if he did not attribute thought to others, or if he did not regard himself as an object of observation by them. The 6-, 8-, and even 10-month-old lack this kind of consciousness of self. Later, dignity becomes one of the constant goals of human life, often taking priority over hunger, sex, even life itself. (Consider the face-saving self-disemboweling of feudal Japan.) Something that important to man, yet of little or no importance to other animals, is a good benchmark to use for the infant's transition from organism to person.[3]

In defining self-consciousness in this way I am admittedly choosing one of many possible points in a continuum. Its advantage for researchers would be that one could apply behavioral criteria to decide when the infant achieves self-consciousness in this sense. Some important facts about its development are already clear. We can fill in the spaces between those facts now to theorize about how the self emerges in the socialization process. We shall see that self-consciousness is inseparable from consciousness of others. And we shall find that both are natural consequences of infants' apprenticeships within parental frames.

Consciousness: Of Rules, of System, and of Self

Socialization begins before the infant's intelligence has progressed to the level of symbolic representation or to the consciousness of rules guiding his own behavior: in short, before he has a mind. By the time he is a member of the social system, he does have a mind. Therefore the conscious mind is not what socialization acts upon; it is what socialization produces. In fact, it is the main product of human infancy. In this section I hope to show that an inseparable part of that mind must be the consciousness of self. To gesture to another is to have an intention with respect to that other's mind, which can happen only to the extent one supposes that other person to have a mind like one's own. That is the same as what I have been calling the consciousness of selves. The consciousness that emerges is at one and the same time the consciousness that makes human behavior rule-governed, the shared consciousness that makes particular groups of people behave as social systems, and the consciousness that forms the essence of personhood or Self. One sees how connected these three kinds of consciousness are as soon as one attempts to examine them separately.

Consciousness of Rules. We find ourselves once more concerned with the problem of what it means to be following a rule. As Toulmin (1974) pointed out, the term *rule* is used in a broad spectrum of ways. At one end of Toulmin's continuum, following a rule merely means conforming to some regularity without necessarily being aware of it. At the other extreme, it means actually referring to the rule mentally when deciding how to proceed. The former definition accepts too much behavior as

---

3. This corresponds nicely with Erikson's (1950) stage of "shame and doubt." From a psychoanalytic point of view, as a necessary condition and, indeed, criterion for self-consciousness, children must experience the evaluating eye of others. Psychotic adults, who have never resolved this transition into the second of Erikson's eight stages of the life cycle, are said to have fixated on "animal" issues of nourishment vs. harm from others, and consequently not to have achieved an integrated sense of self.

rule-governed (am I following a rule when I walk on my feet instead of my hands?); the latter is too restrictive (am I not following a rule when I automatically stop at a red light?). In Chapter 6, I suggested a useful place to divide this continuum. Social interaction is rule-governed if the participants are aware whenever the rule is violated, though not necessarily conscious of it every time it is followed.

We have to make an additional distinction if we mean to restrict ourselves to the kind of rule-following that uniquely characterizes the human mind. By "awareness that a rule has been violated" I do not simply mean awareness in the sense of strikingly altered behavior. This is the kind of reaction that many animals show, for example, when their territory is invaded by a conspecific (an awareness that may also be evident in the behavior of the invader). One would be anthropomorphizing terribly to infer from this that the animals have territorial "rules." My awareness of violating a rule when I fail to reciprocate a proferred handshake is of an entirely different kind. It is more than just my knowledge that I am supposed to extend my hand. I also know that the other person expects me to do so, and I can put myself in his place. My awareness of the violation, and my awareness of his awareness of it, show that I understand what is expected of me: not just that I conform to someone else's knowledge of the regularity in my behavior, but that I myself have internalized those expectations.

Suppose that I am such a boor, or so lost in my own thoughts, as not to notice other people's extended hands at all. They are greatly offended. The rule exists in their social system, but I am unconscious of violating it; so it is not a rule governing my behavior. And if I sometimes do extend my hand in response, perhaps through imitation, there is still no reason to say that I am following a rule on those occasions. I shall have to learn, before being a member of that social system, that I am always *expected* to join in a handshake under certain conditions. That can mean no less than my being aware, when I or others fail to shake hands, that a rule has been violated.

Apprenticeship, however, is another story. We have seen how many ways there are for parents to arrange interactions so that the infant seems to be taking turns; seems to be greeting them; seems to be smiling contingently; seems to be talking. These are the functions of the various spatial and temporal frames organized by adults. Frames facilitate the learning of conventions, including conventional signs. But the important point, illustrated in Chapter 6 with respect to turn-taking conventions, is that this learning process cannot be explained simply in terms of increasing contingencies. Even a 100% contingency may not be a rule. Along with the increasing contingencies—sometimes, in fact, preceding them—there is the dawn of a new kind of awareness in the infant about the meaning of his own and others' behavior. He knows that their interaction is mutually organized toward shared purposes. Once conscious of mutual expectations and once in possession of symbols with which to designate the external reality that the system has to deal with, the child is truly a person, with a mind.

Consciousness of the System. Two points have just been reiterated from earlier chapters: (1) A social system can assimilate an organism's behavior into its own functioning without that organism being conscious of its rules; but (2) the human infant cannot operate in that way for very long without anticipating others' behavior and thereby figuring out many of the system's rules and expectations, both from his own point of view and from the points of view of other members; which makes him a conscious partner. Once again, I emphasize that the extrinsic frames provided by adults are as crucial to the infant's ability to internalize those rules as his own intrinsic learning capabilities are.

Consciousness is an important aspect of social system membership. This is an enormous difference between other kinds of open system—including any organism—and a social system. The organism's communicating parts are physically tied to one another, absolutely dependent for their survival upon the spatiotemporal integrity of the whole. The communicating parts of a social system, on the other hand, are themselves autonomous organisms. If there is an analogy to be made between the members of a social system and the parts of an organism, it is in terms of the information all cells share, deep within their nuclei—not in terms of the glue at the cell walls where they touch. The members of a social system are not physically stuck together the way parts of an organism are. Each system member has its own mouth and stomach and limbs and sense organs; each has its own mind and self. Since there is no family mind or community mind (literally speaking), the sense of the family's identity, purpose, and status can only exist within individual minds. An individual person has a mind and a self; a social system has only the minds and selves of its individual members. Whatever group identity they share must depend upon each one's ability to introject a projection of other people's thinking. The sense of individual identity, self-image, and social intentions also depend upon that same prior ability.

The cell nucleus metaphor is apt in another way. Individual cells do not begin separately, then convene to form an organism. Instead, cells are differentiated by the organism. Similarly, a social system is not a federation of individual selves each of whom retains his or her original identity. Selves are the products of social system membership. This is nowhere more true than it is of the infant, who only comes to be a person for the first time through socialization in the family system. Hence, the consciousness that is involved in following rules, of which the first ones learned are social rules, is closely related to the consciousness of being a person.

Consciousness of Self. Self-consciousness is the child's realization that the world results from the intentional agency of individual persons, among whom he is one. This is something less than the individual's having a theory of himself; and it is not quite what one would call a "decentered" understanding, which allows us to imagine ourselves from other people's points of view. For the purposes of this book, I have described consciousness of self as a realization that comes before decentering and is its prerequisite. It does mean that the child henceforth always operates within two spheres of action: his sphere as an organism and his sphere of action as part of a social system. "An awareness of the intentionality of an act exists when one attributes to others the attribution to oneself of its intentionality" (Tajfel, 1980, p. 80).

In proceeding through the four major periods described in earlier chapters, we have also seen four successive stages of the infant's developing self-consciousness, stages characterized by different kinds of co-opting activities by adults. There is what we might call a *regulating self* inherent in the fact that the newborn is a distinct organism with homeostatic functions. In the next period an *intending self* emerges, onto whose simple intentions parents can project the gestures and thoughts of a real person. Then there is a *remembering self*, consisting of interpersonal roles and learned signals, tying the infant to the particular others who have shared his experiences; and finally the *social self*, the conscious system member. We shall review these four periods once more, from the point of view of the parents' role in the infant's creation of a self, in the next chapter when we can include the related processes of attachment and individuation.

This is only the first stage of self-consciousness, to which a great deal will be added after age 2. The child will learn more about other selves, more about the attributes that bind him to them and make him both similar and dissimilar to them. He will learn to add to the list of actors in his world gods, spirits, story and cartoon characters; and his relations with family members will change. His self-image, beginning as the simple ability to recognize himself in a mirror (Lewis & Brooks-Gunn, 1979), goes on to comprise *self-concept*, a whole set of positively and negatively valued attributes adding up to *self-esteem*.[4] All of that continued development of self-consciousness comes later, relying upon the basic assumptions about the self as agent and perceiver that have been established within the parental frames of infancy.

What we have been concerned with here is the change in I/other consciousness that comes with object permanence and with permanent names for the animate objects in the child's world (including himself). However, because we are considering the self as an aspect of socialization, we can see a parallel, in infancy, to the argument between Vygotsky and Piaget over the preschool child's so-called egocentric speech and its implications for the egocentricity of thought. Two- to 4-year-old children produce a good deal of speech not directed to others (the kind of thing we called "unlinked utterances" in Chapter 6). Piaget (1926) had argued from this that young children are not yet able to adopt the point of view of another, a prerequisite for communication. "One might say that an adult thinks socially even when he is alone, and a child under seven thinks and speaks egocentrically even when he is with others" (Piaget, 1926, p. 56). Vygotsky suggested an opposite interpretation of the meaning of egocentric speech: a transitional phase between social discourse and thought. Language was obviously acquired through social discourse in the first place, and Vygotsky saw thought as internalized discourse. He described the child as first learning to talk, then mimicking dialogue with another in talking to himself, then internalizing that dialogue in thought.

When Piaget had an opportunity to reply to Vygotsky, his reply was ambiguous: "All logical thought is socialized because it implies the possibility of communication between individuals" (1962, p. 13; see note 2, Chapter 7). The word *logical* is important. Piaget continued to see the ability to put oneself in the point of view of another as an outgrowth, or at most a simultaneous development, of the transition to operational thinking from preconceptual egocentric thought. He chose to interpret Vygotsky as saying essentially the same thing.

This was a major flaw in Piaget's vision. It was the reason he could not conceive of imitation, as we saw in Chapter 9, in anything but C-model terms, the reason he described it as though it were not a social process. And it explains why his views on affective development (Piaget, 1969) were so oddly rooted in children's delights and frustrations with

4. An interesting point about self-image is that it is always the image of how we look to other *people*, not just from other vantage points in space; not, for example, how we appear in the eyes of another animal. We love our pets, feel loved by them, talk to them, pretend to be talked to by them. Yet our image of ourselves (even as "the kind of person who takes good care of his dog") comes only from a projection into the minds of other people. That is a process that occurs in real time, in the course of interaction as a member of various social systems.

their own sensorimotor schemas, ignoring the social exchanges that elicit the first smiling, laughter, wariness, and attachments. The conviction that infants had to develop on their own the basic skills necessary to enter into meaningful interactions with others blinded Piaget to some facts that should have been obvious.

Vygotsky, on the other hand, as mentioned earlier in this chapter, had strong ideological reasons for objecting. Piaget seemed to see mental development as a private enterprise and socialization as merely a fettering set of restrictions. To Vygotsky there could be no mind at all except as emergent from the inherently social nature of childhood. Vygotsky and Piaget differed on egocentric speech (ages 3–5) in much the same way they differed on "scientific thinking" (ages 9–13 or so). Vygotsky neither knew of Piaget's work on infancy nor studied infants himself. If he had done either, the debate would have been staged at this age level too. In fact, this book can be regarded as an extension of Vygotsky's ideas down to the years before language. I have argued that parents, in making the child a member of their preexisting system, induce the development of mind.

Socialization: The Infant Joins a Previously Established System

There are several ways a system of interacting organisms can form. One way is through *evolution*. Over many generations, behavior patterns are selected, either within species (e.g., male-female) or across species (e.g., between grazing animals and certain birds such as plovers and cattle egrets, which groom them of ticks and other insects) so that individual members of those species can depend upon one another in predetermined ways. I have already noted that mothers and infants constitute such a system, from an evolutionary point of view, before they know anything about one another as individuals. The newborn has some information—in the form of innate responses—about mothers in general, and his mother has some innate information about babies in general.

A second way is by *mutual adaptation*. This involves the "shared development" I discussed in Chapter 3. It may also involve shared goals among the individuals; but the important thing is that they adjust to one another's behavior as individuals through the course of their experience together. Their social system did not exist before these individuals began to interact. A married couple is a good illustration. A man and a woman adapt to one another as individuals. The basis for their individual relationship is, first of all, the sexual attraction between male and female. There are species-specific ingredients in that attraction, including the secondary sexual characteristics and, literally, "chemical attraction." But these mechanisms only lay a foundation upon which the partners build an individual relationship lasting days or years. The relationship consists of mutual knowledge, expectations, and communication patterns that evolve through shared experience.

A third way is by *enlistment or affiliation*. An individual can be convinced that his goals can be met by being a member of a system. If he chooses to join it and the system chooses to accept him, then he will accommodate to the rules of the system; it will not change for him. This is how one joins the army or enrolls in a university. It is characteristic of the relations between individuals and large institutional systems.[5] There is often an apprenticeship period in this process.

A special type of enlistment, co-optation, provides a better description of what happens between infants and parents. An individual can be brought involuntarily into an already existing system of which he has little knowledge: for example, a new employee joining the group in an office or shop. (He chose to accept the job, but he did not choose his group of co-workers, who already have established a social system with particular rules.) Some preadapted human social mechanisms (e.g., smiling) will play a role in his fitting in, and there will also be some mutual adaptation. But the principal means by which the new member will become part of the system is co-optation: The system will incorporate him in its previously developed ways of functioning. The apprentice accommodates to the system much more than it accommodates to him. It is true that the system will not be exactly the same as it was before this individual became a part of it; he may, in fact, over time, change it significantly. But he will not become a partner in it at all without learning fairly quickly the roles and expectations that are already shared by its present members.

Whereas formal institutional enlistment requires shared purpose between the system and the new member as a condition of joining, co-optation can occur without the apprentice having to share goals of the system beforehand, or to have any understanding of its functioning, or even to conceive of himself as an individual capable of joining a system.

5. This book has almost exclusively concerned interpersonal roles, and what is expected of a person interacting with particular individuals or with people in general. One's relation to an institution, like a school or a profession, is different in a number of important ways—far less stable and less compelling, for example, though perhaps also more abstract. Social skills for interindividual interaction are more internalized than any institutional loyalties and rules an individual learns. When an individual Palestinian and an individual Zionist encounter one another, or when a Catholic encounters a Protestant in Belfast, their need to respond appropriately in dyadic communicative situations often outweighs any allegiance to the less personal role of representing one institution, social class, or political movement against another. Basic interaction processes are primitive, and the mind with its conscious reference to institutional loyalties is a secondary derivative of those processes rather than vice versa.

A human infant is brought into the preexisting adult social system through a process more like co-optation than like mutual accommodation. This does not require much from the infant in the way of initial understanding of the system or of his own relationship to it. That understanding arises only gradually and only as a consequence of his changing behavioral relations with adults.

The infant's preadapted social nature, in the form of specific behavior well-fitted to the social behavior of adults, is crucial to their ability to incorporate him into their system. Socialization means making the child a member of a particular system: of a dyad at the most particular level, of the family to which dyads belong, and of the community to which the family belongs. This view leads to the proposition that socialization proceeds through successive levels of involvement, from evolutionarily determined interaction to a communication based upon shared purpose, shared experience, and shared rules. The evolutionary means of system formation are involved in the period of shared rhythms and regulations; mutual accommodations begin in the period of shared intentions; while the child's enlistment in systems beyond the family does not begin until he shares the community's language. Co-optation into the family itself can be said to begin at birth, but it is most intensely expressed when conventional signs begin to be taught, in what I called the period of shared memory.

> Human beings combine in behavior as directly and unconsciously as do atoms, stellar masses and cells; as directly and unknowingly as they divide and repel. They do so in virtue of their own structure, as man and woman unite, as the baby seeks the breast and the breast is there to supply its need. . . . Associated activity needs no explanation; things are made that way. But no amount of aggregated collective action of itself constitutes a community. . . . Human associations may be ever so organic in origin and firm in operation, but they develop into societies in a human sense only as their consequences, being known, are esteemed and sought for. . . . They demand *communication* as a prerequisite. [Dewey, 1939, pp. 387–388; italics in original]

The change Dewey described was, in fact, the development of a social system. I suggest that this be conceived in a slightly different way: as the *en*velopment of the child by a social system, which in turn causes development in the child himself. The system in which he will become a member already exists prior to his birth. Furthermore, it is larger than the system of the nuclear family.

Transfer. Somewhat paradoxically, the differentiation of social schemas and of conventional signs by the parent-infant system does not have the effect of making the infant increasingly dependent upon the parents. Instead, because the conventions suggested by parents are the conventions of the community, and because the interpretations they have all along projected onto infant gestures are just as if those gestures had been made by other members of the community, the child's adopting the conventions makes it possible for him to engage in discourse with any other member. The first spontaneous use of gestures that have been learned in imitative games is just a matter of stimulus transfer—to the same person in a different context, to the same object with a different person.[6] In effect, to the extent that the child fully assumes a symmetrical role in the social system with his parents, he becomes a member of the whole community. (This statement applies to an increasing symmetry that continues throughout childhood and adolescence. Later, its inverse establishes the opposite sort of asymmetry between the elderly and their middle-aged children: To just the extent that the aged withdraw from the larger community, they become the younger generation's children.)

It is still the case that adults overinterpret the extent to which the child shares the adult's understanding of a gesture's meaning. (In fact, we constantly overestimate the extent to which others share our meaning; we behave as if all the connotations of a word were the same for another person as they are for us.) Shared memories, too, develop gradually. In their case as with shared intentions, much of what the infant and parent share due to their experience together is also shared by the wider community due to the generic nature of experience. So the real significance of the "system" is to be found in what it establishes in the way of a "generalized other" (Mead, 1934) and transfers to interactions with later instructors (Vygotsky, 1962).

Do We Need a "General" System Theory? It is easy to find analogies to the way infants are socialized. Throughout the life span, individuals join existing systems. Their functioning is largely due to patterns previously established by adults or earlier members. These systems—school, club, factory, office, profession—assimilate new members much more than they accommodate to them. We can also think of examples of social systems whose members are not individual persons, such as the system of all nations on earth, or animal systems like a baboon troop. These

6. In fact, Sebeok and Umiker-Sebeok's (1979) criticism of the experiments in training apes to use symbols suggests that one of the principal differences between apes and children is that the responses of the former depend upon their sensitivity to cues from specific trainers.

also assimilate new members. A long list of such examples could then be analyzed and compared to infant socialization.

What purpose would that serve? Even if the process that occurs when infants are socialized is an instance of a general class of similar processes, that fact does not constitute an explanation. To say "the parents comprise a social system and co-opt their infant into becoming a member of it, by the same developmental process always used by social systems to incorporate new members," begs the question why infant socialization happens to be subject to those processes. In fact, it is more likely that some of the later instances of socialization work because of the basic processes established in infancy: in other words, that they are a result rather than a cause of the way parents socialize their infants.[7]

However, it is worth pointing out two distinctive features of the latter process that will not be true in later socialization. One unique feature is that the infant brings innate, evolutionarily preadapted equipment to his socialization: the rhythms allowing adults to anticipate his behavior, the semblance of dialogue built into his sucking behavior and the ups and downs of his arousal, the visual preference for faces, the pretuned sensitivity to distinctive features of human speech sounds, the sign-release mechanisms establishing automatic imitation of certain facial and perhaps hand movements, the sensitivity to contingent feedback, the smile, the ability to activate adults by making and breaking eye contact with them, the unignorable cry, the conflict between watching and doing that sets up turn-taking with adults, and so forth. This list only includes mechanisms that have been revealed and investigated in recent years; there are many more.

Most other systems that an individual joins in the course of his life are cultural products adapted to the nature of human beings and their developmental processes. That is not true of infant socialization, which evolved biologically, not culturally. The very nature of the young human infant and the very nature of the parent evolved so as to facilitate socialization. (We are talking of *universal* human socialization, ignoring the differences among societies in traditional infant-care practices, which, on balance, turn out to have little effect on the basic properties of mind.

7. I suspect, for example, that the sequence "shared rhythms and regulations, shared purpose, shared memory, and shared language" can be applied to a wide variety of cases of socialization into existing systems. The basic point about parent-infant interaction that I have emphasized, the asymmetry allowing adults to project their expectations into the infant's rhythms and intentions, is actually true of adult-child and teacher-learner interaction in general. But that only suggests a research program for the future, whose hypothesis would be that processes of infant socialization are replicated by the human species at other ages and at other levels of social system, not that infant socialization proceeds as it does "because" the infant is joining a social system.

Culture-specific socialization comes into its own later, when particular languages are learned.)

A second difference between infant socialization and later social-ization is related to the fact that the infant originates as output of the very system—the parents—that he will turn around and join. The Adam and Eve story retains that element (in Eve's creation from Adam's rib), but the only time it occurs in real life is in infancy. Parents (especially mothers) are the creators of the organism that they socialize. So the infant begins as a part of the parental system in one sense, a differen-tiated product to be used as instrument to certain ends, and becomes a part of the same system in a very different sense: an actively partici-pating person, both an autonomous organism and a conscious partner in joint enterprise.

The infant, as we saw in Chapter 10, is fantasized by parents as a member of their family even before he is born. While they distinguish their fantasy from reality when required to do so (tolerating all sorts of violations of the interaction rules), they also preserve the fantasy when-ever possible (e.g., by pretending the infant has observed the rules). In a way, then, the "apprentice" is more like an honorary, unconditional member. He can practically do no wrong. He cannot develop as a human being without being socialized, but neither can he normally "flunk out" or be fired for the missteps he makes along the way.

On the other hand, there are at least two basic similarities that extend to socialization throughout the life cycle, and even to the joining of larger systems (though not, I think, to the socialization of animals). One is that language is both the principal product of socialization and a compelling force maintaining one's membership. Once one possesses the means of discourse within a community (whether it is a particular language such as English, or a sublanguage such as the jargon of a life style or a profession), one is strongly bound to those who use the lan-guage and to the particular perspectives on reality it offers. We take up this point in the next chapter.

The second similarity is that socialization may involve unconscious processes, but it always creates or changes consciousness. Changes in an individual's behavior cannot merely be described as changes in the likelihood of certain contingent responses in certain contexts. The in-dividual acquires his own expectations of what the rules are, recognizes violations in himself and others, and makes plans that depend upon rules being followed. Most of all, this consciousness (which in the infant is nothing less than the change from not having to having a mind) includes a sense of self in relation to the system. One knows one is behaving in consistent ways, one is conscious of at least some of those ways, and one is aware that others are also. In fact, one is not a person until one has the basic understanding that social systems are comprised of persons among whom the self is one and to whom, in a sense, the self belongs.

12

Attachment, Individuation, and Personhood

"I can't explain myself, I'm afraid, sir," said Alice, "because I'm not myself, you see."
"I don't see," said the Caterpillar.

Lewis Carroll, *Alice's Adventures in Wonderland,* 1865

The self is an integration of various kinds of differentiated awareness: differentiating between the *I* of "I act" and the *I* of "I see," between the *I* and the *me*, between *I* and *we* (or *me* and *us*), between *I* and *he/she*, between *we* and *they*. Involved in those differentiations are two somewhat competing developmental processes commonly called attachment and individuation.

The individuation (or "separation-individuation") process refers to the infant's gradual emergence from a mere extension or subordinate component of the parents' system to a person with his own autonomous ego functions (Mahler & Gosliner, 1955; Mahler, Pine, & Bergman, 1975). Attachment, on the other hand, refers to the set of processes that create a bond between the infant and particular others, especially those processes that keep the infant working to maintain proximity with the mother and those that enable him to cope with physical separation from her (Ainsworth, 1969; Bowlby, 1969; Sroufe, 1979). Such authors as Erikson (1950) and Sander (1962) have discussed the issues arising between mother and baby over the conflict between individuation and attachment, the seemingly opposite directions that development has to take. The conflict, to the extent there is one, is inherent in the nature of human development. It is not a theoretical conflict: A self, a *person* as distinguished from a human organism, is in fact an individual with particular

222

roles in particular social systems. *Attached individual* means the same as what I have been calling an individual member or full partner. The very young infant does not need to be attached, because he has not yet been detached.

Attachment, then, requires that the early phase of separation has already occurred. To become attached to parents and other principal caretakers—for instance, to be wary of others with whom one has not interacted very much—requires separating *I* from *not-I*, at least to the extent of being aware of goals whose attainment depends upon *not-I*. It requires a certain consciousness about others' bodies and their location in space, though not yet the consciousness that they are selves. And attachment demonstrates the infant's awareness that he is not always in the parental envelope: that there is a difference, in other .words, between the parents' presence and absence, or between the parents' behavior and the behavior of others.

On the other hand, at the later stages attachment is a prerequisite for individuation. Attachment is a set of skills developed in interaction with particular others, investing those others with special meaning and thereby helping to define the self. For the question "Who am I?" only has meaning in relation to the family of significant persons who define the self, both by contrast ("Where is Mommy? Where is Tommy?") and by similarity ("Where is Mommy's nose? Where is Tommy's nose?"). The chronology in the second half-year is therefore something like separation ⟶ attachment ⟶ individuation.

Attachment as a Component of Interpersonal Skills

Attachment behavior, as Sroufe (1979) points out, is one of the best demonstrations of the inseparability of cognitive, social, and affective development. In fact, there is an affective component in every skill. The skilled organism has feelings of pleasure in competence, fear of incompetence, and some degree of confidence tied to each component of any given skill. It is that relative degree of confidence in the adequacy of each subskill for the task at hand that makes those subskills either less or more susceptible to modification. The more attention a skill requires for its execution, the less confidence is associated with it and (for both reasons, the high attention and the low confidence) the more open it is to accommodate. I mentioned examples from our own studies of imitation (Kaye & Marcus, 1978, 1981), where the infants chose to assimilate certain features of the model to their schemas and then accommodated to those features, while other features of the model were ignored in favor of persevering with a previously learned schema on trial after trial.[1]

1. Another example of this phenomenon can be seen in nonnative speakers' retaining the phonology of their original language.

From this point of view, attachment includes the affect associated with interpersonal skills, even before the infant understands those skills as rules of interaction. Thus attachment is really the set of interpersonal skills associated with primary caretakers. What is the infant anxious about when he shows "stranger anxiety?" Not that the stranger will hurt him, or fail to protect him from predatory beasts, or deprive him of nurturance and affection. He is anxious because he is not sure he knows how to act with the unfamiliar person. He attaches himself to his parents and other familiar people because he is "surer of himself" with them. (It might be added that this is the basis of attachment to friends, spouse, co-workers, fellow Lithuanians, and so forth, throughout the life cycle.)

The idea of attachment as the affective component of interpersonal skills underscores Hay's (1980) argument that the early hominid child had better reasons for staying close to parents than merely to protect himself from predators. The social environment is the one in which the most important developmental lessons are taught. The direct lessons Mother Nature offers, to shun the fire and to come in out of the rain, are nothing in comparison with the equally natural lessons of mother, father, and other people. Neither fire nor rain remembers for the child how much he currently knows, what he ought to learn next, what interested him the last time they played together. The adult does all of that. A toddler seems to recognize this, for example, when he uses an adult as a storage place for toys he wants to retain possession of but cannot attend to simultaneously (cf. the 17-month-old I described in Chapter 1). Placing physical things in escrow with an adult is a reenactment of the basic trust that is essential to shared symbolic meaning: Signs, in fact, would not retain their meaning without attachment among family members and, at a broader level, among community members.

Generalization to Others. One of the interesting and important things to notice about attachment behavior is that it is a *relative* preference. It is not, in fact, attachment to a particular person; wariness of strangers is not absolute and neither is proximity-maintaining behavior. The same person from whom a toddler flees into his parent's arms may be, in the parent's absence, the very person to whom the toddler runs when he meets an even more unfamiliar person. So he does not dichotomize people into two categories, "familiar caretaker" and "stranger"; he judges the relative familiarity or strangeness of different people depending on the situation.

For example, a colleague who happened to have his 12-month-old in the office dropped in to see me for a moment. The child, who had only recently taken his first steps, toddled into my office holding his father's hand. Joshua had seen me on a number of occasions but now watched me warily, staying close to his father. A toy near the doorway attracted the child's attention, and he took a couple of steps toward it. Because he retreated to his father when I approached, I made no further attempt to interact, and ignored him while he explored the toy. The father had to do a brief errand and asked me to watch Joshua for a few minutes. When his father told him he would be right back and started to leave, Joshua protested briefly; but once his father was out of sight he was content to return to the toy. I kept my distance, pretending to be involved with something else. A minute later another colleague came to the door, who had not seen the child for a few months. She had barely started to step into the room when he dropped to the floor (being able to crawl faster than walk) and scurried toward me. Without a thought I extended my arms, into which Joshua leaped like a baby monkey, clinging to me and peering warily at the new adult just as though I were his father, mother, and guardian angel all rolled into one.

This anecdote illustrates something that I believe is not widely understood about attachment. The attachment "system" is an evolved one, not a social system developed by each parent-infant pair. It is a skill that allows the infant to survey the alternative people available, choose the one whom he prefers to be near under specific circumstances, and keep that person nearby. The "system" exists in the sense that this kind of behavior fits nicely with adult behavior: My response to Joshua's hasty approach was instinctive. But it is not correct to say that attachment is the seeking of proximity to a specific person. The proximity-seeking behaviors that the infant develops are by no means tied to a specific adult.[2]

In general, a young child assumes that whatever he learns in the course of interaction with his parents will be effective behavior with others. Initial social learning is not person-specific. It only becomes person-specific when a set of experiences leads the child to make the differentiation that certain skills are to be used only with certain people, just as he learns to use them only in certain contexts. The infant takes a broad set of cues as discriminative stimuli, aided by evolved predilections for human faces, human voices, and so forth, then narrows that set down through a learning process. From the start, attachment behavior is not so much a set of attitudes about interacting with particular individuals as it is a set of attitudes about social interaction in general, coupled with relatively more confidence in the infant's skills within

2. The choice of person, however, as in the foregoing anecdote, is based on more than familiarity. Lewis and Michalson (1982) have shown experimentally that a 12-month-old's willingness to interact with a stranger is affected by having seen that stranger warmly greeting and being greeted by his mother. Strangers who had performed the same acts with another stranger were not trusted to the same extent.

familiar interpersonal contexts. However, there is an irony here. At the same time that infants begin to learn conventional signs, which will make them members of the language community at large, they learn them as apprentices to specific individuals. The signals are acquired as interpersonal routines in specific contexts with specific others, so those contexts and significant persons form a part of the consciousness of self.

Parents' Agendas for Attachment and Individuation

The parents' roles in attaching and individuating their infant must change in the course of his socialization. The four periods we have discussed in previous chapters can provide a useful perspective for theorists concerned with attachment and individuation, by emphasizing that what eventually develops is a relationship between parents and infant, or between system and system member, rather than any property of the child himself. In making this point I am once again in strong agreement with Sroufe (1979; Sroufe & Waters, 1977). Bowlby's (1969) and Ainsworth's (1969) descriptions tell us how mother-infant behavior is organized optimally in the human species, how it sometimes breaks down, and about certain situational factors that produce continuity in the manifestations of attachment in individual dyads. There is nothing to suggest that we ought to consider attachment a measurable trait in babies. The same can be said of separation-individuation. In fact, many other so-called traits, such as temperament, may really be properties of the system.

Both the attachment and the individuation literatures are consistent with the view of socialization that was presented in the previous chapter. The infant first is differentiated from the maternal system that gave birth to him—a psychological process lasting some months after the physical severing of the umbilicus—and then he gradually is attached to the parents' preexisting social system as an individual member. The process of that socialization involves an apprenticeship. In the remainder of this concluding chapter, I shall attempt to summarize and integrate all that I have said, under the organizing rubric of the four periods of parent-infant relations. While the infant takes on a slowly increasing share of the responsibility for the interaction, other parts of his role are performed for him, or the parents merely pretend he is performing them. In effect, then, he never really achieves autonomy until he has become a member of the system, taking over functions that had been performed by the parent: intentions, initiatives, and memory of the system's history. The gradualness of this transition is possible just because the infant does not come to the system as an external, voluntary applicant for membership. Instead, he comes directly from being a completely subordinate offshoot to being a still-dependent apprentice partner.

The Regulating Self. The newborn is, after all, only a differentiated sub-system of the reproducing parents. On the other hand, he is also a distinct organism with distinct self-regulating mechanisms governing his metabolism, sleep, arousal, hunger, and growth. The autonomy of those functions is the germ of the self that is later to emerge. Some of the mechanisms are homeostatic ones intrinsic to the infant—tempera-ture control being the classic example. Others take the form of mutual regulatory mechanisms built into the evolved mother-infant system: the innate cycle of hunger, crying, mother's lactation reflex and nursing behavior, rooting, sucking, swallowing. So the regulatory mechanisms of the neonate include preadapted effects on mothers. In addition, they include all the preadapted sensory acuities and attentional preferences that make adult behavior such a salient part of the neonate's stimulus world. In other words, the interpersonal context for the development of skills begins to be established from birth.

As a separate organism, the newborn is equipped with many self-regulating systems; he has to control his own metabolism, his own sleep/wake states, and also his own growth, for "self-regulating" (or "homeo-static") does not mean "staying the same." An open system is both able and compelled to change in order to preserve its balance with its en-vironment. So far as the infant's intrinsic processes of maturation and adaptation are involved, his development is a matter of self-regulation.

At the same time, however, the newborn often finds caretakers reflecting his own state of arousal. When he is asleep in mother's arms, she is calm; when he is fussing, she bounces him or moves him around; when he is crying, she is anxious. Within a given activity such as feeding, we have seen how mothers allow their interventions to be timed by the built-in cycles of sucking. Similarly, the infant's eye movements affect what adults do and say: For example, the baby fixates on a necklace and the parent shakes it, prolonging the interesting event. These kinds of parental accommodation are a matter of reaching out to where the infant is, "getting on his wave length" as we say; so that his otherwise autistic activities can be made a part of their common life. It is a unilateral sharing, at first; but, as described in previous chapters, by 5 or 6 months (already in the period of shared intentions) we begin to see more sym-metrically shared rhythms and regulations.

The mother's attempts to entrain herself to the infant's built-in cycles of sucking, attention, and arousal are a kind of rear-guard action to prevent his defection, to compensate psychologically for the physical detachment. So-called bonding, a natural process in mothers, can be seen as the evolved system's way of guaranteeing their proximity to their infants, even when all physical needs have been met. Why should the species have evolved these particular forms of psychological bonding? What is the adaptive function of rhythm-sharing? Many of the specific behaviors involved have no protective value for the infant's physical survival. If their evolutionary function is reflected at all in their typical consequences, as we should assume it is, it must lie in the establishment of turn-taking and mutual alternation between directing expressions toward the partner and monitoring the partner's expressions toward oneself. The first step in getting him to identify himself as a partner in the social system is for the mother to identify herself, in certain respects, with him.

This is why when we talk of mutual effects between parent and child, we do not necessarily mean simultaneous effects. An account of how self-concepts develop would examine the ways a mother's and father's own self-concepts recapitulate themselves in the child's self-concepts. Although this process belongs to a later period, the parents' role in the process has clearly already begun, because parents never really separate those aspects of their image of the child that pertain to him as an individual from those aspects that are merely projections of themselves. This may be partly because the infant has indeed originated as a part of themselves. The neonate's built-in rhythms, the mother's built-in responses to them, and her ability to adjust the rhythms of her pretend dialogues to those of the infant's actual processing mechanisms, all keep alive the mother's image of the infant as a part of her self. Both parents' sharing of an infant's cycles of attention and arousal enable them to infer his intentions and thus to rearrange objects, to play imitative and other turn-taking games, to respond consistently and contingently to actions that look like meaningful gestures in the adult world.

The Intending Self. The next period permits adults to become instrumental not just in the infant's survival and growth but in purposeful action. Intentionality comes to the infant of its own accord, as it does to all organisms possessed of the capacity to learn about the regularity in their worlds and to reorganize their behavior in the light of that knowledge. It is not the task of a science of human development to explain intention, as it is not our task to explain assimilation, because they are not specifically human phenomena. However, the direction of the infant's intentions, the specific objects of his experience and the objects that become salient through association, are partly products of the ways adults have responded to his rhythms and internal regulations, and then to his apparent interests and intentions.

Beginning in the second month or so, when the infant has become proficient at orienting to sights and sounds and at tracking moving objects, when firm eye contact has become established in face-to-face situations, and when the primary circular reactions have appeared, many of the parents' inferences about his intentions are no longer fantasies. As we saw in earlier chapters, those intentions can be shown on behavioral grounds. Although it is true that an adult not bound by scientific laws of parsimony and objectivity is inclined to flesh out the skeleton intentions more than is strictly justifiable (e.g., saying that a baby whose gaze is following a necklace dangling in front of him "thinks it looks good to eat"), at least the bare bones of the infant's intention really exist and are often perceived accurately by parents. This means that the parents' view of him as a person with intentions of his own has a greater grounding in reality than it had in the first month or so. The adult notion of the infant's personhood is only a step ahead of his actual development. The infant actually does engage in intentional behavior, directing head, body, arms, and legs toward specific objects, practicing actions over and over. What he lacks is an integration of those separate acts into a persisting whole, a conscious agent/perceiver, an ego.

Yet it is crucial that parents project onto their baby's behavior the intentions of a functioning ego. It is crucial both for the maintenance of the parental image of who the baby is and for the interaction frames—instrumental, modeling, discourse, and so forth—in which those intentions will be completed and the infant's skills enhanced. For the parent is invested in more than the isolated advances in the infant's skills that the two of them can achieve together. More important than those achievements is the proof they give to the parent of the baby's agency as well as of their joint partnership in his development.

> She will not be satisfied until it seems to her that he *himself* did it: He must give indications in his actions that he did it as a result of trying to do it; that he knew *what* he was trying to do, that his action was based in some *knowledge of the socially defined requirements of the situation*—he must indicate that he "sees" the situation as she does. [Shotter & Gregory, 1976, p. 6; italics in original]

Apart from the achievements parents notice, we should mention one achievement whose importance few recognize. Darwin (1872), Preyer (1893), Baldwin (1895), Piaget (1951), and Guillaume (1971) all recorded some time between 3 and 5 months that their infants were able to imitate movements of parts of their bodies that they could see; for example, opening and closing the hands. Later (but not much later, under the right conditions, as the Kaye and Marcus [1978, 1981] studies showed) the infant can imitate movements of parts of his own body he cannot see, for example, mouth movements. Both these forms of assimilation of another person's body part, which he sees but cannot control, to his own corresponding part, which he can control, are crucial first steps in the development of a self. As I argued in Chapter 9, they are steps that evolution has provided, in the form of built-in release mechanisms that have been found even in the first month, allowing the infant to imitate certain hand and mouth movements, vocalizations, and perhaps other kinds of actions. The change I am describing here, from "regulating self" to "intending self," reiterates Chapter 9's argument that neonatal imitation is of a lower order, not a higher order than assimilation.

The instrumental frame, the feedback frame, the modeling frame, all are enhanced whenever a parent can accurately interpret the infant's intentions. By helping him achieve self-initiated goals, adults clearly provide the infant with a greater measure of individuation; but at the same time they co-opt him by making it easier for him to do things their way, and by making themselves indispensable partners in his action.

It is not enough to provide the frame. The adult has to keep the infant in the frame. For example, instrumentally completing his action for him is of no benefit if it is done with extraneous movements that distract him, or if it overwhelms him with stimulation so that his sensory system shuts it out, or if it pushes his level of arousal up so high that he cries. An important part of the parental frames is the management of the infant's level of arousal. Without that as a sine qua non, the infant would be unable to benefit from the informative aspect of the frame. Managing arousal and thereby performance is very much a matter of transmitting affect (Sander, 1962; Stern, 1971; Sroufe, 1979; Brazelton et al., 1974; Tronick et al., 1979; Campos & Stenberg, 1981). Smiling and laughing manifest optimal levels of arousal; gaze aversion and crying are consequences of overarousal. Hence problems arise when the parent is insensitive, or overly sensitive, or overly anxious about the infant's states and about his approach and withdrawal during face-to-face interaction, or when the infant is overly sensitive or insensitive to the parent's attempts to increase arousal (Epilogue).

The period of shared intentions begins as asymmetrically as the preceding period, with the adult making interpretations of infant intention rather than the other way around. But imitation actually introduces new intentions, transmitted from adult to baby. So, too, does the adult's memory of what engaged the infant on previous occasions. A parent can introduce familiar objects and novel variations upon familiar objects and be pretty sure that the infant will attempt to reach them, to explore them, to take them apart or put them together. When this happens the infant is receiving an intention from the parent, who in turn received it from the infant's own history. So the parent, in the period of shared intentions, serves as a repository of memory. The adult social system now possesses information that is useful for the infant. It buys his co-operation by making itself the instrument of his blossoming will.

The Remembering Self. Once events begin to signify for the infant, representation having progressed to the comprehension and production of signals, the memory of their mutual past ceases to reside only with the parental partner. The period of shared memory, then, marks the beginning of a symmetrical kind of sharing not found in the two earlier periods. There is a mutual acknowledgment of the meaning of signs. Yet there remains an asymmetry of understanding. The adult partners offer signals as gestures. They intend to produce, and assume they do produce, the same effects in the infant that would be produced in themselves if others were to make those gestures to them. Adults also assume that the infant is gesturing when he uses a signal. But several months pass before comprehended and produced signals cohere into a single reversible lexicon. They do cohere because of the child's intrinsic cognitive drive to make simple sense of reality, but this would not occur if it were not for the alternate role-switching in the dialogue structure, which results from earlier turn-taking created by adults interpretation of infants' rhythms and intentions.

The acquisition of signs, whether comprehended or produced (and also whether indexical or arbitrary), gives the infant a new measure of control over his relation to the behavior of others. Because he remembers what led to what in the past, he can anticipate what others are about to do. Because they have been monitoring the regularity in his behavior, they are able to incorporate him in stereotyped routines. We have already discussed how some of the parental frames function to augment the infant's memory capacity and increase the salience of decision points in skilled action. Now it must be added that there is tremendous emotional energy for the infant in having these needs met. The joy in mastery, which has often been discussed by students of sensorimotor development (Bruner, 1972), is to a large extent an interpersonally shared excitement, the affective side of intersubjectivity between infant and adult. The ability to anticipate what is going to happen next, with the feeling of surprise when expectations are moderately violated, are constituents of humor at all ages, even to the younger infant. But in this period the link between cognitive anticipations and interpersonal affect comes into its own.

> But *by 9 months the infant is an emotional being*. Now the subject-object relationship is primary. In a new way the *meaning* of the event *for the infant* is responsible for the affect. Thus, by about 9 months the infant laughs *in anticipation* of mother's

return in peek-a-boo, rather than in response to the completed sequence. It is angry in the face of an obstacle blocking an *intended* act (a particular relationship and a psychological investment). And it can experience threat in advance of noxious stimulation (fear). This is also the age at which surprise, as opposed to startle, appears. . . .Awareness has become anticipation. While in the second quarter the infant has motor anticipation based on well-established action sequences, by 9 months there is cognitive anticipation. [Sroufe, 1979, p. 488; italics in original]

In fact, games like peek-a-boo and pat-a-cake begin to be supplanted, by this age, by games like "Where's the . . ." whose only point is to demonstrate the infant's memory and comprehension of conventional signs, and then to make shared affect contingent upon a correct answer. A good transition from pat-a-cake to "Where's the . . ." is the game of "So big!" At 5 or 6 months, its rules are essentially the same as pat-a-cake. The parent chants "How big is Jeffrey?" and also answers the question by thrusting Jeffrey's hands heavenward: "So big!" As soon as the baby anticipates and performs this movement himself, the rules become essentially those of "Where's the . . .": Parent asks, child replies, both acknowledge the joy.

Of course, the infant participates in these signal routines without yet understanding them as rule-bound. In the period of shared memory the infant merely begins to learn what works and what does not work with particular others. Immediately, he then begins to learn what to expect of those others in various situations, and what they expect of him (he learns that they will wait for certain actions from him). He is learning to play roles within the parental frames. He does not learn until the next period that the roles are rules, that some contingencies are obligatory, and that some contingencies are reversible (expected of both interactants). But he does become dependent on those individuals who know the significations he himself is learning.

The difference between these routines with signs and the earlier exchanges with objects or merely with body parts is enormous. Earlier (in the discourse, modeling, instrumental, and feedback frames) the parent was facilitating experiences that were instructive with respect to competence in the world at large, whereas the games with signs have no meaning and no utility outside the group whose conventional signs (and games) they are. As his own skills differentiate, the skills make him a hostage to the supporting system in which they were acquired and within which they are effective.

In the anticipation of roles (the twin roles of interpreter and producer of signs) lies the beginning of integration of *I* and *me*. They cannot yet be fully integrated, however, because the child knows some signals as signals to produce and others as signals to comprehend. A fully integrated consciousness of self will require a reversibility of the two roles, in at least some social interaction skills. The child who does not yet use symbols is not truly self-conscious.

It is not accidental that the next transition, to the period of shared language, coincides with the acquisition of nonlinguistic kinds of rules as well as linguistic ones. A contingency can become a rule only when it is brought into consciousness. I have argued that consciousness of rules, system, and self are all interdependent and that all three are involved in the ability to gesture to another.

The Social Self. Because symbols require self-consciousness, symbolic thought is a reflection of the fact that self-consciousness has developed (Charney, 1980a). However, symbols are also the *means* by which self-consciousness develops. And as the acquisition of symbols is a gradual process in the period of shared language (a period that really continues indefinitely), so the dawning awareness of self in relation to others is also a gradual process (Flavell, 1974). Socialization obviously continues throughout childhood, and self-concepts change. Not having investigated those later developments myself, I shall merely suggest a few points for consideration and point to one virgin area in need of exploration.

At the start of this period the infant anticipates, through shared memory, many of the roles other people take when interacting with him. We would not say, however, that he puts himself in those roles, or experiences the interaction intersubjectively from the other's point of view. That is what is achieved in the next year or so. The 2- to 3-year-old will not only recognize what refers to him, he will project his own view of reality into the minds of those with whom he communicates and he will introject their reactions to him into his own view of himself. This change, from recognizing what involves him to internalizing the perspectives of all partners, may not merely transpire in one long continuous development. It appears to occur over and over again, in one domain after another (Donaldson, 1979). This is particularly evident in the learning of deixis.

Deixis, consisting of those elements of language whose meaning depends upon a knowledge of who is speaking to whom and where they are located in time and space, is a universal property of all natural languages. The sentence "The book is in your lap" refers to a particular lap only when one knows who is being addressed; otherwise, there are billions of "your laps" in the world. "This pen" only means a particular pen when the speaker can be seen holding or standing near a pen.[3] It is remarkable that every human language (linguists believe) all the way back to the original Mother Tongue has made use of deixis of person (personal pronouns), place (e.g., *here/there, this/that*), and time (*now/then*). Still more remarkable, every language distinguishes at least three persons in the personal pronoun (*I, you, he*) and at least two numbers (in English, singular and plural as in *I/we* and *he/they*). Yet it is perfectly simple to design artificial languages with all reference in the third person, and without any pronouns:

> Adam: Adam is hungry.
> Eve: Adam can eat an apple. Eve had a bite, and discovered that apples are delicious.
> Adam: Adam prefers not to eat of the forbidden tree.
> Eve: Adam is a fool.

In fact, such a language would have offered advantages to Cain and Abel. They would not have had to learn, as every child in the world has in fact had to learn, the meaning of words that refer to different people every time they are used. Consequently they would not have had to differentiate speech roles and they would not have had to differentiate themselves from others;[4] individuation would not be, as it is in fact, a prerequisite for language learning.

If it is surprising that all languages contain these logically unnecessary deictic features such as personal pronouns, it is equally surprising that normal children have no difficulty learning them. In English (and in other languages so far as we know) children do not confuse *I* and *you* as one would expect them to do on the basis of the data presented to them. They do learn first how the words refer to their own speech roles and only later how those same words refer to others. They learn what *you* and *your* mean when they are being addressed, before being able to use the second person in addressing others; and they learn to say *I* and *my* in formulaic expressions, like "I want X" and "my X," before they understand how to choose which of two objects a speaker must mean by "my X" (Charney, 1980a). But they do not make the error of

---

3. It is a measure of the power of deixis that a word like "this" can force an utterance to be understood as referring to a particular object even when nothing about that object qualifies it for lexical reference by the nondeictic words employed. If I were to hand you a pen and say, "Take this orange," you (or any 3-year-old) would reply, "That's not an orange," showing that you knew exactly what I was referring to, orange or not. The power to refer without having to agree on the lexical meaning of terms may be the reason for the universality of deixis.

4. One can only guess whether this would have made their fraternal relations less acrimonious.

confusing first and second person, even though their second person refers to another speaker's first person and vice versa.[5]

How can normal children pick up deixis so readily from normal adult speech? So far as we know, parents do not make adjustments in deixis as part of "baby talk." What they do, instead, is establish the discourse frame with alternation of turns and hence of roles. That alone creates an initial level of self-consciousness, a differentiation of roles plus imitation of models in those roles. Without this prior groundwork, the acquisition of deictic forms would be impossible. If it were the other way around—that is, if progress in learning language were necessary for this aspect of individuation—the child would make pronoun errors at first, be corrected, and only as the correct deictic shifts were learned would we see the consciousness of self emerging. Instead, children learn the correct usages by imitating the way parents do it, when they find themselves in the role the parents were in when the latter demonstrated that usage. Such imitation requires recognition of the respective roles. So the initial level of self-consciousness, which appears simultaneously and inevitably with the first symbols, must precede any understanding of what *I*, *you*, and other pronouns mean, by several months. Thus pronoun use is one area where social development is clearly an antecedent of the corresponding cognitive/linguistic development.

Self-consciousness can also be seen as a kind of conservation: the conservation of self across transformations of time, space, and roles. Since we are talking about an intuitive (not an operational) level of conservation, it is really a type of permanence: self-permanence as compared to object- or person-permanence. The development of self-permanence has not yet been studied. It would seem to depend upon the shift from understanding roles separately as speaker and as listener, as signer and as interpreter of signs, to understanding them simultaneously from both sides. In any case, it will have several stages or levels of establishment and the child may have to proceed through those levels more than once. Charney (1979) found a similar course of acquisition of *here* and *there* to the one she found for *my* and *your*, except that *here* and *there* came a year or so later. Tracking the self and others through successive displacements of role would seem to correspond to the final stages of infancy. This area is worth exploring. In the meantime, I would add deixis to Sroufe's (1979) list of types of evidence, between 18 and 36 months, of the infant's emerging self-concept.

5. Autistic children do make this error, showing that autism is not a cognitive or linguistic deficit per se (because younger normal children very rarely make the error) but a social incomprehension (Charney, 1980b). Of course, a social deficit can also have organic causes.

Language Forces the Transition to
Full System Membership

The most important truth revealed by the universality of deixis and the surprising ease with which children acquire it is that language, like all other aspects of culture, is adapted to man (not the other way around). The reason all human languages have personal pronouns as well as deixis of place and time is that human thought is inherently interpersonal and inherently grows out of communication. Language universals reflect universals of the human mind, but those in turn reflect universal processes of mental development. In other words, our distant ancestors had to evolve not only language itself but at the same time a set of parent-child and parent-infant communicative forms that would allow language to be passed on. Those forms were bound to have universal effects upon all languages.[6] The mind capable of symbolic communication develops in the first place out of role-switching turns. So it should not be surprising, after all, that the child assumes the existence of speech roles right at the outset of his language learning and, therefore, has no difficulty with deixis.

In earlier chapters, in discussing the beginnings of shared language, we have seen the importance of fully reversible symbols. These signs designate meanings the child can share with a community including, but not limited to, the primary caretaker. We reviewed some ways in which the infant's apprenticeship teaches him both to comprehend and to produce signs. I suggested that signs are introduced in the context of parental frames, which in turn depend upon the parent's ability to share the infant's intentions. The fact that the parents treat the infant as if he were a member of their social system plays a crucial role in his development of symbolic ability in general as well as in his acquisition of the specific language.

Language, then, is a result of socialization. But now let us look at the other side. It turns out that his acquisition of language is what guarantees that the apprentice member becomes a permanent active member of the social system. The reason this is so is easier to understand if we consider what the use of language really involves. Despite the fact that the infant begins with single-word utterances and with the ability to identify the referents of single words, language does not consist of a set of word meanings. Language, in fact, does not exist merely for the sake of naming things. Nor does it exist for the sake of propositions

6. The infant's ability to acquire language evolved along with language functions themselves: The adult brain, the infant brain, adult-infant interaction processes, and language universals all evolved together. Each individual language itself, however, is a cultural product, completely dependent on those universals. There has been no evolution within any population to make it easier for them to learn one language rather than another.

about the world. It consists of interpersonal communication about shared or shareable intentions. This in turn involves propositions about language itself, circular as that may sound. To talk is always to make or imply assertions about the meaning of terms, to a community, in a context. "It is raining" is more than a proposition about precipitation. It means, "I say to you that what we mean by 'It is raining' is the case here and now." In fact, it usually says something more than that: "I have the right or the responsibility to say to you . . . ."

This metalinguistic aspect is an integral part of the child's speech from the beginning. His commentary on the passing scene consists of hypotheses, which adults are expected to confirm or refute. They are hypotheses about language, not about the world. The child says "doggie" time and again, meaning: "Is this a 'doggie' which I see before me?" "What about this, it is one of those things you call 'doggie' too, isn't it?" "There goes another 'doggie,' I think." We can make those interpretations of his one-word utterances partly because of their intonation, partly because the child is satisfied when we respond to them as though that were what he meant ("Yes, that's a doggie. . . . No, that one's a cat"), and partly because one can think of no other sensible reason for his repeating the names of things so assiduously. Even when the child seems to be uttering words for his own entertainment rather than to elicit a reply, a better translation than "There goes a doggie" would be "There—I know what that's called—people call that sort of thing a 'doggie'!"

From the moment the first conventional sign is learned, in the period of shared memory, the child is learning who may say what, to whom, and for what purpose. He does not just learn more signals. The signals he learns are differentiated by social context. Shared memory is involved because what he understands is how certain signals have been used on occasions that are also remembered by his parents. So, in effect, while the symbol frees thought from the here and now, it does so at the price of being conventional. Even in thought, "We cannot be free from parents, teachers, and society because they are the extracerebral sources of our minds" (Delgado, 1969, p. 243). Symbols only have meaning because the child shares with the adult system the memory of their consistent use. This, of course, is equally true of syntax and pragmatics. Symbols could not be used without the community's rules for when to use them and how to combine them so as to convey propositional meaning.

Since this dependence on participation in the social system arises only gradually as conventional signs are acquired and are understood to be reversible (as speech roles are reversible), the relation between language and socialization should not be oversimplified. It is not a matter of one preceding the other. Nor does language either precede or follow thought, or precede or follow self-consciousness. What really happens is that a little language changes the nature of thought a little, advances the socialization process a little, which enables language to advance to a more sophisticated level, and so forth.

> Symbols [both] depend upon and promote communication. The results of conjoint experience are considered and trans-mitted. Events cannot be passed from one to another, but mean-ings may be shared by means of signs. Wants and impulses are then attached to common meanings. They are thereby trans-formed into desires and purposes, which, since they implicate a common or mutually understood meaning, present new ties, converting a conjoint activity into a community of interest and endeavor. [Dewey, 1939, p. 388]

Neither symbols nor propositions have any meaning beyond their conventional use in discourse. Hence they can have no role in thought beyond the internalized discourse. This is a point I stressed earlier, in defining representation as a mental process that can operate with sym-bols and other signs just as it operates with perceived objects and events. There is no evidence of any qualitative change at 12–15 months in the brain's processes of storage and retrieval. But after that age what the human mind thinks *about*, much of the time, are symbols, and this means representing to itself an imagined exchange of meaning with others. Language, then, as well as forcing the child to join the social system so that he can further develop and use his symbolic knowledge of reality, also forces him to internalize the system so that he can think about that reality "independently." In other words, there could be no covert rep-resentation of symbols without a covert representation of the social sys-tem that gives them meaning. So the very creation of mind locks the infant into both overt and covert participation in the language com-munity. This can no longer be an apprenticeship by the sufferance of the adult members. It has to be a full membership, the child anticipating how his own behavior will fit into the ongoing program of the whole. Only a full member (albeit of unequal status in many ways) can gesture to others and interpret the signs of others as gestures to him.

The price at which symbolic knowledge is purchased is the theme of some of the most enduring myths of all societies. For example, Adam and Eve were born naked and ignorant, products of God's system but not privy to it. Their fall from Grace was a loss of the same paradise that an infant enjoys in the first year of life: Their needs had been met and their intentions fulfilled. Not satisfied, however, they tasted of the Tree of Knowledge, with the inevitable consequence that they had to mature and to become participating agents in the world. They lost forever the ignorant bliss of apprenticeship in Eden.

We Are Multilingual. Part of that ignorant bliss of infancy is the potential for learning any human language, with all the different alternative ways of categorizing the world. Sometimes, however, perhaps misinterpreting Whorf (1956), cognitive psychologists and social anthropologists tend to exaggerate the extent to which one loses that potential in the course of acquiring a particular language and growing up in a particular culture. It is important to remember that the sort of difficulty adults experience in second-language-learning is due to maturation of some specific critical parts of the nervous system. It is not due to interference by the first language. Children are quite capable of learning several languages simultaneously. This is also true to a great extent of the learning of other social systems' rules (and not just in childhood). The child does not really give anything up in exchange for that social knowledge. True, it is a knowledge that weds him to the community that shares it. But the infant is promiscuous. His attachment to the family does not preclude his learning the rules of other social systems and becoming a member of them as well. He learns to interact with mother by mother's rules, father by father's rules, grandma by hers, and the nursery school by its rules.

By the time formal schooling starts (and increasingly thereafter), the child will be a member of a multiplicity of systems. Although it is beyond the age domain of this book, this fact raises two additional points bearing on any discussion of socialization, culture, attachment, and individuation. The first point is that there is not a sharp boundary around any social system the child enters. There will always be similarity and overlap of membership among the different systems, so that the more systems the child belongs to the easier it will be to accommodate himself to new ones. Second, there is also bound to be some conflict among these systems. The child will not always be out of the jurisdiction of one while interacting within another. So there are times when the rules of the mother-child dyad, for example, directly conflict with those of the father-child or grandmother-child dyads; and when the family's rules conflict with those of the peer group. As a matter of fact, mother herself will play by different rules when different people are present, or at different times of day (dinner time, playtime, bedtime).

What are the consequences of that kind of inconsistency and conflict? One is that the child must differentiate more and more specialized, context-dependent rules. Another is that he must retain flexibility, not commit himself irrevocably to one system. This is surely the source of some anxiety, and perhaps of that conflict among parts of the self that psychoanalysts call ego-dystonicity. But it is also a source of resilience and adaptability, part of the opportunism that is man. And it helps to explain why people in heterogeneous societies are able to be more opportunistic than in those societies where all family systems are fairly similar.

The fact that socialization goes on throughout life, even into radically different social systems, does not mean that the initial socialization process is unimportant. It does mean, I think, that what the young child learns is never *at the expense of* the alternative cultural rules he might have acquired. In fact, when the child learns what his family does, believes, and talks about, it is often in contrast to what others do, believe, and talk about, which means he learns something about those alternatives too. Much of his socialization constitutes a voluntary acceptance of one set of practices among several sets that he has actually learned about. The learning of sex roles (own and opposite) is only one example of this broader kind of cultural learning, already begun by age 2 or 3. Otherwise, how could children play according to different rules in different contexts—be so malleable as a result of subsequent changing experiences, as when they go off to school, and invent dramas in which dolls refuse to obey the rules of home and instead behave as members of imaginary communities (Piaget, 1951, obs. 89–92)? And how could they identify with significant others throughout the life span, introjecting self-images that are imitative and therefore selective?

There is a lot that the 3-year-old still does not know about different possible and actual viewpoints. His parents therefore remain the senior partners. But at least some of what had been the parents' fantasy has become reality. The infant's psychological autonomy has been traded for dependence upon a particular language and particular sets of social rules, at the same time that his physical dependence has given way to more physical autonomy. Socialization, then, is the development of dependence and autonomy at the same time. On the one hand, it is the learning of a particular set of rules that only work because others share them. On the other hand, those rules create a permanence in the world far greater, and offer more cognitive power to the individual, than anything that could have been deduced from solitary experience.

A Short Summary

Mysterious in the light of day,
Nature will not be denied her veil,
And what she does not make manifest to your spirit
Cannot be forced from her with levers and screws.

Johann Wolfgang von Goethe, *Faust*, 1808

The evidence my students and I gathered has been combined with other evidence to reject two fashionable hypotheses, one having to do with the young infant and his mother as comprising a social system from birth, the other having to do with a mutual intersubjectivity beginning in the first or second month.

In place of those hypotheses, and in place of any theory based purely upon developmental processes intrinsic to the infant, I have offered a theory of early human development as an apprenticeship. I conceive of the intrinsic rhythms and self-regulatory processes of the infant as being marshaled by some extrinsic functions residing in the adults of the species, including a variety of parental frames brilliantly adapted to the tutelage of an organism that must be transformed into a person. Central to this theory is a new theory of imitation, which also embodies both the intrinsic cognitive functions and the extrinsic contributions of adults. With respect to the kinds of information shared between parent and infant (rhythms, intentions, memory, and language), and again with respect to the semiotic levels en route to symbols (assimilation, representation, signification, designation), and finally with respect to stages of the self (regulating, intending, remembering, social), I have organized the course of infancy into the same four major periods. Stages are not in themselves an explanation, but these have helped us to keep various causal sequences straight.

241

A Short Summary

At the end of any colloquium, most of the audience immediately vanishes (unless there is wine and cheese, in which case some people hang around for about 10 minutes). A few colleagues and students remain behind: One or two are enthused, most are dissatisfied. The speaker himself feels a mixture of both sentiments. He has shared a good deal of what was closest to him intellectually, yet he has not said enough. The audience has listened politely, smiled and nodded, asked some challenging questions, yet they have not said enough either. In this case, I imagine one of the stragglers blurting out rudely, "So what?" Momentarily unbalanced, I might recover my poise and then unburden myself of a few thoughts on practical matters.

Epilogue: Clinical Implications

There is no finer investment for any community than putting milk into babies.

Winston Churchill, radio broadcast, 1943

Dost thou not see my baby at my breast,
That sucks the nurse asleep?

William Shakespeare, *Antony and Cleopatra*, 1607

Much of the impetus for conceiving of mothers and infants as partners in a system came from clinicians who reacted against what Chess (1971) described as the *"mal de mere"* interpretation of developmental deficits. It had been an unattractive idea, blaming mothers for their children's problems. Building up parental guilt did not ameliorate the problems, nor was it good public relations for pediatricians. Besides, it was unfair, for all mothers are not presented with equally easy infants. Just as theoreticians were shifting from a passive to a more active view of the infant, who was now seen as an organizer of his own stimulus world, clinicians were arguing that different infants have different effects on caretakers. Therefore an extremely difficult baby would elicit negative reactions from some parents that could only increase the baby's difficulties. On the other hand, when the infant's cycles were easy to interpret and anticipate, the parent's behavior too would be more consistent, and communication would become easier and more effective. This is the "transaction model" described by Sameroff and Chandler (1975). Essentially the same idea has been expressed by many other investigators including Thomas, Chess, and Birch (1968), Sander (1977), Sroufe and Waters (1977), and Brazelton, Yogman, Als, and Tronick (1979).

The two aspects of this model, the "system" idea and the amplification of deficits idea, seem at first glance to be related. They both give

243

the infant a more active role than that of a receptacle of experience, and they both emphasize moment-to-moment interaction. However, if we take the concept of an open system seriously, it suggests that deficits in interaction should correct themselves. Only if mother and infant constituted a *closed* system, or if they were not members of the same open system, would we expect amplification of their failures at communication (Bateson, 1949). So the transaction model does not really grow out of the particular notions about the mother-infant system that its advocates have generally espoused. In fact, the transaction model is not incompatible with the idea of the *mal de mere*.

Since the theory and findings presented in this book have led to the conclusion that infants take some time to become members of social systems, what practical implications follow? It seems to me that we can make three main generalizations.

1. *It is the parents' attitudes that matter.* It is not the infant's membership in the system that matters but the parents' pretense that he is a member. If they shut him out, he does not have the resources or the status to establish his own role in their system. On the other hand, so long as they believe him to be a member of the family, he can almost be an automaton and still be involved in dialogues, play, and other meaningful interactions that will eventually apprentice him to the family system.

2. *The more organized the baby's innate cycles, the better.* If the infant is able to offer his caretakers smooth, organized behavior in feeding, play, and so forth, the adults will just naturally fit parental frames into and around those cycles. This is because the frames evolved precisely in adaptation to the general organization of infant behavior, and vice versa.

3. *Managing the baby's affect keeps him in the frame.* Social exchanges, even when they appear to have no substantive content, serve a vital function in keeping the infant involved in the adult's world. Most babies are fairly easy to tune up to the point where they are alert and engaged in the greeting behavior we described in the face-to-face situation, or where they try to solve problems like the detour task, or to imitate sounds and words; and they can be kept at that level for some time without becoming so highly aroused that they have to turn away, withdraw from the interaction, or cry. However, some infants are slow to arouse; others quickly become overexcited, or become distressed at a level of excitement that would be comfortable for most babies. This is often difficult for parents to sense, or difficult for them to accept. It looks too much like rejection.

With these principles in mind, we should reconsider the *mal de mere* argument. Unpopular as it is, might it not be true? Given that some babies are more difficult than others, is it not still true that some parents would have more difficulty than other parents, no matter what baby they were presented with? As a concrete case for discussion, take the following detailed transcript by Sander (1962). I chose this particular vignette because Sander's article inspired many of the more recent studies I have cited in this book, and because it places the problems of face-to-face interaction in the larger context of daily life. In fact, Mrs. C. is by no means an extreme case. She could be any of us, at one time or another, with our own firstborns. The infant is 4 weeks old.

> After about a half hour there was a slight whimpering sound from the other room. Mrs. C. immediately alerted to this, although it was only the faintest sound and then said that she had better wait until he really cried as she half got out of her seat, then sat down again, and then immediately got up and went to the baby. I followed her into the bedroom to look at him. The infant was lying in prone, head to the right, with some slight frown which did not seem like crying to me particularly. Mrs. C. turned him over and he lay quiet again. Again Mrs. C. said, looking at me questioningly, "I'd better wait until he really wakes up" and came back into the kitchen and sat down again. At another slight sound she got up again almost immediately, picked the baby up and brought him out, holding him first against her arm. He looked very sleepy and as though discomforted at being moved and he closed his eyes again. Mrs. C. then put him back in the bassinet; soon after this he began to cry, and she picked him up again. The whole sequence had a quality of a kind of disorganized indecision about it, as though Mrs. C. never once settled on any kind of action for more than a minute. Almost before she decided on one move, she was already reversing it.
>
> Once it was definitely ascertained that the baby was awake, Mrs. C. took him into the kitchen and held him against her arm in a sitting position. As he quieted, she tapped his nose and chin; this seemed to be an irritant that set him off crying, and Mrs. C. now shifted him against her shoulder. He looked very cozy in this position, his legs drawn up under him so that he was curled up in a kind of little ball, and cuddled against his mother's shoulder, very quiet now.
>
> As Mrs. C. had not given the baby his bath yet, she now decided to do this, taking him to a shelf by the sink and lying him down in supine. Actually there were a few moments of indecision again as she thought that she would give him his bath, then looked at me questioningly, and then continued to hold him, and finally got up and made the actual decision to bathe him. The baby began to cry as she laid him down, and

Mrs. C. shifted him about, tapped his chin and nose—all of
this with a kind of uncertainty. It seemed to me that she made
a great many small movements that gave me the sense of acute
discomfort in watching and seemed to have a similar effect on
the baby.

As the baby activated his arms, he seemed to try to get his
hand to his mouth. He seemed not able to do this, and cried
briefly and then quieted. Mrs. C. spoke to him, tapped his
nose, and he again began to cry and Mrs. C., looking very
distressed, pushed a pacifier into his mouth. She said that he
was hungry and that he didn't like the pacifier, but the baby
quieted again. As he yawned and stretched his arms a bit, the
pacifier dropped out and Mrs. C. immediately put it back in.
It would drop out again soon and the baby would seem to be
yawning and stretching. But Mrs. C. seemed to take this as the
beginning of a cry, although the baby looked quite content to
me, and pushed the pacifier in his mouth again. This was repeated several times. Mrs. C. said to me, "I'll let you watch
him and go finish my cigarette." [Sander, 1962, p. 149]

Where is the "mother-infant system" in this description? Baby C.
was playing his role correctly, so far as we conceive of the human infant
having *evolved* as part of a system. He whimpered on awakening, cried
when he was irritated, cuddled when he was held, and so forth. The
problem was his mother. Her "great many small movements" and "in-
decision" and "looking very distressed" were simply failures to tune in
to his rhythms and self-regulations.[1] For whatever reason, her behavior
seems to have been motivated by her own needs and reactions more
than by his. (Specifically, her own needs for a pacifier, as we learn at
the end.)

So, if this incident turned out to be characteristic of Mrs. C. over
many weeks and even years, and if her case were representative of a
sizable group of parents, I would be ready to go back to the *mal de mere*
interpretation, even if this conclusion put me at odds with prevailing
recommendations to clinicians. However, it does not. Even when invoking the "system," most other authors continue to emphasize prevention work, coaching, and therapy with the mother. It turns out that
their recommendations, embodied in some successful intervention programs with mothers and infants, are actually more consistent with the

1. Obviously, this mother's anxiety and sense of incompetence were amplified by the
observer's presence in her home. Today, we know how to establish rapport, to be less
obtrusive, and to reduce our subjects' self-consciousness; but the problem is always there
to some extent. Keep in mind that one is not trying to make an estimate of what Mrs. C.'s
behavior is like when she is alone; instead, one is comparing her with other mothers who
were observed under equally obtrusive conditions, yet were not affected as she was.

three conclusions listed above than they are with the concept of "system" or with the notion of intersubjectivity in the young infant.

To put this another way, my theory of the young infant and his relation to the parental system is significantly different from that of Brazelton et al. (1979), for example, yet I cannot disagree with their recommendations. Does this mean the theory does not matter? No. A false theory can lead to good recommendations sometimes, but it cannot do so as often or as specifically as a more correct theory can. The truth is that the notion of mother-infant "system" did not really generate those intervention models. Pediatricians and psychologists generated them intuitively, then reached back into the literature of general systems theory (rather superficially, I have argued) for some rhetoric in support of their intuitions. The acceptance of a given intervention model by practitioners depends upon empirical demonstrations of its results in controlled studies; so in that sense the source of the model does not matter. The danger lies in the possibility that some authors may come to believe that the success of such interventions lends support to the romantic notions about babies that were used to justify them.

Is Intervention Necessary?

All of my own investigations concerned normal development among American babies and normal mother-infant interaction, with special reference to phenomena—notably the many forms of turn-taking—that we believed to be species-universal. For that reason, this work has little or no consequence for the majority of parents and infants. The things I have been describing are robust: They normally happen without any experts' intervention.

Some might argue that parents need new techniques today because our world is to some extent an "unnatural" one, our survival problems are different from those of our ancestors, and our society is changing more rapidly than ever before. But these facts only strengthen my conviction that most of the practical recommendations one might fabricate would be likely to do more harm, if adopted, than good. Furthermore, most books and magazine articles aimed at parents are self-serving nonsense, shaped more by what it is popular to say than by any actual results of research.

On one hand, it is hard to imagine a significant revision in theories of human development not having any implications at all. On the other hand, a little knowledge about some of our studies could actually be detrimental to normal parent-infant interaction. For example, we discovered that mothers' jiggling does not have quite the effect mothers think it has on their babies' sucking. Suppose we therefore tell mothers, "Don't keep jiggling; just give a brief jiggle and stop. Then wait for the baby to respond." Is it wise to tell people things nature has contrived for them to learn on their own? I assume that my own understanding of the phenomenon is only partially correct, that there is more to this business than we yet understand. The way most mothers adjust to the feeding task is undoubtedly more adaptive, more suited to their individual infants, and more effective than any instructions I could give them.

To take another example, one of the things I have said in this book is that a baby is more organism than person, has neither a mind nor a self until late in the first year, but that adults are tricked into treating babies as communicating partners. If that is true, then psychology should keep it as a trade secret. There is good reason for letting parents deceive themselves in this regard, and nothing to be gained by taking the debate into the public arena.[2] The trend over the past 10 or 20 years to regard newborns and young infants as intelligent, gesturing persons has been entirely benign, from the point of view of the popular lore. Its only deficiency has been in terms of a rigorous theory; it is only as scholars, not as parents, that we need to know the truth.

Despite these disclaimers, one is tempted to translate what one finds to be the "normal" patterns of parent-infant interaction within a given culture into diagnostic and prescriptive recommendations. There must be some mothers who adjust their jiggling better than others do—some who treat their babies as people more consistently than others do, who play with them more effectively, talk to them more intelligently, derive more joy from them, or pump more into them. If these kinds of behavior have indeed evolved for a reason, if they are important for the infant's development, then surely more is better; or, perhaps, a moderate amount of such activity is best, and either too much or too little is bad.

The main problem with that argument is that it is an oversimplification. It can only be applied on a case-by-case basis; the very meaning of "a moderate amount" is different with each case. If we cannot afford to counsel parents individually and in depth, we certainly have no business making ambiguous generalizations. When we are prepared to take upon ourselves the responsibilities of therapists, we can make interpretations of the kind implicit in Sander's commentary above. But when we are tempted to write prescriptions for the readers of Sunday supplements, we had better limit ourselves to harmless bromides.

Attempting to translate a theory of normal development, based on processes that are seen in all parent-infant interactions, into an explanation of developmental problems along the "continuum of caretaking casualty" (Sameroff & Chandler, 1975) faces two major difficulties. First,

2. In fact, Cohler (1975) has found that mothers hospitalized for postpartum depression tend to be those who do not see their babies as capable of reciprocal social interaction.

the universal processes need not correspond to dimensions of individual differences. Second, dimensions of individual differences in the normal range need not correspond to the important discrimination between normal and abnormal interaction processes.

We have already said some things about the first question. We tested that hypothesis when we analyzed continuity among our many measures of infant behavior, maternal behavior, and interaction contingencies across the different domains and across time (Chapter 3). We concluded that there are not, in fact, enduring patterns of interaction established in the early months, as many authors had speculated there would be on the basis of the idea of the mother-infant system. We concluded that (in a "low-risk" sample like ours) each new domain of interaction gives parent and infant a new chance,[3] and there is no evidence their interaction in that new domain (e.g., in the instruction situation at 6 months) is any different than it would be if they were meeting for the first time. (Perhaps the most graphic way to express this is that one should not hesitate to adopt a 6-month-old just because one has not shared his "crucial" first 6 months of interaction.) In short, the various phenomena we focused upon seem to be overdetermined. So many intrinsic and extrinsic factors determine them that they do not depend upon "how well" the interaction proceeded at earlier stages. This explains how there can be individual differences within each domain, yet little or no continuity from one to the next.

Does this mean that the various phenomena are unimportant? No. I think they are like vitamin C. We all need some vitamin C. Yet individual differences in vitamin C intake—say, whether we get 100 milligrams a day or 500—may not be correlated with health, because it is only the difference between 0 and 30 milligrams that matters. Most of us get more than we need, and our kidneys eliminate the excess. This does not make it unimportant. It may be vital to human life and growth. In the research described in this book, we have looked at phenomena that are vital to human life and growth. They are universally present (though not in equal amounts), I believe, because they are a crucial part of the process by which an organism endowed with a remarkable nervous system and a very slow timetable of maturation is transformed into a creature with language and a mind. Precisely because of their importance, they are so overdetermined that individual differences in their

---

3. By contrast, Goldberg, Brachfeld, and Divitto (1980) concluded that this may be precisely where the problems of high-risk infants and parents lie. They followed a sample of sick, premature babies through the first year, comparing them with a full-term and a healthy preterm sample: "The major differences between groups may be the ease with which they adapt to new developmental stages. Although most preterm dyads eventually establish a harmonious relationship, they may take longer to make a successful adaptation" (p. 149).

prevalence at different times or in different domains, and minor deprivations that an infant may suffer in one experience or another, happily cannot stop the larger process from running its course.

There is a common misconception among developmental psychologists that causation entails correlation. Everyone knows that the opposite is not the case, that correlation need not entail causation (two variables can be correlated without either of them having any effect upon the other), but many people's notions about causal factors in development automatically translate to an assumption about correlations. For example, they assume that if parents' baby talk helps children's language development, there ought to be a correlation between how extensively parents resort to baby talk and how rapidly their children acquire language. This is not necessarily true. If some baby talk is necessary, and if all parents use some, and if the excess beyond that necessary amount is simply harmless, then there will be no correlation at all between the two variables. That is how it is with vitamin C and with most of the phenomena I have discussed in this book. They are as important as they can be, yet their importance simply does not take the form of a dimension of individual differences that society ought to concern itself about.

The rest of this Epilogue deals with three exceptions to that disclaimer, under the headings of prevention, coaching, and therapy. Preventive programs are indicated for "high-risk" groups of mothers and infants, in whom we know there is a significant likelihood of developmental deficits that have been shown to be related either to maternal attitudes (my point 1 above) or to the baby's behavioral disorganization making it difficult to engage him in normal interaction (points 2 and 3). Coaching is indicated when such risk is based on individual assessment of interactions (point 3) and difficulties can be traced to special characteristics or needs of the baby (point 2), which can be communicated to his parents (point 1). Therapy (I shall argue, *family* therapy) is indicated when we can diagnose consistent dysfunctional styles in parents. However, I am not at all sure we can yet distinguish symptoms of serious disturbance in parental behavior from mere personality differences, which are none of a clinician's business. Sander's case of Mrs. C., for example—for all that we might agree in criticizing her indecisive style, she certainly did not behave in bizarre enough fashion to warrant therapy. Only if her apparently dysfunctional interactions were observed in the course of a workup with converging indications of ambivalence about the infant, depression, unrealistic fears, or the like, would we have reason to recommend therapy. In other words, we would do so because of problems in the mother herself or in the adult system including her spouse and their parents (point 1) rather than because of the so-called mother-infant dyad.

Indications for either coaching or therapy require that the clinician have had sufficient opportunity to observe parents and infant together over a substantial period of time and also that he or she be in a position to counsel them. This might happen when a pediatrician examines the infant whose parent reports feeding or sleeping problems, colic, or the like, or when a social worker investigates a report of abuse or neglect. Since these complaints are only likely to detect a small proportion of all dysfunctional parent-infant dyads, we ought to precede our consideration of coaching and therapy with a discussion of preventive treatments applied to high-risk groups.

The High-Risk Newborn

To be precise, we call an infant "high-risk" on the basis of a medical diagnosis at birth, whereas a mother may be "high-risk" on the basis of her condition at that time, her history, or merely her socioeconomic status. The use of the same term for several different categories can be confusing. But it turns out that the two kinds of risk, medical and socioeconomic, co-occur more often than chance. For example, a premature infant is medically at risk if (as is often the case) the respiratory system is vulnerable to infection. A teenage mother is socially at risk if (as is often the case) she is not yet emotionally or cognitively ready to assume the responsibilities of motherhood. Teenage mothers have more than their share of preterm deliveries, partly because of stressful pregnancies and partly because they themselves may not yet be physiologically mature. The transaction model (a P-model, by the way) explains how the baby's frailty and lack of responsiveness elicits a natural reaction of withdrawal on the mother's part, how her own immaturity and ambivalence accentuate this reaction, which is precisely the opposite of what she would need to do to elicit more optimal responses from the baby.

Let us begin with what happens to babies who are diagnosed as at risk. These are essentially all babies who are kept in intensive care in the hospital nursery for 2 or more days (about 1 in 10 live births in American hospitals at the present time). Intensive care is indicated at birth for a wide variety of reasons: low birthweight, heroin withdrawal symptoms, fetal alcohol syndrome, apnea, cardiac arhythmia, preeclamptic toxemia, anoxia, infections, and so forth. Many of these infants have been shown to have a significant likelihood of developmental deficits in the first year of life, even when gestational age is controlled statistically (Drage & Berendes, 1966; Fisch, Gravem, & Engel, 1968; Fitzhardinge, Pape, Arstikaitis, Boyle, Ashby, Rowley, Netley, & Swyer [!], 1976). Field, Dempsey, and Shuman (1979) found that mothers were as sensitive to these deficits as trained clinicians were. Although motor delays have been reported more often than mental delays, Goldstein, Caputo, and Taub (1976) found deficits among preterm infants in Bayley mental scores at 12 months, and Field et al. (1979) also found language delays and social-behavioral problems such as irritability and hyperactivity in their respiratory-distress sample as late as age 24 months.

However, once a high-risk infant survives what Clement Smith (1951) called "the valley of the shadow of birth," he tends to catch up gradually, so that there are relatively few deficits that continue with any high probability into the school years. This fact—that pre- and perinatal problems do not lead with any certainty to developmental deficits—is a principal reason for supposing that those infants who do show deficits must have suffered from poor subsequent interactions with their environments on top of their initial problems (Drage, Berendes, & Fisher, 1969; Sameroff & Chandler, 1975; Sigman & Parmelee, 1979).

In those studies where deficits are found in follow-up studies of these infants, the deficits are not specific disabilities (as they are with other birth defects such as chromosomal anomalies or specific central nervous system damage). Instead, the deficits appear in gross measures such as IQ, and the categories of infants in whom they are found are global categories (e.g., premature birth, which occurs for many different reasons). This makes sense, because the global measures and combinations of predictors are likely to tap chronic problems that in turn lead to cumulative deficits (Parmelee & Michaelis, 1971; Parmelee & Haber, 1975; Sameroff & Chandler, 1975), while acute, transitory traumas such as anoxia are compensated for by the growing organism (MacKinney, 1958; Stechler, 1964). In short, an infant of more than 1500 grams born to a middle-class family, who spends the first few weeks of life in an intensive care unit for any reason, will probably be indistinguishable from any other child of his age before he starts school. But when an infant suffers from hyaline membrane disease on top of his prematurity, for example, and his mother is an unmarried inner-city teenager, one can begin to make statistically significant predictions of developmental problems. There is apparently enough resiliency in human development so that an infant has to start life with two strikes against him, one of which is economic or educational disadvantage among his caretakers, before there is a significant likelihood of his striking out. Even then, we cannot predict in advance whether his problem will be in terms of growth, motor development, language, or being battered by his parent (Klein & Stern, 1971).

The best predictor of whether a high risk infant will show later deficits is socioeconomic status (Pasamanick, Knobloch, & Lilienfeld, 1956; Drillien, 1964; McDonald, 1964; Illsley, 1966; Werner, Bierman, &

French, 1971; Birch & Gussow, 1970). For example, Werner et al. found that preterm and dysmature infants weighing between 1500 and 2500 grams, if they survived, were, by the time they reached age 10, no different on the average from those who had been of normal weight.[4] Their social class, however, was a highly significant predictor of deficits. Thus the deficits were not determined by the low birthweight per se, but by how well or poorly the child and his caretakers were able to make up for the initial risk factor over the next few years.

Recurring results of that kind are consistent with the idea of post-partum environmental factors: Economically or educationally disadvantaged mothers fail to do something middle-class mothers do, or they do something middle-class mothers refrain from doing. Unfortunately, the results do not allow us to rule out congenital factors. Pregnancy disorders are more predictive of later deficits than any perinatal factors, and pregnancy disorders are also far more common among lower-class women (Pasamanick & Knobloch, 1966). The incidence of low birthweight among American blacks is twice that among whites (Niswander & Gordon, 1972). So socioeconomic status is not only a predictor of recovery from newborn risk factors, it is a predictor of whether the infant will be born at risk in the first place.

Socioeconomic status has little explanatory power since it confounds at least a half-dozen distinguishable factors: nutrition, age of mother, education, stability of home, life style, and genetic factors. It is, however, the most practical variable we can use to identify that group in which perinatal problems are most likely to be magnified rather than compensated for by caretakers.

Separation. In many cases, the only "risk" we can predict is that the mother may not form the strong attachment to her newborn that would normally keep her closely involved in handling and playing with him. The infant is adequately cared for in the intensive care unit, but for that very reason—that someone else is caring for him—we should be concerned about the mother. Sick or premature babies are, in fact, exposed to all the critical sensory experiences to which a newborn must be exposed. No critical attachment has to occur in the baby at this age to any particular caretaker. The baby who receives the stimulation that is now routine in a hospital nursery is not put at risk by being denied the chance to get it from one primary caretaker or to form a lifelong attachment to her in the first weeks of life. He is at risk because *she* has been denied the chance to form an attachment to *him*. That is what all the currently

4. Normal weight at birth would be between 2500 and 4000 grams. About 50%–60% of low-birthweight infants are small for gestational age ("dysmature") rather than premature births (Chase, Erhardt, & Nelson, 1973).

fashionable talk about "bonding" is about: bonding the mother to her baby.

Klaus and Kennell (1976) have assembled evidence that in humans, as in many other mammals, early contact with her infant facilitates the mother's formation of psychological attachment. They theorize that there is a critical period for bonding, and that the routine separation of mother and infant in hospitals interferes with the natural attachment process that would otherwise occur.[5] This hypothesis inspired a series of experiments providing extra sensuous, emotionally gratifying contact between mothers and babies, usually naked skin-to-skin contact, in the first few days of life. These studies provide some evidence that extra contact makes a difference—but only in high-risk mothers.[6] The studies do not consistently show that an average group of mothers would form any stronger attachments to their *healthy* babies or behave in any way differently with them after having extra contact with them in the hospital room. The literature has sometimes been summarized as though this were what it indicated, but only because those citing it were eager to justify what they already believed, namely, that hospital procedures are dehumanizing and that anything that enhances sensuousness or makes the lying-in period more of a family affair must be good. (Their valid point is that the vast majority of babies ever born were born at home, not in hospitals.)

Even with babies who are premature or otherwise "at risk," no one has shown that fully prepared mothers who are unambivalent about wanting their babies and economically capable of caring for them are in any danger of withdrawing from those babies if they do not receive an extra-contact intervention in the first day or so after delivery. It is true that the infant who is kept in the intensive care nursery is even more separated from his mother than usual, both in terms of quality of contact and in terms of length of stay (Kennell, 1978). But the majority of babies who have to remain in intensive care for a few weeks or even months after their mothers go home from the hospital are received into their

5. Seashore, Leifer, Barnett, and Liederman (1973) found that the lack of opportunity to interact with their infants during the first few days postpartum reduced mothers' confidence in their caretaking abilities. Fanaroff (reported in Kennell, 1978) found that the incidence of mothering disorders (essentially, lack of attachment) was 25 times as high among mothers who visited the intensive care unit less than three times per week as among those who visited three or more times.

6. The principal extra-contact experiments that succeeded in bringing maternal attachment up to normal and significantly increasing a number of interaction measures during the first year were by Ringler, Kennell, Jarvella, Navojosky, and Klaus (1975) with inner-city black mothers; Hales, Lozoff, Sosa, and Kennell (1977) with Guatemalan Indian mothers; and deChateau (1979) in Sweden. In a follow-up of the Ringler et al. study, consequences were found in the children's language development at age 5 (Ringler, Trause, Klaus, & Kennell, 1978). On the other hand, with white middle-class mothers, Ottaviano, Campbell, and Taylor (1979) found no effect on infant-mother attachment at 1 year.

families with at least as much rejoicing when they finally go home as would have been their due had they come on time. Exceptions tend to be among highly disadvantaged families or families in crisis.

Early contact interventions, carefully compared with control groups, have achieved striking differences among disadvantaged mothers, for example, inner-city black unwed teenagers. Even without extra contact, Vietze, O'Connor, Falsey, and Altemeier (1978) showed that rooming-in alone greatly reduced failure to thrive and child abuse in an inner-city sample. At this point, one can only speculate about the mechanisms involved. There is certainly nothing in the studies to suggest any phys-iological effects of the naked tactile experience, which would justify the comparisons to what occurs in animals (Schneirla, Rosenblatt, & Tobach, 1963). A more plausible theory is that a high-risk mother is one who has many needs conflicting with her need to mother. Babies normally have the power to intensify the latter need and to satisfy it, to make us feel wonderful about ourselves. Once adults reach the stage in their own life cycle when they are ready to embark on the task of parenthood, practically any warm little body will do, so long as it is "our baby." These same processes affect an inner-city teenager, too; but they may work a little more slowly. Perhaps extra time with the baby allows them to do so.

Mothers' perceptions of their infants by age 1 month have been found to predict developmental disorders at age 10 years (Broussard, 1976). This study and others do not really establish how much the ma-ternal perceptions are due to experiences a mother has with her infant in the first few weeks and how much to attitudes she had before he was born (Cohler, 1975; Bibring, Dwyer, Huntington, & Valenstein, 1961). But the important point is that those perceptions can be altered. The early contact procedures of Klaus and Kennell are clearly not the only procedures that can be used to set normal interaction in motion: Any-thing that helps to overcome the effects of separation, anxiety, or acute depression during the lying-in period will continue to affect the infant's cognitive growth through his continuing social involvement with the mother. When the Klaus and Kennell procedures are impossible because the infant is incapable of surviving an hour or more of naked contact with his mother, other procedures may accomplish the same effects: make the mother familiar with her infant not as an object but as a highly significant person. Indeed, steps are now being taken to involve mothers (and fathers) in the care of their sick newborns in the intensive care nurseries in many hospitals in the United States, England, Sweden, and elsewhere.

The basis for all such concerns is the assumption that parents' con-ceptions about the child—those attitudes they will begin reflecting back to him—come in part from their reaction to his infancy. The impressions parents gather from their infant are bound to vary greatly with individual differences in infant temperament, intelligence, attractiveness, ease of handling, and so forth. They will continue to apply their conclusions later, when evaluating and labeling him. Although some of the parents' fantasies about their baby are well entrenched before they ever see him, there is certainly a great deal that comes as a reaction to the baby's behavior. While I doubt that these reactions have much *immediate* effect on the infant's personality, they affect him by enduring into the later years when they are transmitted to the child in verbal as well as non-verbal ways.

The Pragmatics of Intervention. Intervention programs have been aimed at many different groups of high-risk infants and/or high-risk mothers. A remarkable and promising feature of these studies is that the interventions involved are often relatively small. In the Hales et al. study (1977) mentioned above, all the mothers had their babies by the bedside from 9 A.M. to 5 P.M. each day, the difference between treatment and control group amounting to only a 45-minute period of skin-to-skin contact. Klaus and Kennell do not suggest that any effects—least of all the complex effects on children's language by age 5—occur as a direct result of the 45-minute experience. Whatever the initial effect of the experience on the mother might be (e.g., releasing her from certain inhibitions regarding intimacy with the fragile infant), it is multiplied a thousandfold as it leads to more rewarding caretaking and play experiences with the infant over the succeeding weeks. The same point has been made about preschool intervention projects such as Levenstein's (1971) and Slaughter's (1979). A home visitor does not alter the child's IQ by means of a 30-minute interaction with certain toys; she introduces subtle changes that affect subsequent transactions between mother and child. The only effective intervention is one with a "multiplier effect" that carries beyond the program, as if one had infiltrated a secret agent into the home to continue the work (Deutsch & Deutsch, 1967). No one has found or even suggested a single crucial interactive process that, once learned, sets everything else in motion automatically. But the human capacity for nurturance and sensitivity to infants seems to be sufficiently universal so that parents' skills begin to develop once their attitudes have been affected. (And in the family system, affecting one caretaker often affects other members' behavior with the infant as well.)

Field and her colleagues at the University of Miami have conducted a number of intervention studies with significant results. In one, Widmayer and Field (1980) let teenaged disadvantaged mothers watch Brazelton examinations of their preterm newborns and then asked them to fill out weekly rating scales similar to the Brazelton ratings. This experience alone apparently produced more optimal face-to-face inter-action scores (rated from videotaped play sessions at 1 and 4 months) and smoother feedings than in the control group. (Control group mothers had also been asked to fill out questionnaires weekly, but had not had the experience of seeing their babies' capacities brought out by the Brazelton procedure.) Almost as important as the positive results of this experiment is the fact that the intervention cost virtually nothing, since the Brazelton assessments were already being performed routinely in the nursery. The intervention consisted simply in including the mothers in the assessment and allowing them to see that their babies could track moving objects, orient to stimulation, quiet themselves, and, perhaps most important, engage the intense interest of an adult for half an hour. I recall that in our own project, when we asked the mothers at 6 months what they had liked most about our visits, the most frequent answer was, with no hesitation, "When they were examining him the first time they came to the house, and they had him looking at that red ball"—referring to item 5 of the Brazelton exam.

Coaching and Therapy

The foregoing conclusions with respect to preventive programs—that they exert their effects by altering the mother's ideas about her infant rather than by affecting the infant directly—are consistent with the views that I have presented throughout this book. The newborn is not really a member of any social system, except in his parents' fantasies. However, this does not mean that all infants are alike, or that sick infants elicit the same degree of parental involvement in their rhythms of feeding, attention, and arousal as normal infants do.

Disorganization. Another set of studies suggests that healthy full-term neonates provide important kinds of feedback while their mothers are feeding and handling them, and that a disorganized neonate either fails to do so or elicits such overcompensations from his mother that his interaction is set off on an increasingly disturbed course (Bakeman, 1978; Field, 1982). "Disorganization" means an incapacity for sustained response to the caretaker's face and voice; poor integration of the motor and kinesthetic systems with the thermal regulating system of skin, lungs, and heart; and an inability to calm down to an awake, calm state after handling. Gorski, Davison, and Brazelton (1979) have proposed a model for treating such infants and their mothers prior to discharge from the nursery: (1) The disorganized neonate requires quiet, gentle handling, on a "demand" schedule (waiting for the infant's own state changes without attempting to hasten or delay them). Nurses and physicians examining the baby can help him to marshal his integrative processes by supporting his limbs during handling, avoiding sudden movements and changes, and limiting nearby traffic in the nursery. (2) As important as the standard neurological and physical examinations is the assessment of the degree and nature of disorganization, including the infant's recovery from periods of handling and stimulation. (3) Assessment must include finding each infant's strengths, not just weaknesses: the conditions under which he is best able to attend and to give reinforcing feedback to a caretaker rather than withdrawing from the interaction. (4) The results of these assessments can and should be communicated to each mother, which itself requires sensitive interaction so as to meet her emotional needs and counter her fears with specific information about the baby. (5) Both patients (mother and infant) must be treated on a case-by-case basis rather than prescriptively or categorically. The variance among high-risk infants is greater than the difference between them and normal infants.

With older infants, organization of behavior is surely no less important. The studies discussed in Chapters 3-6 suggest that (1) the word *organization* can be used meaningfully to describe more and more aspects of the infant's behavior, in an increasing variety of situations, between ages 2 and 6 months; (2) parental frames capitalize on whatever degree of cyclicity and predictability the infant makes available at a given age. The largest number of observational studies happen to have focused on the face-to-face situation, which we think manifests important features of other kinds of interaction as well.

The maintenance of mutual gaze during face-to-face interaction is a universal goal among mothers, but in its intensity it is a source of variance from one dyad to another. Several investigators have noticed that mutual gaze is also a variable distinguishing disordered infants from normals, and indeed the reaction of mothers who consistently fail to attract their infants' gaze indicates their awareness that something is wrong. Gaze aversion is one of the symptoms of autism, and infant gaze aversion may be an early sign of autism before other symptoms appear (Hutt & Ounsted, 1966). Robson (1967) pointed out the importance of eye-to-eye contact in establishing the mother's attachment to her infant and perception of him as a "real person." Greenberg (1971), Brazelton et al. (1974), Stern (1974), and Field (1982) have described how some mothers resort to overstimulation in reaction to infants who resist eye contact—thus driving the infants into even more prolonged gaze aversion. Beckwith and Cohen (1978) found that mutual gaze between mothers and preterm infants was one predictor of cognitive development at 2 years, while a full battery of neurological assessments on the infant alone did not predict. Of course, the behaviors during interaction that predicted complete recovery from the risky birth included many of the same behaviors that Cohen and Beckwith (1976) found more prevalent among middle-class mothers. So we cannot say whether successful attempts at maintaining mutual gaze were really a factor in preventing deficits, or were merely a characteristic of those mothers who *also* managed to prevent deficits. For example, mutual gaze might be easier to achieve when nutrition is optimal.

It is not only the mothers of preterm and dysmature infants who sometimes have problems achieving mutual gaze. All parents do at some time or other, and they naturally differ in their acceptance of the infant's increasing interest in other objects of attention. In Chapter 5 I quoted Richards's description of the "constant and unphased barrage of stimulation" to which some of his mothers subjected their infants. Nor is mutual gaze the whole story; it is merely one manifestation of how adult and infant behavior fit together appropriately, or can fail to fit together if a parent is out of tune with the infant's cycles.

The large number of published descriptions of the face-to-face situation make it clear that infant attention is related to the adult's activity in the following way. Infants avert their gaze from a still face, but they also avert their gaze from a face that is trying too hard to be animated and to hold their attention. Moderately active faces are the most successful in holding the infant; for example, when Tronick, Als, Adamson, Wise, and Brazelton (1978) asked mothers to count slowly, when Field (1982) asked them to imitate their infants, or when she asked them to become silent each time the infant looked away. These interventions simply produce the kind of behavior that an average mother most typically does with a normal infant in face-to-face interaction, as we saw in earlier chapters (Kaye & Fogel, 1980). The clinical problem, then, is to identify parents who are too anxious or impatient, or whose infants have low thresholds of overstimulation, and teach them to slow down or "cool it" when the baby seems to be backing off from them.

The Family System. A great deal more goes on in the mental-social world of the family than simply "parent-infant interaction." The matrix of development is the family, not the mother-infant dyad. The family system exists before the infant's birth, forces him to become an apprentice to it, and slowly makes him into a full member. A mother is not free to behave in any way she wishes with her baby, nor to hold any view of him that we might suggest to her. Any changes that a clinician can hope to produce in her (or in a father, for that matter) are constrained by the structure and functioning of the family.

One of the first appearances of systems concepts in psychology was in the field of family therapy (Bateson, 1949; Bateson, Jackson, Haley,

& Weakland, 1956; Watzlawick, Beavin, & Jackson, 1967). Workers in that field have become expert at spotting boundaries between subsystems within the family, describing coalitions and competitions that occur among them, and intervening so as to alter the boundaries, coalitions, and patterns of interaction. In a troubled family—for example, one that is avoiding confrontation with one member's alcoholism, or one that is structured primarily to serve the members' neurotic needs rather than to facilitate their development through the life cycle—the fact that the infant's role exists so much in the parents' fantasies can make him particularly vulnerable. On the positive side, it can also make the infant a useful instrument for family change.

There are many ways the baby's arrival can be used by a dysfunctional family to make various boundaries rigid or diffuse. One of the most common patterns is to reject the prior child, now obsolete or expendable, exaggerating his or her shortcomings in comparison with the new improved model. The opposite also occurs, where the baby is invidiously compared with memories, real or distorted, about what a "good baby" the elder sibling was. Both of these maneuvers become extremely dangerous in a stepfamily situation, where the different children represent different fathers or different mothers.

Another dysfunctional structure is the use of an infant to establish coalitions and boundaries among adults in the extended family. (The "he says" phenomenon described in Chapter 4 serves this purpose nicely.) For example, sometimes an unmarried mother and her family of origin may use the baby to lure the father into the family. The grandmother can help by temporarily taking charge of other children who are not his. Conversely, the birth of an infant can also be used to drive the father away, or used by him as an excuse to be driven away. There were families illustrating each of these patterns in our "normal" sample. Of course, they can be functional structures for some families; there is more than one normal model.

My point here is that pediatricians and psychologists ought to be asking more than simply, "How well are these parents meeting the baby's developmental needs?" Even if the child's needs are met for the time being, a family may be at risk in the future if the developmental needs of *all* members are not being met. Some people, unfortunately, have babies just so as not to develop. A young woman who is ambivalent about leaving her parents' nest may get pregnant so as to give them a reason to continue taking care of her (even if she is married); another woman gets pregnant for the opposite reason, so as to prove that she has come of age; another so as to give her parents a child in place of her, or her husband's parents a child in exchange for him. These immature adults want to be seen as grown up, but they do not yet really want to be parents. Tragically, they deny themselves (or are denied by their families) the stage of independent adulthood before parenthood.

Parents' fantasies about who their baby is play a large role in his cognitive and social development, but they play just as large a role in the functioning of the family itself. I suspect it is inevitable that a baby will be used instrumentally, as a factor in altering or maintaining particular subsystem relations, just as it is inevitable that he will be seen as a person and communicated with as if he were a full partner. A clinician who sought to prevent the infant from being used in that way, out of a misguided advocacy of the infant, would only fail and perhaps precipitate even worse abuses. Instead, family therapists can try to achieve a balance between adults' uses of the baby for their own purposes and their willingness to allow him to develop even if that requires them to change with him.

Conclusion. This Epilogue has suggested some changes in the way a psychologist, pediatrician, or other practitioner might view the "mother-infant system." First, while recognizing that the newborn will be a member of the family in the minds of other family members, we must also see him objectively as an organism lacking any real understanding of that system, any real communication with other members, any role in the planning or restructuring of the system as a whole. This puts the infant at risk of being used for ends that may not be in his own interest. On the other hand, it ensures some initial flexibility with respect to the particular adults who take on the parental role.

Second, though I, like most other investigators, have focused upon the interaction between infants and their mothers, in reality the mother is only one component of the family system. By the time the infant has become a member of a social system, it will be of that family system rather than merely of the dyad. Attempting to change his destiny by intervening only in the dyad will have limitations. It can only succeed to the extent the "multiplier effect" can be set into motion. This clearly depends upon the mother's relation to the family as a whole, and upon her broader support system beyond the family.

References

Abravanel, E., Levan-Goldschmidt, E., and Stevenson, M. Action imitation: the early phase of infancy. *Child Development*, 1976, 47, 1032–1044.

Ainsworth, M. Patterns of attachment behavior shown by the infant in interaction with his mother. *Merrill–Palmer Quarterly*, 1964, 10, 51–58.

———. *Infancy in Uganda*. Baltimore: Johns Hopkins Press, 1967.

———. Object relations, dependency, and attachment: A theoretical review of the infant-mother relationship. *Child Development*, 1969, 40, 969–1026.

Anderson, B., Vietze, P., and Dokecki, P. Reciprocity in vocal interactions of mothers and infants. *Child Development*, 1977, 48, 1676–1681.

Austin, J. *How to Do Things with Words*. New York: Oxford University Press, 1962.

Bakeman, R. High–risk infant: Is the risk social? Presented to the American Psychological Association, Toronto, August 1978.

Baldwin, J. M. *Mental Development in the Child and the Race*. New York: Macmillan, 1895.

———. *Social and Ethical Interpretations in Mental Development* (4th edition). New York: Macmillan, 1906. (First edition published in 1897)

Bandura, A. *Psychological Modeling: Conflicting Theories*. Chicago: Aldine Atherton, 1971.

Bandura, A., and Huston, A. Identification as a process of incidental learning. *Journal of Abnormal and Social Psychology*, 1961, 63, 311–318.

Bartlett, F. *Remembering*. London: Cambridge University Press, 1932.

Bates, E., Camaioni, L., and Volterra, V. The acquisition of performatives prior to speech. *Merrill-Palmer Quarterly*, 1975, 21, 205–226.

Bateson, G. Bali: The value system of a steady state. In M. Fortes (ed.), *Social Structure*. Oxford: Clarendon Press, 1949.

Bateson, G., Jackson, D., Haley, J., and Weakland, J. Toward a theory of schizophrenia. *Behavioral Science*, 1956, 1, 251–264.

Bateson, M. C. "The epigenesis of conversational interaction": A personal account of research development. In M. Bullowa (ed.), *Before Speech: The Beginning of Interpersonal Communication*. Cambridge: Cambridge University Press, 1979.

Beckwith, L., and Cohen, S. Preterm birth: Hazardous obstetrical and postnatal events as related to caregiver-infant behavior. *Infant Behavior and Development*, 1978, 1, 1–17.

Beckwith, L., Cohen, S., Kopp, C., Parmelee, A., and Marcy, T. Caregiver-infant interaction and early cognitive development in preterm infants. *Child Development*, 1976, 47, 579–587.

Bell, R. A re-interpretation of the direction of effects in studies of socialization. *Psychological Review*, 1968, 75, 81–95.

Belsky, J. Mother-father-infant interaction: A naturalistic observational study. *Developmental Psychology*, 1979, 15, 601–607.

Berger, P., and Luckmann, T. *The Social Construction of Reality*. Garden City, N.Y.: Doubleday, 1966.

Bernal, J. Crying during the first ten days of life and maternal responses. *Developmental Medicine and Child Neurology*, 1972, 14, 362–372.

Bernshtein, N. *The Coordination and Regulation of Movement*. New York: Pergamon Press, 1967. (Collection of papers originally published in Russian, 1935–1960)

Bibring, G., Dwyer, T., Huntington, D., and Valenstein, A. A study of the psychological processes in pregnancy and of the earliest mother-child relationship. *Psychoanalytic Study of the Child*, 1961, 16, 9–72.

Birch, H., and Gussow, G. *Disadvantaged Children*. New York: Grune & Stratton, 1970.

Bloom, L., Rocissano, L., and Hood, L. Adult-child discourse: Developmental interaction between information processing and linguistic knowledge. *Cognitive Psychology*, 1976, 8, 521–552.

Boden, M. *Purposive Explanation in Psychology*. Cambridge: Harvard University Press, 1972.

Booth, W. Kenneth Burke's way of knowing. *Critical Inquiry*, 1974, 1, 1–22.

Bornstein, M. Visual behavior of the young human infant: Relationships between chromatic and spatial perception and the activity of underlying brain mechanisms. *Journal of Experimental Child Psychology*, 1978, 26, 174–192.

Bower, T. G. R. Slant perception and shape constancy in infants. *Science*, 1966, 151, 832–834.

———. *Development in Infancy*. San Francisco: Freeman, 1974.

———. Infant perception of the third dimension and object concept development. In L. Cohen and P. Salapatek (eds.), *Infant Perception: From Sensation to Cognition* (Vol. 2). New York: Academic Press, 1975.

Bower, T. G. R., and Paterson, J. The separation of place, movement and object in the world of the infant. *Journal of Experimental Child Psychology,* 1973, 15, 161–168.

Bowerman, M. Semantic factors in the acquisition of rules for word use and sentence construction. In D. Morehead and A. Morehead (eds.), *Normal and Deficient Child Language.* Baltimore: University Park Press, 1976.

Bowlby, J. *Attachment.* London: Hogarth Press, 1969.

Brazelton, T. B. The early mother-infant adjustment. *Pediatrics,* 1963, 31, 931–937.

Brazelton, T. B., Koslowski, B., and Main, M. The origins of reciprocity. In M. Lewis and L. Rosenblum (eds.), *The Effect of the Infant on Its Caregiver.* New York: Wiley, 1974.

Brazelton, T. B., Yogman, M., Als, H., and Tronick, E. The infant as a focus for family reciprocity. In M. Lewis and L. Rosenblum (eds.), *The Child and its Family.* New York: Plenum Press, 1979.

Bronson, G. *Infants' Reactions to Unfamiliar Persons and Novel Objects. Monographs of the Society for Research in Child Development,* 1972, 47, No. 148.

Broussard, R. Neonatal prediction and outcome at 10–11 years. *Child Psychiatry and Human Development,* 1976, 7, 85–93.

Brown, J. Non-nutritive sucking in great ape and human newborns. In J. Bosma (ed.), *Oral Sensation and Perception: Development in the Fetus and Infant.* Bethesda, Md.: U.S. Department of Health, Education and Welfare, 1973.

Brown, R. The development of WH questions in child speech. *Journal of Verbal Learning and Verbal Behavior,* 1968, 7, 279–290.

Browne, G., Rosenfeld, H., and Horowitz, F. Infant discrimination of facial expressions. *Child Development,* 1977, 48, 555–562.

Bruner, J. The growth and structure of skill. In K. J. Connolly (ed.), *Motor Skills in Infancy.* New York: Academic Press, 1971.

———. The nature and uses of immaturity. *American Psychologist,* 1972, 27, 688–704.

———. From communication to language: A psychological perspective. *Cognition,* 1975, 3, 255–287.

———. Early social interaction and language acquisition. In H. R. Schaffer (ed.), *Studies in Mother-Infant Interaction.* London: Academic Press, 1977.

Bryan, W., and Harter, N. Studies in the telegraphic language: The acquisition of a hierarchy of habits. *Psychological Review,* 1899, 6, 345–375.

Burd, A., Milewski, A., and Camras, L. Matching of facial gestures by young infants: Imitation or releasers? Presented to the Society for Research in Child Development, Boston, April 1981.

Butterworth, G. Object disappearance and error in Piaget's stage IV task. *Journal of Experimental Child Psychology,* 1977, 23, 391–401.

Callaghan, J. Anglo, Hopi, and Navajo infants and mothers: newborn behaviors, interaction styles, and child–rearing beliefs and practices. Ph.D. Dissertation, University of Chicago, 1981.

Campos, J., Emde, R., Gaensbauer, T., and Henderson, C. Cardiac and behavioral interrelationships in the reactions of infants to strangers. *Developmental Psychology*, 1975, 11, 589–601.

Campos, J., and Stenberg, C. Social referencing: An appraisal process crucial for infant emotional development. Presented to the Society for Research in Child Development, Boston, April 1981.

Caron, A., Caron, R., and Carlson, V. Do infants see objects or retinal images? Shape constancy revisited. *Infant Behavior and Development*, 1978, 1, 229–243.

Carpenter, G. Visual regard of moving and stationary faces in early infancy. *Merrill-Palmer Quarterly*, 1974, 20, 181–194.

Chappell, P., and Sander, L. Mutual regulation of the neonatal-maternal interactive process: Context for the origins of communication. In M. Bullowa (ed.), *Before Speech: The Beginning of Interpersonal Communication*. Cambridge: Cambridge University Press, 1979.

Charney, R. The comprehension of "here" and "there." *Journal of Child Language*, 1979, 6, 69–80.

———. Speech roles and the development of personal pronouns. *Journal of Child Language*, 1980, 7, 509–528. (a)

———. Pronoun errors in autistic children: Support for a social explanation. *British Journal of Disorders of Communication*, 1980, 15, 39–43. (b)

Chase, H., Erhardt, C., and Nelson, F. A study of risks, medical care, and infant mortality. *American Journal of Public Health*, Supplement, 1973, 63, 1–56.

Chess, S. Genesis of behavior disorder. In J. Howells (ed.), *Modern Perspectives in International Child Psychiatry*. New York: Brunner/Mazel, 1971.

Chomsky, N. Review of *Verbal Behavior* by B. F. Skinner. *Language*, 1959, 35, 26–58.

Clark, R. The transition from action to gesture. In A. Lock (ed.), *Action, Gesture, and Symbol: The Emergence of Language*. New York: Academic Press, 1978.

Clarke-Stewart, A., and Hevey, C. Longitudinal relations in repeated observations of mother–child interaction from 1 to 2½ years. *Developmental Psychology*, 1981, 17, 127–145.

Cohen, L., and Strauss, M. Concept acquisition in the human infant. *Child Development*, 1979, 50, 419–424.

Cohen, S., and Beckwith, L. Maternal language in infancy. *Developmental Psychology*, 1976, 12, 371–372.

———. Preterm infant interaction with the caregiver in the first year of life and competence at age 2. *Child Development*, 1979, 50, 767–776.

Cohler, B. Character, mental illness and mothering. In H. Grunebaum, J. Weiss, B. Cohler, C. Hartman, and D. Gallant (eds.), *Mentally Ill Mothers and Their Children*. Chicago: University of Chicago Press, 1975.

Collis, G. Visual co-orientation and maternal speech. In H. R. Schaffer (ed.), *Studies in Mother-Infant Interaction*. London: Academic Press, 1977.

Cooley, C. *Human Nature and the Social Order*. New York: Scribner's, 1902.

Corsaro, W. The clarification request as a feature of adult interactive styles with young children. *Language and Society*, 1977, 6, 183–208.

Cox, D., and Lewis, P. *Statistical Analysis of Series of Events*. New York: Halsted, 1966.

Craik, K. *The Nature of Explanation*. London: Cambridge University Press, 1943.

Darwin, C. *On the Various Contrivances by which British and Foreign Orchids are Fertilised by Insects, and on the Good Effects of Inter–crossing*. London: Murray, 1862.

———. *The Expression of the Emotions in Man and Animals*. London: Murray, 1872.

deChateau, P. Long-term effects of early postpartum contact. Presented to the Society for Research in Child Development, San Francisco, March 1979.

Delacroix, H. De l'automatisme dans l'imitation. *Journal de Psychologie Normale et Pathologique*, 1921, XVIII, 97–139.

Delgado, J. *Physical Control of the Mind: Toward a Psychocivilized Society*. New York: Harper & Row, 1969.

Deutsch, C., and Deutsch, M. Brief reflections on the theory of early childhood enrichment programs. In M. Deutsch and Associates (eds.), *The Disadvantaged Child*. New York: Basic, 1967.

Deutsch, J. *The Structural Basis of Behavior*. London: Cambridge University Press, 1960.

DeVore, I., and Konner, M. Infancy in hunter-gatherer life: An ethological perspective. In N. White (ed.), *Ethology and Psychiatry*. Toronto: University of Toronto Press, 1974.

Dewey, J. *Democracy and Education*. New York: Macmillan, 1916.

———. The recovery of philosophy. In J. Dewey et al. (eds.), *Creative Intelligence: Essays in the Pragmatic Attitude*. New York: Holt, 1917.

———. *Intelligence in the Modern World*. New York: Modern Library, 1939.

Donaldson, M. *Children's Minds*. New York: Norton, 1979.

Drage, J., and Berendes, H. Apgar scores and outcome of the newborn. *Pediatric Clinics of North America*, 1966, 13, 635–643.

Drage, J., Berendes, H., and Fisher, P. The Apgar score and four-year psychological examination performance. *WHO Scientific Publications*, 1969, No. 185, 222–226.

Drillien, C. *The Growth and Development of the Prematurely Born Infant.* Baltimore: Williams & Wilkins, 1964.

Duncan, S. Some signals and rules for taking speaking turns in conversation. *Journal of Personality and Social Psychology,* 1972, 23, 283–292.

Duncan, S., and Fiske, D. *Face-to-Face Interaction.* Hillsdale, N.J.: Erlbaum, 1977.

Dunn, J., and Kendrick, C. The arrival of a sibling: Changes in patterns of interaction between mother and first-born child. *Journal of Child Psychology and Psychiatry and Allied Disciplines,* 1980, 21, 119–132.

Durkheim, E. Education: its nature and its role. In *Education and Sociology.* New York: Free Press, 1956. (Originally published in French, 1922)

Eckerman, C., Whatley, J., and McGehee, L. J. Approaching and contacting the object another manipulates: A social skill of the 1-year-old. *Developmental Psychology,* 1979, 15, 585–593.

Elliott, J., and Connolly, K. Hierarchical structure in skill development. In K. Connolly and J. Bruner (eds.), *The Growth of Competence.* New York: Academic Press, 1973.

Emde, R., Campos, J., Reich, J., and Gaensbauer, T. Infant smiling at five and nine months; analysis of heart rate and movement. *Infant Behavior and Development,* 1978, 1, 26–35.

Emde, R., Gaensbauer, T., and Harmon, R. Emotional expression in infancy: A biobehavioral study. *Psychological Issues Monograph Series,* 1976, 10, No. 37.

Emde, R., and Koenig, K. Neonatal smiling, frowning and rapid eye movement states. *Journal of the American Academy of Child Psychiatry,* 1969, 8, 637–656.

Epstein, S. The stability of behavior. II: Implications for psychological research. *American Psychologist,* 1980, 35, 790–806.

Erikson, E. *Childhood and Society.* New York: Norton, 1950.

Ervin-Tripp, S. Some features of early child-adult dialogues. *Language and Society,* 1977, 7, 357–373.

Fantz, R. The origin of form perception. *Scientific American,* 1961, 204, 66–72.

Field, T. Differential and cardiac responses of 3-month-old infants to mirror and peer. *Infant Behavior and Development,* 1979, 2, 179–184.

———. Affective displays of high-risk infants during early interaction. In T. Field and A. Fogel (eds.), *Emotion and Interaction: Normal and High-Risk Infants.* Hillsdale, N.J.: Erlbaum, 1982.

Field, T., Dempsey, J., and Shuman, H. Developmental assessments of infants surviving the respiratory distress syndrome. In T. Field, S. Sostek, S. Goldberg, and H. Shuman (eds.), *Infants Born at Risk.* New York: Spectrum, 1979.

Field, T., Woodson, R., Greenberg, R., and Cohen, D. Discrimination and imitation of facial expressions by neonates. *Science*, 1982 (in press).

Fisch, R., Gravem, H., and Engel, R. Neurological status of survivors of neonatal respiratory distress syndrome. *Journal of Pediatrics*, 1968, 73, 395–403.

Fischer, K. A theory of cognitive development: The control and construction of hierarchies of skills. *Psychological Review*, 1980, 87, 477–531.

Fitzgerald, H., and Brackbill, Y. Classical conditioning in infancy: Development and constraints. *Psychological Bulletin*, 1976, 83, 353–376.

Fitzhardinge, P., Pape, K., Arstikaitis, M., Boyle, M., Ashby, S., Rowley, A., Netley, C., and Swyer, P. Mechanical ventilation of infants of less than 1501 grams birth weight. *Journal of Pediatrics*, 1976, 88, 531–541.

Flavell, J. The genesis of our understanding of persons: Psychological studies. In T. Mischel (ed.), *Understanding Other Persons*. Totowa, N.J.: Rowman & Littlefield, 1974.

Fogel, A. Gaze, face and voice in the development of the mother-infant face-to-face interaction. Ph.D. dissertation, University of Chicago, 1976.

———. Temporal organization in mother-infant face-to-face interaction. In H. R. Schaffer (ed.), *Studies in Mother-Infant Interaction*. London: Academic Press, 1977.

———. Peer vs. mother directed behavior in 1- to 3-month-old infants. *Infant Behavior and Development*, 1979, 2, 215–226.

———. Affect dynamics in early infancy: Affective tolerance. In T. Field and A. Fogel (eds.), *Emotion and Interaction: Normal and High-Risk Infants*. Hillsdale, N.J.: Erlbaum, 1982.

Fouts, G. T., Waldner, D., and Watson, M. Effects of being imitated and counterimitated on the behavior of preschool children. *Child Development*, 1976, 47, 172–177.

Fraiberg, S. Blind infants and their mothers: An examination of the sign system. In M. Lewis and L. Rosenblum (eds.), *The Effect of the Infant on Its Caregiver*. New York: Wiley, 1974.

Freedman, D. *Human Infancy: An Evolutionary Perspective*. Hillsdale, N.J.: Erlbaum, 1974.

Gardner, J. The development of object identity in the first six months of human infancy. Ph.D. dissertation, Harvard University, 1971.

Gardner, J., and Gardner, H. A note on selective imitation by a 6-week-old infant. *Child Development*, 1970, 42, 1209–1213.

Garvey, C. The contingent query: A dependent act in conversation. In M. Lewis and L. Rosenblum (eds.), *Interaction, Conversation, and the Development of Language*. New York: Wiley, 1977.

Garvey, C., and Berninger, G. Timing and turn-taking in children's conversations. *Discourse Processes*, 1981 (in press).

Gibson, E. *Principles c,ᶜ Perceptual Learning and Development*. New York: Appleton-Century-Crofts, 1969.

Gibson, J. *The Senses Considered as Perceptual System*. Boston: Houghton-Mifflin, 1966.

Goffman, E. *Frame Analysis: An Essay on the Organization of Experience*. New York: Harper & Row, 1974.

Goldberg, S., Brachfeld, S., and Divitto, B. Feeding, fussing, and play: Parent-infant interaction in the first year as a function of prematurity and perinatal medical problems. In T. Field, S. Goldberg, D. Stern, and A. Sostek (eds.), *High Risk Infants and Children: Adult and Peer Interactions*. New York: Academic Press, 1980.

Goldin-Meadow, S., Seligman, M., and Gelman, R. Language in the two-year-old. *Cognition*, 1976, 4, 189–202.

Goldstein, K., Caputo, D., and Taub, H. The effects of prenatal and perinatal complications on development at one year of age. *Child Development*, 1976, 47, 613–621.

Golinkoff, R., and Ames, G. A comparison of fathers' and mothers' speech with their young children. *Child Development*, 1979, 50, 28–32.

Goodman, N. Symposium on innate ideas: The epistemological argument. In D. Reidel (ed.), *Boston Studies in the Philosophy of Science* (Vol. 3). New York: Humanities Press, 1968.

Gorski, P., Davison, M., and Brazelton, T. B. Stages of behavioral organization in the high-risk neonate: Theoretical and clinical considerations. *Seminars in Perinatology*, 1979, 3, 61–72.

Gratch, G. Recent studies based on Piaget's view of object concept development. In L. Cohen and P. Salapatek (eds.), *Infant Perception: From Sensation to Cognition* (Vol. 2). New York: Academic Press, 1975.

Greenberg, N. A comparison of infant–mother interactional behavior in infants with atypical behavior and normal infants. In J. Hellmuth (ed.), *Exceptional Infant* (Vol. 2). New York: Brunner/Mazel, 1971.

Grice, H. Meaning. *Philosophical Review*, 1957, 66, 377–388.

Guillaume, P. *Imitation in Children*. Chicago: University of Chicago Press, 1971. (Originally published in French, 1926)

Gustafson, G., Green, J., and West, M. The infant's changing role in mother-infant games: The growth of social skills. *Infant Behavior and Development*, 1979, 2, 301–308.

Haith, M. Visual competence in early infancy. In R. Held, H. Leibowitz, and H. Teuber (eds.), *Handbook of Sensory Physiology* (Vol. 8). Berlin: Springer-Verlag, 1977.

Hales, D., Lozoff, B., Sosa, R., and Kennell, J. Defining the limits of the maternal sensitive period. *Developmental Medicine and Child Neurology*, 1977, 19, 454–461.

Hamlyn, D. Epistemology and conceptual development. In T. Mischel (ed.), *Cognitive Development and Epistemology.* New York: Academic Press, 1971.

Hamm, M., Russell, M., and Koepke, J. Neonatal imitation. Presented to the Society for Research in Child Development, San Francisco, March 1979.

Harding, C., and Golinkoff, R. The origins of intentional vocalizations in prelinguistic infants. *Child Development,* 1979, 50, 33–40.

Harnick, F. The relationship between ability level and task difficulty in producing imitation in infants. *Child Development,* 1978, 49, 209–212.

Hay, D. Multiple functions of proximity seeking in infancy. *Child Development,* 1980, 51, 636–645.

Hayes, L., and Watson, J. Neonatal imitation: Fact or artifact? *Developmental Psychology,* 1981, 17, 655–660.

Head, H. *Studies in Neurology.* Oxford: Oxford University Press, 1920.

Heider, F. Perceiving the other person. In R. Tagiuri and L. Petrullo (eds.), *Person Perception and Interpersonal Behavior.* Stanford: Stanford University Press, 1958.

Held, R. Plasticity in sensorimotor systems. *Scientific American,* 1965, 213, 84–94.

Held, R., and Hein, A. Movement-produced stimulation in the development of visually-guided behavior. *Journal of Comparative and Physiological Psychology,* 1963, 56, 872–876.

Hinde, R. Control of movement patterns in animals. *Quarterly Journal of Experimental Psychology,* 1969, 21, 105–126.

Holding, D., and Macrae, A. Guidance, restriction, and knowledge of results. *Ergonomics,* 1964, 7, 289–295.

Husserl, E. *Cartesian Meditations: An Introduction to Phenomenology.* The Hague: Martinus Nijhoff, 1960. (Originally published in German, 1950)

Hutt, C., and Ounsted, T. The biological significance of gaze aversion with particular reference to the syndrome of infantile autism. *Behavior Science,* 1966, 11, 346–356.

Huttenlocher, J. The origins of language comprehension. In R. Solso (ed.), *Theories in Cognitive Psychology.* Hillsdale, N.J.: Erlbaum, 1974.

Huttenlocher, J., and Higgins, E. T. Issues in the study of symbolic development. In W. A. Collins (ed.), *Eleventh Minnesota Symposium on Child Psychology.* Hillsdale, N.J.: Erlbaum, 1978.

Illsley, R. Early prediction of perinatal risk. *Proceedings of the Royal Society of Medicine,* 1966, 59, 181–184.

Jackson, E., Campos, J., and Fischer, K. The question of decalage between object permanence and person permanence. *Developmental Psychology,* 1978, 14, 1–10.

Jacobson, S. Matching behavior in the young infant. *Child Development*, 1979, 50, 425–430.

Jaffe, J., and Feldstein, S. *Rhythms of Dialogue*. New York: Academic Press, 1970.

Jakobson, R. *Child Language, Aphasia, and Phonological Universals*. The Hague: Mouton, 1968.

James, W. *The Principles of Psychology* (Vol. 1). New York: Holt, 1890.

Kagan, J. *Change and Continuity in Infancy*. New York: Wiley, 1971.

————. Structure and process in the human infant. In M. Bornstein and W. Kessen (eds.), *Psychological Development from Infancy*. Hillsdale, N.J.: Erlbaum, 1979.

Kagan, J., Lapidus, D., and Moore, M. Infant antecedents of cognitive functioning: A longitudinal study. *Child Development*, 1978, 49, 1005–1023.

Kawai, M. Newly-acquired pre-cultural behavior of the natural troop of Japanese monkeys on Koshima Islet. *Primates*, 1965, 6, 1–30.

Kaye, K. Maternal participation in infants' acquisition of a skill. Ph.D. Dissertation, Harvard University, 1970.

————. Milk pressure as a determinant of the burst–pause pattern in neonatal sucking. *Proceedings of the 80th Annual Convention of the American Psychological Association*, 1972, 8, 83–84.

————. Infants' effects upon their mothers' teaching strategies. In J. Glidewell (ed.), *The Social Context of Learning and Development*. New York: Gardner Press, 1977. (a)

————. Toward the origin of dialogue. In H. R. Schaffer (ed.), *Studies in Mother-Infant Interaction*. London: Academic Press, 1977. (b)

————. *CRESCAT: Software System for Analysis of Sequential or Real-time Data*. Chicago: University of Chicago Computation Center, 1977. (c)

————. Discriminating among normal infants by multivariate analysis of Brazelton scores: Lumping and smoothing. In A. Sameroff (ed.), *Organization and Stability in Newborn Behavior. Monographs of the Society for Research in Child Development*, 1978, 43, No. 177.

————. The development of skills. In G. Whitehurst and B. Zimmerman (eds.), *The Functions of Language and Cognition*. New York: Academic Press, 1979. (a)

————. Thickening thin data: The maternal role in developing communication and language. In M. Bullowa (ed.), *Before Speech: The Beginning of Interpersonal Communication*. Cambridge: Cambridge University Press, 1979. (b)

————. Estimating false alarms and missed events from inter-observer agreements. *Psychological Bulletin*, 1980, 88, 458–468. (a)

————. The infant as a projective stimulus. *American Journal of Orthopsychiatry*, 1980, 50, 732–736. (b)

————. Why we don't talk "baby talk" to babies. *Journal of Child Language*, 1980, 7, 489–507. (c)

Kaye, K., and Brazelton, T. B. Mother–infant interaction in the organization of sucking. Presented to the Society for Research in Child Development, Minneapolis, March 1971.

Kaye, K., and Charney, R. How mothers maintain "dialogue" with two-year-olds. In D. Olson (ed.), *The Social Foundations of Language and Thought*. New York: Norton, 1980.

————. Conversational asymmetry between mothers and children. *Journal of Child Language*, 1981, 8, 35–50.

Kaye, K., and Fogel, A. The temporal structure of face–to–face communication between mothers and infants. *Developmental Psychology*, 1980, 16, 454–464.

Kaye, K., and Marcus, J. Imitation over a series of trials without feedback: Age six months. *Infant Behavior and Development*, 1978, 1, 141–155.

————. Infant imitation: The sensorimotor agenda. *Developmental Psychology*, 1981, 17, 258–265.

Kaye, K., and Wells, A. Mothers' jiggling and the burst–pause pattern in neonatal sucking. *Infant Behavior and Development*, 1980, 3, 29–46.

Keenan, E., and Schieffelin, B. Topic as a discourse notion. In C. Li (ed.), *Subject and Topic*. New York: Academic Press, 1976.

Kennell, J. Parenting in the intensive care unit. *Birth and the Family Journal*, 1978, 5, 223–226.

Kessen, W., Levine, J., and Wendrich, K. The imitation of pitch in infants. *Infant Behavior and Development*, 1979, 2, 93–100.

Kessen, W., Salapatek, P., and Haith, M. The visual response of the human newborn to linear contour. *Journal of Experimental Child Psychology*, 1972, 13, 19–20.

Killen, M., and Uzgiris, I. Imitation of actions with objects: The role of social meaning. *Journal of Genetic Psychology*, 1981, 138, 219–229.

Klaus, M., and Kennell, J. *Maternal-Infant Bonding*. St. Louis: Mosby, 1976.

Klein, M. *Our Adult World, and Other Essays*. New York: Basic, 1963.

Klein, M., and Stern, L. Low birthweight and the battered child syndrome. *American Journal of Diseases of Children*, 1971, 122, 15–18.

Korner, A. The effect of the infant's state, level of arousal, sex, and ontogenetic stage on the caregiver. In M. Lewis and L. Rosenblum (eds.), *The Effect of the Infant on Its Caregiver*. New York: Wiley, 1974.

Kuhn, T. Postscript—1969. In *The Structure of Scientific Revolutions* (2d edition). Chicago: University of Chicago Press, 1970.

Lamb, M. Father-infant and mother-infant interaction in the first year of life. *Child Development*, 1977, 48, 167–181.

Langer, S. *Philosophy in a New Key*. Cambridge: Harvard University Press, 1942.

Lashley, K. The accuracy of movement in the absence of excitation from the moving organ. *American Journal of Physiology,* 1917, 43, 169–194.

Levenstein, P. The Verbal Interaction Project. Final report to the Children's Bureau, U.S. Department of Health, Education, and Welfare, 1971.

Levi-Strauss, C. *The Savage Mind.* Chicago: University of Chicago Press, 1966. (Originally published in French, 1962).

Lewis, M., and Brooks-Gunn, J. *Social Cognition and the Acquisition of Self.* New York: Plenum, 1979.

Lewis, M., and Michalson, L. The socialization of emotions. In T. Field and A. Fogel (eds.), *Emotion and Interaction: Normal and High-Risk Infants.* Hillsdale, N.J.: Erlbaum, 1982.

McCall, R., Eichorn, D., and Hogarty, P. *Transitions in Early Mental Development. Monographs of the Society for Research in Child Development,* 1977, 42, No. 177.

McDonald, A. Intelligence in children of very low birth weight. *British Journal of Preventive and Social Medicine,* 1964, 18, 59–74.

McDougall, W. *An Introduction to Social Psychology.* London: Methuen, 1908.

————. *Psychology: The Study of Behavior.* London: Williams & Norgate, 1912.

MacKinney, L. Asphyxia neonatorum in relation to mental retardation. In W. Windle (ed.), *Neurological and Psychological Deficits of Asphyxia Neonatorum.* Springfield, Ill.: Thomas, 1958.

Macnamara, J. From sign to language. In J. Macnamara (ed.), *Language Learning and Thought.* New York: Academic Press, 1977.

McNeill, D. *The Acquisition of Language.* New York: Harper & Row, 1970.

Mahler, M., and Gosliner, B. On symbiotic child psychosis: Genetic, dynamic, and restitutive aspects. *Psychoanalytic Study of the Child,* 1955, 10, 195–212.

Mahler, M., Pine, F., and Bergman, A. *The Psychological Birth of the Human Infant.* New York: Basic, 1975.

Malinowski, B. The problem of meaning in primitive languages. In C. Ogden and I. A. Richards, *The Meaning of Meaning.* London: Kegan, Paul, 1923.

Martinez, M. Conversational asymmetry between Mexican mothers and children. *Hispanic Journal of Behavioral Sciences,* 1981, 3, 329–346.

Marx, K. *Economic and Philosophical Writings of 1844.* New York: International, 1964. (Originally published in German, 1930)

Matsuda, S. Effects of mother–child relationships on the imitative behaviors of young children. *Japanese Journal of Psychology,* 1973, 44, 79–84.

Mead, G. H. *Mind, Self, and Society.* Chicago: University of Chicago Press, 1934.

Meicler, M., and Gratch, G. Do 5-month-olds show object conception in Piaget's sense? *Infant Behavior and Development,* 1980, 3, 265–282.

Meltzoff, A., and Moore, M. K. Imitation of facial and manual gestures by human neonates. *Science*, 1977, 198, 75–78.

Merleau-Ponty, M. *Signs*. Evanston, Ill.: Northwestern University Press, 1964. (Originally published in French, 1960)

Millar, W., and Watson, J. The effect of delayed feedback on infant learning reexamined. *Child Development*, 1979, 50, 747–751.

Miller, G. The magical number seven, plus or minus two: Some limits on our capacity for processing information. *Psychological Review*, 1956, 63, 81–96.

———. Four philosophical problems of psycholinguistics. *Philosophy of Science*, 1970, 37, 183–199.

Miller, G., and Buckhout, R. *Psychology: The Science of Mental Life* (2d edition). New York: Harper & Row, 1973.

Miller, G., Galanter, E., and Pribram, K. *Plans and the Structure of Behavior*. New York: Holt, Rinehart, & Winston, 1960.

Mueller, E., and Lucas, T. A developmental analysis of peer interaction among toddlers. In M. Lewis and L. Rosenblum (eds.), *Friendship and Peer Relations*. New York: Wiley, 1975.

Mundy-Castle, A. Perception and communication in infancy: A cross-cultural study. In D. Olson (ed.), *The Social Foundations of Language and Thought*. New York: Norton, 1980.

Murphy, C., and Messer, D. Mothers, infants, and pointing: A study of a gesture. In H. R. Schaffer (ed.), *Studies in Mother–Infant Interaction*. London: Academic Press, 1977.

Murray, A. Infant crying as an elicitor of parental behavior: An examination of two models. *Psychological Bulletin*, 1979, 86, 191–215.

Neisser, U. *Cognition and Reality*. San Francisco: Freeman, 1976.

Nelson, C., Morse, P., and Leavitt, L. Recognition of facial expressions by 7-month-old infants. *Child Development*, 1979, 50, 1239–1242.

Nelson, K. Explorations in the development of a functional language system. In W. A. Collins (ed.), *Twelfth Minnesota Symposium on Child Psychology*. Hillsdale, N.J.: Erlbaum, 1979.

Nelson, K., Rescorla, L., Gruendel, J., and Benedict, H. Early lexicons: What do they mean? *Child Development*, 1978, 49, 960–968.

Newport, E., Gleitman, L., and Gleitman, H. Mother, I'd rather do it myself: Some effects and non-effects of maternal speech style. In C. Snow and C. Ferguson (eds.), *Talking to Children: Language Input and Acquisition*. Cambridge: Cambridge University Press, 1977.

Newson, J. An intersubjective approach to the systematic description of mother-infant interaction. In H. R. Schaffer (ed.), *Studies in Mother-Infant Interaction*. London: Academic Press, 1977.

———. The growth of shared understandings between infant and caregiver. In M. Bullowa (ed.), *Before Speech: The Beginning of Interpersonal Communication*. Cambridge: Cambridge University Press, 1979.

Ninio, A. The naive theory of the infant and other maternal attitudes in two subgroups in Israel. *Child Development*, 1979, 50, 976–980.

Niswander, K., and Gordon, M. *The Collaborative Perinatal Study of the National Institute of Neurological Disease and Stroke: The Women and their Pregnancies.* Philadelphia: Saunders, 1972.

Ottaviano, C., Campbell, S., and Taylor, P. Early contact and infant-mother attachment at one year. Presented to the Society for Research in Child Development, San Francisco, March 1979.

Papoušek, H., and Papoušek, M. Mothering and the cognitive head-start: Psychobiological considerations. In H. R. Schaffer (ed.), *Studies in Mother-Infant Interaction.* London: Academic Press, 1977.

Parke, R. Perspectives on father–infant interaction. In J. Osofsky (ed.), *The Handbook of Infant Development.* New York: Wiley, 1979.

Parmelee, A., and Haber, A. Who is the "risk infant"? In H. Osofsky (ed.), *Clinical Obstetrics and Gynecology* (Vol. 18). New York: Harper & Row, 1975.

Parmelee, A., and Michaelis, R. Neurological examination of the newborn. In J. Hellmuth (ed.), *Exceptional Infant* (Vol. 2). New York: Brunner/Mazel, 1971.

Parsons, T., and Bales, R. *Family, Socialization, and Interactive Processes.* Glencoe, Ill.: Free Press, 1954.

Pasamanick, B., and Knobloch, H. Retrospective studies on the epidemiology of reproductive casualty: Old and new. *Merrill-Palmer Quarterly,* 1966, 12, 7–26.

Pasamanick, B., Knobloch, H., and Lilienfeld, A. Socio-economic status and some precursors of neuropsychiatric disorders. *American Journal of Orthopsychiatry,* 1956, 26, 594–601.

Pawlby, S. Imitative interaction. In H. R. Schaffer (ed.), *Studies in Mother-Infant Interaction.* London: Academic Press, 1977.

Peirce, C. S. The fixation of belief. *Popular Science Monthly,* 1877. (Reprinted in J. Buchler [ed.], *Philosophical Writings of Peirce.* New York: Routledge & Kegan Paul, 1940)

————. Logic as semiotic: The theory of signs. In J. Buchler (ed.), *Philosophical Writings of Peirce.* New York: Routledge & Kegan Paul, 1940.

Pepitone, A. Lessons from the history of social psychology. *American Psychologist,* 1981, 36, 972–985.

Piaget, J. *The Language and Thought of the Child.* New York: Harcourt, Brace, 1926. (Originally published in French, 1923)

————. *The Psychology of Intelligence.* London: Routledge & Kegan Paul, 1950. (Originally published in French, 1947)

————. *Play, Dreams, and Imitation in Childhood.* New York: Norton, 1951. (Originally published in French, 1945)

————. *The Origins of Intelligence in Children.* New York: International Universities Press, 1952. (Originally published in French, 1936)

————. *The Construction of Reality in the Child.* New York: Basic, 1954. (Originally published in French, 1937)

————. Preface to L. Vygotsky, *Thought and Language*. Cambridge: M.I.T. Press, 1962.

————. *Six Psychological Studies*. (D. Elkind, ed.) New York: Basic, 1969.

Poppei, J. Toddlers' use of peer imitation for problem-solving. Ph.D. dissertation, University of Chicago, 1976.

Popper, K. *Objective Knowledge: An Evolutionary Approach*. Oxford: Oxford University Press, 1972.

Preyer, W. *Mental Development in the Child*. New York: Appleton, 1893. (Originally published in German, 1888)

Richards, M. Social interaction in the first weeks of human life. *Psychiatry, Neurology, and Neurochirurgy*, 1971, 14, 35–42.

Riegel, K., and Rosenwald, G. (eds.) *Structure and Transformation*. New York: Wiley, 1975.

Ringler, N., Kennell, J., Jarvella, R., Navojosky, B., and Klaus, M. Mother-to-child speech at 2 years—effects of early postnatal contact. *Journal of Pediatrics*, 1975, 86, 141.

Ringler, N., Trause, M., Klaus, M., and Kennell, J. The effects of extra postpartum contact and maternal speech patterns on children's IQs, speech, and language comprehension at five. *Child Development*, 1978, 49, 862–865.

Robson, K. The role of eye-to-eye contact in maternal-infant attachment. *Journal of Child Psychology and Psychiatry and Allied Disciplines*, 1967, 8, 13–27.

Rodgon, M., and Kurdek, L. Vocal and gestural imitation in 8-, 14-, and 20-month-old children. *Journal of Genetic Psychology*, 1977, 131, 115–123.

Roth, V. Infant learning through imitation. M.A. thesis, University of Chicago, 1980.

Sameroff, A. Non-nutritive sucking in newborns under visual and auditory stimulation. *Child Development*, 1967, 38, 443–452.

Sameroff, A., and Chandler, M. Reproductive risk and the continuum of caretaking casualty. In F. Horowitz (ed.), *Review of Child Development Research* (Vol. 4). Chicago: University of Chicago Press, 1975.

Sander, L. Issues in early mother-infant interaction. *Journal of the American Academy of Child Psychiatry*, 1962, 1, 141–166.

————. The regulation of exchange in the infant-caretaker system. In M. Lewis and L. Rosenblum (eds.), *Interaction, Conversation, and the Development of Language*. New York: Wiley, 1977.

Sander, L., Stechler, G., Julia, H., and Burns, P. Regulation and organization in the early infant-caretaker system. In R. J. Robinson (ed.), *Brain and Early Behavior*. New York: Academic Press, 1969.

de Saussure, F. *Course in General Linguistics*. New York: Philosophical Library, 1959. (Originally published in French, 1916)

Scaife, M., and Bruner, J. The capacity for joint visual attention in the infant. *Nature*, 1975, 253, 265–266.

Schaefer, E., and Bayley, N. *Maternal Behavior, Child Behavior, and Their Intercorrelation from Infancy through Adolescence. Monographs of the Society for Research in Child Development*, 1963, 28, No. 87.

Schaffer, H. R. Some issues for research in the study of attachment behavior. In B. Foss (ed.), *Determinants of Infant Behavior* (Vol. 2). London: Methuen, 1963.

Schaffer, H. R., Collis, G., and Parsons, G. Vocal interchange and visual regard in verbal and pre-verbal children. In H. R. Schaffer (ed.), *Studies in Mother-Infant Interaction*. London: Academic Press, 1977.

Schaffer, H. R., and Crook, C. Maternal control techniques in a directed play situation. *Child Development*, 1979, 50, 989–996.

Schleidt, W. Tonic communication: continual effects of discrete signs in animal communication systems. *Journal of Theoretical Biology*, 1973, 42, 359–386.

Schneirla, T., Rosenblatt, J., and Tobach, E. Maternal behavior in the cat. In H. Rheingold (ed.), *Maternal Behavior in Mammals*. New York: Wiley, 1963.

Schutz, A. *Collected Papers* (Vol. 1). The Hague: Nijhoff, 1962.

Seashore, M., Leifer, A., Barnett, C., and Leiderman, P. The effects of denial of early mother-infant interaction on maternal self–confidence. *Journal of Personality and Social Psychology*, 1973, 26, 369–378.

Sebeok, T., and Umiker-Sebeok, D. J. (eds.) *Speaking of Apes: A Critical Anthology of Two-Way Communication with Man*. New York: Plenum, 1979.

Sherrod, K., Crawley, S., Petersen, G., and Bennett, P. Maternal language to prelinguistic infants: Semantic aspects. *Infant Behavior and Development*, 1978, 1, 335–345.

Shipley, E., Smith, C., and Gleitman, L. A study in the acquisition of language free responses to commands. *Language*, 1969, 45, 322–342.

Shotter, J., and Gregory, S. On first gaining the idea of oneself as a person. In R. Harre (ed.), *Life Sentences: Aspects of the Social Role of Language*. New York: Wiley, 1976.

Sibulkin, A., and Uzgiris, I. Imitation by preschoolers in a problem–solving situation. *Journal of Genetic Psychology*, 1978, 132, 267–275.

Siegman, A., and Feldstein, S. *Of Speech and Time*. Hillsdale, N.J.: Erlbaum, 1979.

Sigman, M., Cohen, S., and Forsythe, A. The relation of early infant measures to later development. In S. Friedman and M. Sigman (eds.), *Preterm Birth and Psychological Development*. New York: Academic Press, 1981.

Sigman, M., and Parmelee, A. Longitudinal evaluation of the preterm infant. In T. Field, A. Sostek, S. Goldberg, and H. Shuman (eds.), *Infants Born at Risk*. New York: Spectrum, 1979.

Skinner, B. F. *The Behavior of Organisms*. New York: Appleton-Century-Crofts, 1938.

———. Selection by consequences. *Science*, 1981, 213, 501–504.

Skutch, A. *Parent Birds and Their Young*. Austin: University of Texas Press, 1976.

Slaughter, D. Modernization through education of mother–child dyads. Final report to the National Institute of Child Health and Human Development, 1979.

Slobin, D., and Welsh, C. Elicited imitation as a research tool in developmental psycholinguistics. In C. Ferguson and D. Slobin (eds.), *Studies of Child Language Development*. New York: Holt, Rinehart, & Winston, 1973.

Smith, C. *Physiology of the Newborn Infant* (2d edition). Springfield, Ill.: Thomas, 1951.

Snow, C. The development of conversation between mothers and babies. *Journal of Child Language*, 1977, 4, 1–22.

Snow, C., and Ferguson, C. (eds.) *Talking to Children: Language Input and Acquisition*. Cambridge: Cambridge University Press, 1977.

Sonnenschein, S., and Whitehurst, G. The development of communication: When a bad model makes a good teacher. *Journal of Experimental Child Psychology*, 1980, 29, 371–390.

Spelke, E. Perceiving bimodally specified events in infancy. *Developmental Psychology*, 1979, 15, 626–636.

Spitz, R. The derailment of dialogue: Stimulus overload, action cycles, and the completion gradient. *Journal of the American Psychoanalytic Association*, 1964, 12, 752–775.

Spitz, R., and Wolf, K. The smiling response: A contribution to the ontogenesis of social relations. *Genetic Psychology Monographs*, 1946, 34, 57–125.

Sroufe, L. A. Socioemotional development. In J. Osofsky (ed.), *The Handbook of Infant Development*. New York: Wiley, 1979.

Sroufe, L. A., and Waters, E. The ontogenesis of smiling and laughter: A perspective on the organization of development in infancy. *Psychological Review*, 1976, 83, 173–189.

———. Attachment as an organizational construct. *Child Development*, 1977, 48, 1184–1199.

Stechler, G. A longitudinal follow–up of neonatal apnea. *Child Development*, 1964, 35, 333–348.

Stechler, G., and Latz, E. Some observations on attention and arousal in the human infant. *Journal of the American Academy of Child Psychiatry*, 1966, 5, 517–525.

Stern, D. A microanalysis of mother-infant interaction: Behavior regulating social contact between a mother and her 3½ month old twins. *Journal of the American Academy of Child Psychiatry*, 1971, 10, 501–517.

————. Mother and infant at play: The dyadic interaction involving facial, vocal, and gaze behaviors. In M. Lewis and L. Rosenblum (eds.), *The Effect of the Infant on Its Caregiver.* New York: Wiley, 1974.

Stern, D., Beebe, B., Jaffe, J., and Bennett, S. The infant's stimulus world during social interaction. In H. R. Schaffer (ed.), *Studies in Mother-Infant Interaction.* London: Academic Press, 1977.

Stern, D., Jaffe, J., Beebe, B., and Bennett, S. Vocalizing in unison and alternation. *Transactions of the New York Academy of Sciences,* 1975, 263, 89–101.

Strain, B., and Vietze, P. Early dialogues: The structure of reciprocal infant-mother vocalization. Presented to the Society for Research in Child Development, Denver, March 1975.

Strawson, P. *Individuals: An Essay in Descriptive Metaphysics.* London: Methuen, 1959.

Sylvester-Bradley, B., and Trevarthen, C. "Baby-talk" as an adaptation to the infant's communication. In N. Waterson and C. Snow (eds.), *Development of Communication.* New York: Wiley, 1978.

Tagiuri, R. Person perception. In G. Lindzey and E. Aronson (eds.), *The Handbook of Social Psychology.* Reading, Mass.: Addison–Wesley, 1969.

Tajfel, H. The "New Look" and social differentiations: A semi-Brunerian perspective. In D. Olson (ed.), *The Social Foundations of Language and Thought.* New York: Norton, 1980.

Tarde, G. *The Laws of Imitation* (2d edition). New York: Holt, 1903. (Originally published in French, 1895)

Terrace, H., Petitto, L., Sanders, R., and Bever, T. Can an ape create a sentence? *Science,* 1979, 206, 891–899.

Thelen, M., Dollinger, S., and Roberts, M. On being imitated: its effects on attraction and reciprocal imitation. *Journal of Personality and Social Psychology,* 1975, 31, 467–472.

Thoman, E., Acebo, C., Dreyer, C., Becker, P., and Freese, M. Individuality in the interactive process. In E. Thoman (ed.), *Origins of the Infant's Social Responsiveness.* Hillsdale, N.J.: Erlbaum, 1979.

Thomas, A., Chess, S., and Birch, H. *Temperament and Behavior Disorders in Children.* New York: New York University Press, 1968.

Tillich, P. *Systematic Theology.* Chicago: University of Chicago Press, 1951.

Tolman, E. Behaviorism and purpose. *Journal of Philosophy,* 1925, 22, 36–41.

Toulmin, S. The concept of stages in psychological development. In T. Mischel (ed.), *Cognitive Development and Epistemology.* New York: Academic Press, 1971.

————. Rules and their relevance for understanding human behavior. In T. Mischel (ed.), *Understanding Other Persons.* Totowa, N.J.: Rowman & Littlefield, 1974.

Trevarthen, C. Descriptive analyses of infant communicative behaviour. In H. R. Schaffer (ed.), *Studies in Mother–Infant Interaction.* London: Academic Press, 1977.

————. Modes of perceiving and modes of acting. In H. Pick and E. Saltzman (eds.), *Modes of Perceiving and Processing Information.* Hillsdale, N.J.: Erlbaum, 1978.

————. Communication and cooperation in early infancy: A description of primary intersubjectivity. In M. Bullowa (ed.), *Before Speech: The Beginning of Interpersonal Communication.* Cambridge: Cambridge University Press, 1979.

Trevarthen, C., and Hubley, P. Secondary intersubjectivity: Confidence, confiding, and acts of meaning in the first year. In A. Lock (ed.), *Action, Gesture, and Symbol: The Emergence of Language.* New York: Academic Press, 1978.

Tronick, E., Als, H., and Adamson, L. Structure of early face-to-face communicative interactions. In M. Bullowa (ed.), *Before Speech: The Beginning of Interpersonal Communication.* Cambridge: Cambridge University Press, 1979.

Tronick, E., Als, H., Adamson, L., Wise, S., and Brazelton, T. B. The infant's response to entrapment between contradictory messages in face-to-face interaction. *Journal of the American Academy of Child Psychiatry,* 1978, 17, 1–13.

Tronick, E., Ricks, M., and Cohn, J. Maternal and infant affective exchange: patterns of adaptation. In T. Field and A. Fogel (eds.), *Emotion and Interaction: Normal and High-Risk Infants.* Hillsdale, N.J.: Erlbaum, 1982.

Tulkin, S., and Cohler, B. Childrearing attitudes and mother-child interaction in the first year of life. *Merrill-Palmer Quarterly,* 1973, 19, 95–106.

Tulkin, S., and Kagan, J. Mother-child interaction in the first year of life. *Child Development,* 1972, 43, 31–41.

Turnure, C. Response to voice of mother and stranger by babies in the first year. *Developmental Psychology,* 1971, 4, 182–190.

Uzgiris, I. Organization of sensorimotor intelligence. In M. Lewis (ed.), *Origins of Intelligence.* New York: Plenum, 1976.

————. The many faces of imitation in infancy. In L. Montado (ed.), *Fortschritte der Entwicklungs Psychologie.* Stuttgart: Kuhlhammer, 1979.

————. Two functions of imitation during infancy. *International Journal of Behavioral Development,* 1981, 4, 1–12.

Valentine, C. The psychology of imitation with special reference to early childhood. *British Journal of Psychology,* 1930, 21, 105–132.

Vietze, P., O'Connor, S., Falsey, S., and Altemeier, W. Effects of rooming-in on maternal behavior directed towards infants. Presented to the American Psychological Association, Toronto, August 1978.

von Bertalanffy, L. *General System Theory.* New York: Braziller, 1968.

von Humboldt, A. *Aspects of Nature.* Philadelphia: Lea & Blanchard, 1849.

von Uexkull, J. A stroll through the worlds of animals and men. In C. H. Schiller (ed.), *Instinctive Behavior: The Development of a Modern Concept*. New York: International Universities Press, 1957. (Originally published in German, 1934)

Vygotsky, L. *Thought and Language*. Cambridge: M.I.T. Press, 1962. (Originally published in Russian, 1934)

Watson, J. Memory and contingency analysis in infant development. *Merrill-Palmer Quarterly*, 1967, 13, 55–76.

Watson, J. B. *Behaviorism*. New York: Norton, 1925.

Watzlawick, P., Beavin, J., and Jackson, D. *Pragmatics of Human Communication*. New York: Norton, 1967.

Welford, A. *Fundamentals of Skill*. London: Methuen, 1968.

Werner, E., Bierman, J., and French, F. *The Children of Kauai*. Honolulu: University Press of Hawaii, 1971.

Werner, H., and Kaplan, B. *Symbol Formation*. New York: Wiley, 1963.

West, M., and Rheingold, H. Infant stimulation of maternal instruction. *Infant Behavior and Development*, 1978, 1, 205–215.

White, R. Motivation reconsidered: The concept of competence. *Psychological Review*, 1959, 66, 297–333.

Whorf, B. *Language, Thought, and Reality*. (J. B. Carroll, ed.) Cambridge: M.I.T. Press, 1956.

Widmayer, S., and Field, T. Effects of Brazelton demonstrations on early interactions of preterm infants and their teenage mothers. *Infant Behavior and Development*, 1980, 3, 79–89.

Willatts, P. Adjustment of reaching to change in object position by young infants. *Child Development*, 1979, 50, 911–913.

Wittgenstein, L. *Philosophical Investigations*. Oxford: Blackwell, 1953.

Wolff, P. Observations on the early development of smiling. In B. Foss (ed.), *Determinants of Infant Behavior* (Vol. 2). New York: Wiley, 1963.

———. The causes, controls, and organization of behavior in the neonate. *Psychological Issues*, 1966, 5, Monograph No. 17.

———. The natural history of crying and other vocalizations in infancy. In B. Foss (ed.), *Determinants of Infant Behavior* (Vol. 4). London: Methuen, 1969.

Yarrow, L., and Goodwin, M. Some conceptual issues in the study of mother-infant interaction. *American Journal of Orthopsychiatry*, 1965, 35, 473–481.

Index

Abuse, 252, 255, 261

Accommodation, 47, 61, 90, 116, 122, 125–26, 160, 165–77, 187, 205–6, 216–18, 223, 227

Action, 12–13, 18, 56, 59–61, 79, 125, 129, 135, 158, 167, 171, 207–9, 213, 229–30. *See also* Intention; Skills

Adoption, 31

Adult behavior, 3, 24–27, 32, 46–47, 52, 54–55, 68, 83, 145–46, 155, 172, 217, 225, 227, 248; effects of infants on, 30–53, 71–72, 84, 88–93, 95, 185, 197, 243. *See also* Evolution, parent-infant system; Frames; Interaction; Speech to infants; System, mother-infant

Affect, 30, 32, 66, 141–42, 147, 200, 203–4, 214, 223–24, 230–31, 244. *See also* Anxiety; Facial expressions

Anxiety, 77, 223–25, 239; in mothers, 246n, 250, 255

Apes taught sign-language, 133, 136–37, 177, 181, 184–85, 218n

Apprenticeship, 8, 54–70, 103, 109, 116, 119, 122, 131, 151–52, 180, 185, 204, 210–11, 216, 220, 226, 236, 238, 241, 244, 259–61

Arousal, 30, 46, 51, 66, 71–73, 145, 147, 150, 200, 219, 227, 230, 244, 257

Assimilation, 61, 72, 77, 81, 116, 120, 122, 125–27, 151, 158–67, 173–74,

179, 183, 187, 218–19, 223, 228–30, 241; reciprocal, 62, 166, 179, 181–82, 185

Attachment (infant to mother), 6, 31–32, 46, 59, 72, 116, 180–81, 213, 215, 222–40, 253

Attention, 62–64, 66, 71–75, 79, 88, 99, 115–16, 147–48, 150, 158, 176, 209, 223, 227–29, 257–59; to mother's face, 27, 41–47, 91–96, 143–45, 190, 195, 228, 258

Basic trust, 224

Behaviorism, 12, 135, 166n

Behavior modification, 80–81. *See also* Reinforcement

Biology, 11–14, 24, 28, 53n, 56, 64, 126, 159, 219

Bonding (mother to infant), 47, 53, 227, 253–56, 258

Brain, 3, 19, 32, 86, 138–39, 148, 184–85, 236n, 238–39

Categorical knowledge. *See* Equivalence

Certainty (vs. intelligent guesses), 36, 129, 134n, 136, 137n, 184

Circular reaction, 58, 66, 125, 162, 187, 228

C-models, 19–24, 123–27, 209, 214. *See also* P-models

Cognitive development, 3, 8, 15, 25–27, 29, 32, 55, 76–77, 89, 115, 118, 123–27, 131, 160, 180, 223,